THE COMPLETE IDIOT'S GUIDE® TO

The Founding Fathers

and the Birth of Our Nation

by Ray Raphael

ALPHA

A member of Penguin Group (USA) Inc.

ALPHA BOOKS

Published by the Penguin Group

Penguin Group (USA) Inc., 375 Hudson Street, New York, New York 10014, USA

Penguin Group (Canada), 90 Eglinton Avenue East, Suite 700, Toronto, Ontario M4P 2Y3, Canada (a division of Pearson Penguin Canada Inc.)

Penguin Books Ltd., 80 Strand, London WC2R 0RL, England

Penguin Ireland, 25 St. Stephen's Green, Dublin 2, Ireland (a division of Penguin Books Ltd.)

Penguin Group (Australia), 250 Camberwell Road, Camberwell, Victoria 3124, Australia (a division of Pearson Australia Group Pty. Ltd.)

Penguin Books India Pvt. Ltd., 11 Community Centre, Panchsheel Park, New Delhi—110 017, India

Penguin Group (NZ), 67 Apollo Drive, Rosedale, North Shore, Auckland 1311, New Zealand (a division of Pearson New Zealand Ltd.)

Penguin Books (South Africa) (Pty.) Ltd., 24 Sturdee Avenue, Rosebank, Johannesburg 2196, South Africa

Penguin Books Ltd., Registered Offices: 80 Strand, London WC2R 0RL, England

Copyright © 2011 by Ray Raphael

International Standard Book Number: 978-1-61564-061-4
Library of Congress Catalog Card Number: 2010913757

13   12   11   8   7   6   5   4   3   2   1

Interpretation of the printing code: The rightmost number of the first series of numbers is the year of the book's printing; the rightmost number of the second series of numbers is the number of the book's printing. For example, a printing code of 11-1 shows that the first printing occurred in 2011.

Printed in the United States of America

Most Alpha books are available at special quantity discounts for bulk purchases for sales promotions, premiums, fund-raising, or educational use. Special books, or book excerpts, can also be created to fit specific needs.

For details, write: Special Markets, Alpha Books, 375 Hudson Street, New York, NY 10014.

Publisher: *Marie Butler-Knight*

Associate Publisher: *Mike Sanders*

Senior Managing Editor: *Billy Fields*

Acquisitions Editor: *Tom Stevens*

Development Editor: *Jennifer Moore*

Senior Production Editor: *Janette Lynn*

Copy Editor: *Daron Thayer*

Cover Designer: *William Thomas*

Book Designers: *William Thomas, Rebecca Batchelor*

Indexer: *Brad Herriman*

Layout: *Brian Massey*

Proofreader: *John Etchison*

Contents

Appendixes

Introduction

Let's imagine it's the tenth anniversary of our nation's birth, July 4, 1786. The Revolutionary War is over, but the Constitution has yet to be written and adopted. At this critical juncture, smack in the middle of what we now call the Founding Era, we decide to take a poll. We ask a sampling of Americans, "Who do you think are the ten most important founders of your young nation, the people who will be remembered in the history books?"

Two names will be on everybody's list: George Washington and Benjamin Franklin. After that there will be some variation, but most respondents will probably list the Farmer (John Dickinson) and the Financier (Robert Morris). Dickinson's famous *Letters from a Farmer in Pennsylvania* galvanized opposition to imperial policies in the 1760s, and after independence he penned the Articles of Confederation, the nation's constitution in 1786. Morris personally saved the country from financial ruin and ran it almost single-handedly from 1781 to 1784.

After naming these four nationally prominent figures, Founding Era Americans would probably display regional bias. Virginians might put forth Peyton Randolph, Patrick Henry, Richard Henry Lee, George Mason, George Wythe, Edmund Pendleton, or Thomas Jefferson, but few would include James Madison, a little-known state legislator. New Yorkers might mention John Jay, Robert R. Livingston, George Clinton, or Philip Schuyler, but I doubt any at this date would include Alexander Hamilton, Washington's former aide-de-camp and Schuyler's son-in-law. We could go down the states, one-by-one, to get more names. Some lists would probably include martyrs like Joseph Warren (killed at Bunker Hill) and Richard Montgomery (lost in the attack on Quebec) or folk military heroes like Old Put (Israel Putnam), the Swamp Fox (Francis Marion), the Carolina Gamecock (Thomas Sumter), or Lighthorse Harry (Henry Lee).

Now, more than two centuries later, our sense of history has narrowed and a poll would yield few candidates—Washington, Franklin, Adams, Jefferson, Madison, Hamilton, and just a small number of others. In this book, those nominees will take their rightful places on history's stage, but here you will also become acquainted with leaders who were recognized in their time, if not in ours. You will even meet an entire founding generation—"the body of the people," in the language of that day. Intersecting at critical moments, debating and quarreling or uniting, all struggled to create a new nation.

That nation was like no other. There would be no kings or lords. The government would be rooted exclusively in the people, a concept called popular sovereignty. Any American who wanted a seat at the political table had to buy into that basic ideal.

But the Founding Fathers were not like a team of high-bred horses pulling a carriage in sync. Although they shared a common goal, the good of their nation, they had different answers to the hard nuts-and-bolts questions of nation-building. How, and how much, should government tax the people? Should the wealthy wield political power? Should government and religion intermingle? Who should be the final arbiter of the laws? How can government provide security and stability without interfering with personal liberties? Replies mattered. With one founder responding one way and the next founder another, they could be a contentious lot.

The nation's founding didn't happen in a day or even a decade but over the course of a third of a century. The story is vast, and it is both powerful and entertaining. *The Complete Idiot's Guide to the Founding Fathers* will take you through the years.

With a tale this grand, there is only one place to start: the beginning.

How This Book Is Organized

Part One, Independence, follows the colonists as they forge a new identity. People who would later be founders are Brits at the start, and proud of it. But they have no representatives in Britain's government, so when Parliament taxes them to pay for the expanding empire in North America, they resist. In 1774, after years of protest, Britain strips colonists of rights they have always known. Throughout the Massachusetts countryside, rebels respond by casting off tyrannical British rule. The King's Army retaliates by marching on Lexington and Concord, and war breaks out. Finally, after more than a year of fighting, Congress bows to popular pressure and declares independence.

Part Two, First Drafts, tells of the country's early efforts to act like one. The states form governments, but the first attempt at a federal constitution, the Articles of Confederation, leaves Congress with little power. Systems break down. War debts are huge, and the struggling nation almost goes belly-up.

Part Three, A New Plan, discusses a remarkable revolution, this one in favor of a strong national government. But what will such a government look like? At the Constitutional Convention in 1787, delegates argue long and hard over what powers should be given to a congress, a president, or a supreme court—and what powers should be left with the states.

Part Four, The Launch, reveals that the Constitution is not an easy sell. Each state has to decide whether it will approve, or ratify, a plan that was conceived behind closed doors. The debate is rancorous and the outcome in doubt. In the end, the Constitution barely passes in three key states. To assure people that the new government will not take away the people's liberties, a reluctant Congress finally proposes a Bill of Rights.

Part Five, Partisan Divide, tracks the political maneuvering during the administrations of our first three presidents. People argue about the legitimate powers of government and who within government should wield those powers. It's partisan politics all the way, complete with name-calling, press wars, and competing Fourth of July parades.

Part Six, The American Way, showcases men and women who struggled for ideals we now embrace—political democracy, social equality, and economic opportunity for all. This brings the founding era more up-to-date. We conclude by watching successive generations of Americans venerate one group of founders or another, even if facts must be altered in the process. The manufactured stories are sometimes imaginative, but they help unite the nation.

Extras

To lead you through a treasure-trove of information, *The Complete Idiot's Guide to the Founding Fathers* offers pointers of various kinds. An appendix takes you to Internet sites that provide readily accessible primary sources. These allow you to learn history straight from the people who were actually making things happen. Consulting first-hand materials is both more exciting and more accurate than relying on secondhand accounts written decades or centuries later.

Four types of sidebars will help you get the main points. They offer meanings of important concepts and glimpses of key people. They also present original quotations and reveal particular facts that bring out the story. Look for:

FOUNDER ID

In these thumbnail biographical sketches, you'll meet famous people and some you never knew. Treat these like introductions at a party. You won't learn all there is to know about the people you meet here, but you'll learn enough to decide whom you want to get to know better.

DEFINITION

Some words that appear in the text are critical to understanding the material. When these require further explanation, they are defined and discussed in sidebars.

THEIR OWN WORDS

Here you'll find what our founders actually said, and some of it is startling. These flavorful quotations convey a sense of this amazing time and its people.

BY THE NUMBERS

How many gallons of beer, wine, and rum-punch did 26-year-old George Washington supply so his 301 supporters could party on election day, the first time he ran for public office? Each "By the Numbers" sidebar paints a vivid, precise picture, and a picture is worth a thousand words.

Acknowledgments

My wife Marie is a writer and an educator, and from beginning to end she has been a true partner on this project. She conducted research and contributed mightily as an editor, suggesting more accurate wording or ways of reshaping a chapter or a section. She was there with me through hours of conversation about freedom of religion, judicial review, the peculiar intersection of slavery and politics, the strained relationships among various founders, and so on. We took the journey together.

I would also like to thank the countless editors and compilers, mostly unheralded, who have made so many documentary materials readily available. Without their efforts, the task of synthesizing the history of our founding into a coherent and reasonably accurate narrative would be absolutely impossible. Because of their efforts, researchers and writers can meet our founders face-to-face, as I have done. I encourage readers to do so as well.

Special Thanks to the Technical Reviewer

The Complete Idiot's Guide to the Founding Fathers was reviewed by an expert who double-checked the accuracy of what you'll learn here, to help us ensure that this book gives you everything you need to know about our founding fathers and the birth of this nation. Special thanks are extended to Woody Holton. One of the premier historians of the Founding Era, he gave the manuscript a careful reading. His insightful comments sharpened the focus and made the book more precise.

Trademarks

All terms mentioned in this book that are known to be or are suspected of being trademarks or service marks have been appropriately capitalized. Alpha Books and Penguin Group (USA) Inc. cannot attest to the accuracy of this information. Use of a term in this book should not be regarded as affecting the validity of any trademark or service mark.

Prelude to Independence

We start as Brits; we end as Americans. That is the story in brief.

The men we know today as America's Founding Fathers spent their childhood years saying nightly prayers to the popular King George II. They hailed King George III, who succeeded him in 1760, as their new "Patriot King." On King's Street in Boston, when George III ascended to the throne, a great throng proclaimed "with full voice and consent of tongue and heart" that the new king was their "only lawful and rightful Liege Lord" and pledged "all faith and constant obedience."

Obedience? That would soon change. When Parliament and the king's ministers tried to tax colonists without their consent, they protested. When Parliament revoked the Massachusetts Charter because colonists protested too much, the people rose up as a body and toppled British rule throughout the Bay Colony. Then the King's Army fought back, marching on Lexington and Concord.

It took more than a year of fighting before colonial leaders, following the will of the people, finally broke ties with their king and their mother country. On that day, July 2, 1776, a nation was born.

We're Brits, and Proud of It

In This Chapter

- The Magna Carta and the Glorious Revolution
- The Age of Enlightenment
- Diverse backgrounds of colonial Americans
- Colonists' allegiance to British monarchs
- The young George Washington

Long before the American Revolution, British subjects had stood up to monarchs and stood up for their rights, as this chapter shows. Politically speaking, they were not a downtrodden people, but relatively confident, as far as those things went centuries ago. If pushed to the edge of frustration, they might even challenge the authority of their superiors. Colonists knew their history well. Its lessons would inspire them to lay claim to new freedoms.

By the middle of the eighteenth century, a philosophy had taken hold that could in the end make spirited, rambunctious subjects question even a king's authority. People now lived in the Age of Enlightenment. More and more, they relied on rational thinking, observation, and investigation and less on tradition and custom or on automatic compliance to fixed rules.

History Lessons: The British Tradition

English people had deposed kings in their time and even beheaded one in 1649. That was Charles I, who asserted that God, not people, bestowed monarchical powers and that the king could therefore do no wrong. Some thought he could. The new rulers not only beheaded Charles, but they also abolished monarchy after his death, at least for a time. England became the Commonwealth of England, a republic, with Oliver Cromwell its leader. But civil unrest was still rampant, and after Cromwell died, Charles II, son of the previous king, returned to the throne to usher in a period known as The Restoration. Nine of the "regicides" (people who had killed King Charles I) were executed.

Beheading aside, kings and their subjects clashed. Colonists paid close attention to two struggles that had advanced the legal rights of a king's subjects.

The Magna Carta

Centuries earlier, back in 1215, during the reign of King John, English barons who were frustrated by the King's horrendous taxes and his overbearing treatment captured him and forced him to sign the *Magna Carta*, Latin for "Great Charter." According to that document, a committee of 25 barons could overrule the king. King John actually had to take an oath of loyalty to the committee.

The Magna Carta was reissued and modified three separate times under different kings, and each time those who were supposedly subservient to a monarch were making sure he did not overreach.

One of the Magna Carta's later and most famous clauses declared that no freeman could be jailed, exiled, or killed unless his peers decided that he was guilty. No longer could someone be chained to a wall in a hidden dungeon and left to wither and die at a king's whim. Imagine what a leap forward that must have felt like to a medieval populace. Quite literally, it assured that a king could no longer get away with murder. This protection, called *habeas corpus*, would in due time become one of America's treasured Constitutional rights (see Chapter 16).

> **DEFINITION**
>
> **Habeas corpus** is Latin for "You [shall] have the body." If given a writ of *habeas corpus,* a prison authority must bring the actual prisoner, the living body, forward so a court can decide if he is being legally held. If not, the court will release him.

The Glorious Revolution

Succeeding King Charles II, King James II assumed the throne in 1685. Supposedly, James was to rule with the help of England's legislative body, called Parliament, which took the lead in raising and spending money. But the new king, a particularly forceful ruler, decided that Parliament's supposed *assistance* was simply interference. He attempted to dispense with acts of Parliament, and he dismissed any judges who opposed him.

James was deposed in 1688, and those who toppled him called their move the Glorious Revolution. Parliament, asserting that James had tried to destroy "the laws and liberties of this kingdom," passed a Bill of Rights, which forced the king to seek the consent of the people's representatives in Parliament if he wanted to suspend any laws, levy taxes, or make royal appointments. He could not interfere in legal proceedings by establishing his own courts or acting as a judge. As you can see, some of its provisions resemble our own Bill of Rights, and this is no mere coincidence:

- "That it is the right of the subjects to petition the king."

- "That election of members of Parliament ought to be free."

- "That the freedom of speech and debates or proceedings in Parliament ought not to be impeached or questioned in any court or place out of Parliament."

- "That excessive bail ought not to be required, nor excessive fines imposed, nor cruel and unusual punishments inflicted."

- "That the raising or keeping a standing army within the kingdom in time of peace, unless it be with consent of Parliament, is against law."

- "That the subjects which are Protestants may have arms for their defence."

- "That levying money for … the use of the Crown by pretence of prerogative, without grant of Parliament … is illegal."

This Bill of Rights was revolutionary in its own right. Forever after, people would insist on the rights that were accorded them by this document. When colonists later protested that they were being taxed without representation and controlled by a standing army in time of peace, they were demanding rights that had been promised to all Englishmen a century before.

New rulers—Mary, daughter of King James, and her husband, William of Orange—did ascend to the throne of England, but not until the Bill of Rights was read to them and William said, "We thankfully accept what you have offered us."

After the enactment of the English Bill of Rights in 1689, power was divided between Parliament and King. Over time two political parties emerged in Parliament and, as political parties do, they squabbled. Trumpeting individual liberties, the *Whigs* viewed themselves as the upholders of the Glorious Revolution and pushed back against any hint of monarchical abuse. At times they would side with North America's colonists in their struggles with the king. The *Tories*, on the other hand, were all for stability and often sided with the king in the inevitable tug-of-war between king and Parliament.

DEFINITION

Whigs and **Tories** belonged to competing political camps during the late seventeenth and eighteenth centuries in England. The Whigs emphasized liberty and the Tories stressed stability. Both believed in a mixed monarchy, with the Crown and Parliament sharing power. In America, during the years leading up to the Revolutionary War, those who resisted British imperial authority called themselves Whigs, after the party in England, and they branded their opponents as Tories.

Philosophy Lessons: The European Enlightenment

In the eighteenth century, scientific discoveries demonstrated the power of evidence and proof. Throughout Europe, spellbound audiences attended demonstration lectures in experimental physics or the other sciences. Excluded from universities and scientific societies but eager to be part of this new movement, women often attended. Excitement was in the air.

All in all, enlightened people were less inclined to take matters on faith and instead looked at their world through the microscope of intellect and reason. Innovations in printing brought periodicals and books into wider circulation. More and more, people were gaining an education and could read. Technical dictionaries made an appearance, alongside massive encyclopedias. The 35 volumes of the French *Encyclopédie, ou Dictionnaire Raisonné des Sciences, des Arts et des Métiers* (in English, *Encyclopedia, or a Systematic Dictionary of the Sciences, Arts, and Crafts*) contained 71,818 articles and 3,129 illustrations.

In English coffee houses or debating societies, in the salons of famous women in France, and in American taverns where men raised glasses of hard cider, people talked and pondered and examined the issues of the day far into the night. One could say that in the colonies, far from a king who thought he ruled them, colonists were practicing democracy as they argued back and forth.

Enlightenment philosophers like John Locke in England, or Jean-Jacques Rousseau in France, proclaimed that people had natural rights, which included a say in their own governance. By the mid-eighteenth century these ideas had taken hold in America. Here are some of their "enlightened" beliefs:

- In what was then called a "state of nature," without any type of government or any established community, men (women were not at that time considered citizens) must protect themselves in a war of all against all.

- So they do not have to go it alone, men enter a social contract to join a political state. The state, like a neutral judge, will protect *everyone's* life, liberty, and property. In exchange, citizens will submit to laws. If they don't, they can be punished.

- This social contract can be changed when people petition a king or their legislators or declare their will in an election. People have powers.

- A king is bound by the contract. If he turns into a tyrant, refusing to cede to its regulations, rebellion is permitted.

It is easy to see why potential revolutionaries in America liked this philosophy, especially the *rebellion is permitted* part. Thomas Jefferson wrote, "Bacon, Locke, Newton … I consider them as the three greatest men that have ever lived, without any exception, and as having laid the foundation of those superstructures which have been raised in the physical and moral sciences." Jefferson wanted busts of these three men copied "on the same canvas, that they may not be confounded at all with the herd of other great men."

We're *All* Brits? Diversity from the Start

While the majority of the free colonists were of British descent, inspired by this history and philosophy, it goes without saying that native people inhabited North American lands before colonial peoples did. In Chapter 5 you will meet Dragging Canoe and White Eyes, and consider native struggles. You also will meet African slaves. Their history is the greatest incongruity in our founding story and our celebration of liberty.

Some colonists came from regions in the British Isles—Ireland, Wales, and Scotland—that had once resisted English rule or occupation, and in some cases still did. Ireland, in fact, was itself essentially a colony in the eighteenth century. If English people carried a proud history to America, these newcomers often carried old grievances. Other immigrants were German, Swiss, Dutch, and French. By their very numbers, they would exert influence—the Germans and Scots-Irish in Pennsylvania, where they outnumbered the English, and the Dutch in New York.

Yet even those who came from Germany, Ireland, or elsewhere voluntarily placed themselves within the British realm when they arrived in the British colonies. Injustices from the past would have to be laid aside. Immigrants could take their religions with them, and many did, such as Presbyterians, Puritans, Quakers, and Catholics. But they had to leave their old governments behind and go with the British one. That meant, at the very least, they needed to pledge their allegiance to the king. One man, or one woman, was their monarch. They would have to be okay with that.

BY THE NUMBERS

America was diverse even in Revolutionary times, as the following statistics illustrate:

- 481,000 enslaved blacks (20 percent of the overall population) lived in the 13 British colonies in 1774. This is an estimate, as the first official census was in 1790.

- 18,000 free blacks (1 percent of the population) lived in 13 colonies in 1774.

- 105,000 to 150,000 Indians (estimates vary) lived outside of white settlements but east of the Mississippi in 1768.

- In Pennsylvania, according to the first federal census in 1790, 38 percent of the people were of German descent, 7 percent Irish, and 15 percent Scots-Irish. People of English descent accounted for only 26 percent of the population. Most of the remainder were Welsh and Scottish.

- In the colonies combined, less than 60 percent of the free population was of English descent, with 16 percent Irish or Scots-Irish and 9 percent German.

Long Live the King!

Viewed from our twenty-first century perch, the relationship between British-American subjects (whether English or Irish, German, or Dutch) and their monarch may seem submissive, but at the time the king's subjects were convinced they received as much as they gave. They knew they had rights that protected them from tyrannical interference. They knew their monarch had to seek the consent of elected representatives. And they knew, too, that the king was duty-bound to protect his subjects. Not only did he have the power to do so, but he was *required* to do so. That was part of the deal.

While Native Americans and enslaved blacks stood on the sidelines, excluded and distrustful, for the rest, the bond between king and subject was mutually beneficial. They had entered into the social contract willingly. The power of the state, as exerted through *the Crown*, kept them from regressing into that violent state of nature, where only the strongest few would survive. "Allegiance is the tie … which binds the subject to the king, in return for that protection which the king affords the subject," wrote Sir William Blackstone in *Commentaries on the Laws of England*, which was used at the time as the definitive source on British law.

DEFINITION

The Crown refers to the property or power of the government embodied in a ruling monarch, not actually his personal power or property. Here's a simple example: A king might own a walking stick. It's his. The Crown owns the crown that will pass from king to king, not belonging to any one, but to the state. It's a term that was, and is, commonly used to describe the authority and power of the government of Britain.

Through the seventeenth and eighteenth centuries, the British Crown was called on to stand behind its colonists in North America. British colonials desired regions of land that were inhabited by Native Americans, worked by French fur trappers, or claimed by the French government. Britain and France were often at war during this period, and America served as one of the wartime theaters. Colonial militias might have done most of the fighting along the borderlands, but the power of the Crown stood behind them, which counted for a lot. If push came to shove, the King was the colonials' protector and could dispatch his army to help them out.

One such instance is worthy of special note.

George Washington's First War

"In a heavy rain, and in a night as dark as pitch, along a path scarce broad enough for one man," 22-year-old George Washington wrote in his diary, 40 militiamen from Virginia "were frequently tumbling one over another, and often so lost that 15 or 20 minutes search would not find the path again." This was Ohio country on the night of May 27, 1754, and Washington was leading his men to attack a French exploring party that his Indian allies had said was camped nearby.

Why this adventure? The Ohio Company of Virginia wanted to speculate on lands west of the Appalachian Mountains, but the French were already building forts there.

The previous year the company's surveyor, George Washington, had traveled west with a note to the French from the Governor of Virginia: cease and desist, the note said, to which the French responded, no way! So this time Washington came accompanied by a ragtag group of militiamen, whom Governor Robert Dinwiddie had placed under his charge. They were "loose, idle persons, that are quite destitute of house, and home," Washington groused, but these were the only recruits he could muster.

At dawn, Washington and his militiamen and their Indian allies surprised the French party and massacred all who could not escape. Accounts differed as to what actually happened. The French said their leader, the Sieur de Jumonville, unarmed and defenseless, was trying to read a prepared message to Washington when he was fired upon and killed. Governor Dinwiddie spun the official version: the Indians were responsible for the killings, while Washington and his men were just "auxiliaries." Washington himself was more forthright. He said his Indian allies "scalped the dead," but he himself took responsibility for the attack. He had given the order to fire, he admitted publicly, because he was convinced the French party was spying.

FOUNDER ID

George Washington (1732–1799). Virginia surveyor, planter, and land developer. Leader of Virginia forces, French and Indian War, 1754–1758. Delegate, House of Burgesses, 1758–1776. Delegate, Continental Congress, 1774–1775. Commander-in-Chief, Continental Army, 1775–1783. President, Constitutional Convention, 1787. President of the United States, 1789–1797.

Washington's father died when the boy was 11, and he was raised after that by his mother and his half-brother Lawrence, 14 years his senior. He received the formal equivalent of only a grade school education. At age 16 he learned surveying, and in his excursions into the woods, he mixed with backcountry types and picked up real-life survival skills. On his first trip out, he slept under "one thread bare blanket with double its weight of vermin such as lice fleas." Here were life's lessons, delivered far from civilized classrooms and of great value to a young man who soon would be a soldier. When George was 20 Lawrence died, leaving his half-brother a plantation at Mount Vernon and a rank in the colonial militia. At this stage in his life, military adventure had more appeal than staying at home to farm, and he accepted the task of challenging the French in the West. Perhaps he sought glory or honor, or perhaps he was simply doing his duty to King and country. In any case, Washington was not yet prompted by notions of home rule or republican virtue, which would come into play at a later date. (More information can be found in Chapter 15.)

In the aftermath of the attack at Jumonville Glen, as the place of the massacre came to be called, Jumonville's brother led French troops to seek revenge against the Virginians. Washington and his men erected a makeshift fort to defend themselves, but they were defeated at "Fort Necessity." The government in London ordered the king's troops to come to the aid of the besieged colony. The shots fired by Washington's men in the Ohio Valley, a preemptive strike, provoked a war that would spread throughout the colonies. Here it was called the French and Indian War, and in Europe, the Seven Years War. By either name, it was war indeed.

Twenty-two years before the United States of America declared its independence, events were set in motion. One episode would follow upon another in an almost predictable fashion. An astute observer in 1754 might have guessed the outcome. "Britain will win the war, but it will cost a great deal, and she will not want to bear the entire burden," he or she might say. "Britain will tax her colonies to cover the cost of an expanded empire, but the colonies will resist." Such an observer might correctly guess that one war would lead directly to another, that there was a revolution in the making.

But not even a soothsayer could have prophesized that ordinary citizens acting in concert—*We, the People*—would go on to forge a new nation that would endure for centuries, with no monarch at all.

The Least You Need to Know

- English citizens asserted their rights through the Magna Carta, the Glorious Revolution, and the English Bill of Rights.
- According to Enlightenment philosophy, governments are established through "social contracts," and if any government violates its contract, it can be overthrown.
- Except for Native Americans and enslaved blacks, all colonial Americans offered allegiance to the British monarch, even though they had political, religious, economic, and geographic differences.
- Whether New Englanders or Virginians, rich or poor, Quaker or Episcopalian, Tory or Whig, slave or Indian, a war would affect all.
- George Washington drew first blood in the French and Indian War, which triggered events that would lead to the American Revolution.

Resist Authority— But How?

In This Chapter

- Smugglers, the first American patriots
- The Stamp Tax, and how protestors made it go away
- Townshend Duties and the nonimportation movement
- The Boston Massacre and the Boston Tea Party
- Power to the people, eighteenth-century style

Colonists enjoyed liberties and protections granted to them under a British constitution that was the envy of many. But they did face abuses, often at the hands of royal governors, who were appointed by their monarch and given sweeping powers. According to the 1612 "Laws Divine, Morall and Martiall" for the Virginia Company, for instance, anyone who caught a sturgeon was to "bring unto the Governour" all the fish's caviar "upon perill for the first time offending herein, of losing his eares."

A century and a half later, increasingly proud and self-reliant colonists might defy such an order. By then, living so far from England's shores, they were well versed in local self-governance. But how far would they take defiance and self-reliance? Would they petition? Boycott British goods? Disobey laws? Destroy property? Take lives? Go to war? Declare independence?

Yes, they would do all of these things. This chapter follows the increasingly insubordinate colonists from the early 1760s, when the war that George Washington started was winding down, to the Boston Tea Party in 1773, when resistance reached a fever pitch.

Smugglers: The First American Patriots

As the French and Indian War wound down, the British government realized it would be very expensive to defend and administer the vast addition to its empire. In response, it acted on two fronts. With the Royal Proclamation of 1763, King George III prohibited any white settlement in the newly acquired territory west of the Appalachian Mountains. There, Indians who had been allies of the French were still resisting white advancement. Because defense of the area was too costly, the Crown decided to simply place these lands off-limits in spite of the fact that some white British-Americans hoped to live there or profit from land speculation. (George Washington, for example, was promised 28,000 acres in Ohio country for his service in the French and Indian War, but that would do him no good until the ban on settlement was lifted.)

Simultaneously, Parliament tried to get Americans to shoulder some of the burden. This should have been easy enough, just collect the taxes that were already on the books on imported items, in particular molasses. Over time, however, colonial importers had learned how to bribe customs inspectors and avoid paying what was legally due. Now, the government gave those inspectors increased power, arming them with blanket search warrants called Writs of Assistance. Customs officials could search anywhere they pleased at any time for any type of good, even if there were no particular cause for suspicion.

BY THE NUMBERS

In 1770 the colonies produced 4,807,000 gallons of rum, drinking 3,871,000 gallons and exporting the rest. Boston was the major producer with 36 rum distilleries, far more than any other city. However, making rum required molasses, which was mostly smuggled from the French West Indies. Producing and drinking rum would get more costly if the tax on molasses, passed back in 1733, was indeed collected.

"Not so fast," said Boston's merchant-smugglers, our first patriotic resistors. Refusing to comply with the customs crackdown, 63 Boston-area merchants took the matter to court, claiming the searches violated the British Constitution. They hired James Otis, Jr., a fiery lawyer, to represent them, and Otis did their bidding in grand style. On a cold winter day in the third week in February 1761, Otis faced officious judges in their ceremonial garb and delivered an eloquent tirade against the blanket searches. Otis lost the case, but his argument resounded across the land. John Adams, a young attorney with a front-row seat for the trial, jotted in his notes the essence of

Otis's revolutionary speech: "As to acts of Parliament. An act against the Constitution is void. An act against natural equity is void. The executive courts must pass such acts into disuse."

But if the courts failed to "void" a law, could the people themselves do so? That would be the next step, a huge one.

FOUNDER ID

James Otis (1725–1783). Deputy Advocate General for the Vice Admiral Court, 1757–1760. Pleaded Writs of Assistance case, 1761. Massachusetts House of Representatives, 1761–1768, 1771. Stamp Act Congress, 1765. Author, *The Rights of the British Colonies Asserted and Proved* (1764) and *A Vindication of the British Colonies* (1765).

A Mayflower descendent, James Otis had the perfect patriot pedigree. When the time came, he went to Harvard, where he seemed more interested in parties than in classes. Then, upon hearing evangelist George Whitefield preach, life suddenly acquired profound meaning, and so did his studies. He quickly passed the bar. After his celebrated Writs of Assistance case, Otis was elected to the Massachusetts Assembly, where he espoused patriotic principles. But the stances he took were inconsistent, saying with one breath that acts of Parliament could be voided and with the next that Parliament must be obeyed. In the late 1760s his mental state faltered. Prone to manic episodes, he engaged a customs commissioner in a widely publicized fight and was badly battered. In 1769 John Adams wrote, "He has been, this afternoon, raving mad." Although he dabbled in politics after that, his effectiveness was greatly diminished. Some 14 years later, Otis was struck by lightning, his death as eerily intense as was his life.

The Stamp Act Riots

At dawn on Wednesday, August 14, a man identified by the initials "A. O." dangled from a limb of a majestic elm tree on the outskirts of Boston, along the main road to town. Attached to his breast was a short poem: "A goodlier sight who e'er did see? / A Stamp-Man hanging on a tree!" Here was Andrew Oliver, who had just been appointed Distributor of Stamps. Lucky for "A.O.," this hanged man was made of straw.

In November 1765, according to the Stamp Act recently passed by Parliament, government-issued stamps were to be issued, sold, and applied to "every skin or piece of vellum or parchment, or sheet or piece of paper" that passed into common use. This measure, which reached deep into everyday life and thereby riled up nearly every colonist, has to rank as one of the greatest political blunders ever. The tax would apply to anyone who surveyed land, acquired a deed, made a will, received an inheritance, collected a debt, posted bail, read a newspaper, consulted an almanac, or played cards.

At the hanging tree in Boston, organizers staged a great piece of street theater to bring this point home. As farmers bearing produce to market passed by, each in turn submitted to a mock stamping of his goods by the effigy. Continuing into town, these farmers spread the news, and soon all of Boston was abuzz.

By afternoon several thousand people had gathered at the spot. "So much were they affected with a Sense of Liberty, that scarce any could attend to the Task of Day-labour, but all seemed on the Wing of Freedom," the *Boston Post-Boy* reported. Late in the afternoon, the throngs paraded past the State House, where the Governor and his Council were huddled. Bearing the effigy, they chanted "Liberty and Property! No stamps!" That was only the beginning of the evening's events. By the end, the crowd had pulled down a building erected by Andrew Oliver, beheaded the effigy before his home, and broken into the house looking for Oliver, who of course had fled.

This demonstration produced results. Governor Bernard retreated to Castle William, an island in Boston harbor, where the crowd couldn't reach him, and Andrew Oliver announced he would resign.

Twelve days later, on August 26, ax-wielding laborers and seamen attacked the home of Thomas Hutchinson, the lieutenant governor and the chief justice of Massachusetts. They arrived at his home during the dinner hour, smashed in the front door, and drove the terrified family out. Then they ransacked the house, even tearing down interior walls and carrying valuables away.

They got into Hutchinson's personal papers, and historians now suspect they were looking for documents that incriminated smugglers. But their anger extended beyond that. Hutchinson, who once praised poverty for producing "industry and frugality" among the poor, was not very popular with the lower classes, and these angry fellows, emboldened by the events of August 14, were taking protest to the next level. A contemporary of the rioters wrote, "Gentlemen of the army, who have seen towns sacked by the enemy, declared they never before saw an instance of such fury." While patriot leaders condoned the "hanging" of Andrew Oliver and related protest events on August 14, and some had even helped plan it, they condemned the destruction of Hutchinson's home. There were limits to protest, they insisted, although commoners did not always heed their words. The decision of how far to go was made group-by-group, household-by-household, and individual-by-individual. What was the right thing to do? What was out-of-bounds?

Most colonists deemed the first riot acceptable, the later one not. From New Hampshire to South Carolina people staged theatrical demonstrations similar to the August 14 event in Boston, and fearful stamp distributors in 13 colonies either agreed to resign or abandoned office. In the end, Parliament repealed the Stamp Act.

To celebrate their newfound powers, patriot activists affixed a copper plaque bearing the golden letters "TREE OF LIBERTY" to the elm tree where "A.O." had been hanged. Soon patriots in dozens of other towns christened their own "liberty trees" or erected "liberty poles," giant flagstaffs that were often simply trees stripped of their limbs. Officials might meet in dignified assembly rooms or "in-chambers," to use the terms of the times, but common people, meeting "out-of-doors," claimed the territory surrounding liberty trees or liberty poles as their designated quarters. Like their counterparts in-chambers, *the body of the people* could influence Parliament and the Crown. The people were inspired.

DEFINITION

Calling themselves **the body of the people,** Revolutionary Era Americans gathered in large numbers to protest British policies and organize resistance measures. In Boston, the body of the people met at Faneuil Hall, or when the crowd was too large, Old South Meeting House. In Philadelphia, the body gathered in the open area outside the State House. In New York, people met on the Commons. In Charleston, South Carolina, it was a huge live oak–their liberty tree—in Isaac Mazyck's pasture. Everywhere, the body superceded governmental functions. Whereas only men of property could vote, the body of the people did not exclude anybody. Often, the body determined the agenda, driving so-called leaders to take more radical actions.

Rebuffing the Townshend Duties

In 1767, not long after repealing the Stamp Act, Parliament came back with a new round of taxation. Known by the name of its primary promoter, Chancellor of the Exchequer Charles Townshend, the Townshend Act levied new duties on imported paper, paint, glass, lead, and tea. But colonists had a plan for dealing with this. If nobody purchased the taxed items, they reasoned, Parliament would raise no money and the taxes would prove useless. So in all the major ports, merchants entered into *"nonimportation agreements,"* pledging not to import British goods. Consumers, for their part, vowed not to buy goods from any merchants who violated the nonimportation agreements.

Seeing the opportunity for an increase in local manufacturing, skilled craftsmen and laborers welcomed these moves. So did George Washington, who observed that the boycott would give indebted planters like himself "a pretext to live within bounds." So too did women, who were often denied political expression but could and did participate this time. Fine ladies denied themselves London's gloves and gowns. Common women gave up British cloth and wove their own by hand. "The industry and frugality of American ladies must exalt their character in the eyes of the world and serve to show how greatly they are contributing to bring about the political salvation of a whole continent," wrote a contributor to the *Boston Evening Post*.

DEFINITION

Nonimportation agreements, when signed by merchants to protest taxation without representation, were pledges not to import certain goods from Britain. Consumers, meanwhile, refused to buy British goods or even buy anything from those who sold such goods, a program they called **nonconsumption.** Starting in 1775, most free Americans refused to send key items to Britain, a practice they called **nonexportation.** Today, such actions are called **boycotts,** but eighteenth-century colonials had a very good reason for not using this term: it did not enter the English language until 1880, more than a century later, when tenant farmers in Ireland, to protest high rents, refused to do any business with Charles Boycott, the estate agent for the landlord.

Enforcement, Soft and Hard

But what about those who refused to get with the program, merchants who continued to import and consumers who purchased their goods?

In tight-knit colonial communities, where everybody knew everybody else, shame forced folks who didn't want to participate in boycotts to do so. In Lancaster, Pennsylvania, advocates of *nonimportation* pledged "never to have any fellowship or correspondence" with an importer or consumer of imported goods and to "publish his or their names to the world as a lasting monument to infamy." In the major cities and many towns, the body of the people would meet to determine who was obeying and what to do about those who were not.

If holdouts resisted public pressure, they were threatened with retaliation. In July 1769, the erection of a scaffold finally convinced Thomas Richardson, a New York jeweler, to comply with nonimportation. In Boston the "Signs, Doors and Windows" of those who were known to import British goods "were daub'd over in the Night time with every kind of Filth." Nonimportation, originally touted as a nonviolent alternative to rioting, and still offering that option, came to embrace mob actions, too. A few defiant characters were tarred and feathered; more, however, gave in at the mere sight of a steaming bucket of tar.

THEIR OWN WORDS

What, exactly, was tarring and feathering? Here is one "recipe" from those times: "First, strip a person naked, then heat the tar until it is thin & pour it upon the naked flesh, or rub it over with a tar brush. After which, sprinkle decently upon the tar, while it is yet warm, as many feathers as will stick to it. Then hold a lighted candle to the feather, & try to set it all on Fire."

Washington's Last Resort

And if nonimportation didn't work? What then?

Enter George Washington, making his public debut as an American patriot. Washington had sat out the Stamp Act protests and would later sit out the Tea Crisis, but he played a role when the Townshend duties appeared.

Back in 1758, when he returned home from the French and Indian War, Washington ran for a seat in Virginia's Assembly, called the House of Burgesses. Once elected, he was expected to represent his constituents' interests, dole out patronage, and help Virginia govern itself in all local matters; in return for his services, he would earn respect, deference, and some degree of power. He certainly did not expect to engage in heated disputes with the British Parliament.

BY THE NUMBERS

In colonial days, before revolutionary unrest, candidates were expected to throw parties for the voters. Here's what George Washington supplied to the 301 voters who sent him to his first term in the House of Burgesses in 1758: 33 gallons of beer, 28½ gallons of wine, 40 gallons of "rum punch," and "1 hogshead & 1 barrel of punch, consisting of 26 gals. Best Barbados rum and 12 lbs refd sugar." A decade later, political life was taken more seriously.

But by 1769, Washington had come to resent British interference with his western land schemes and British trade policies, including taxation without representation. With his neighbor George Mason, he drafted a nonimportation agreement, which he then presented before the House of Burgesses. When the royal governor got wind of this, he dissolved the Burgesses, but Washington and the other representatives just moved down the street to the Raleigh Tavern and continued with their business.

For Washington, economic warfare was the last peaceful option; after that, he believed, the colonial Americans might have to resort to force to get their way. "That no man shou'd scruple, or hesitate a moment to use a—ms [arms] in defence of so valuable a blessing, on which all the good and evil of life depends, is clearly my opinion," he asserted, "yet a—ms I wou'd beg leave to add, should be the last resource, the denier resort."

A Snowball in Hell: The Boston Massacre

Economic warfare caused the British government to back off, at least for a while. In London on March 5, 1770, Parliament repealed the Townshend duties on all items except tea.

But that very same day, across the Atlantic in Boston, a crowd composed largely of rowdy apprentices taunted Redcoat soldiers by throwing frozen snowballs and chunks of ice. One soldier broke discipline and fired into the crowd, and other shots followed. When smoke from the muskets cleared, five men had been killed or mortally wounded—a rope maker, a leather worker, an apprentice ivory turner, and two sailors, including Crispus Attucks, who was part Indian and possibly part black. Another six had received serious wounds.

The next day at Faneuil Hall, where the city's public business transpired, the body of the people gathered. The meeting sent an ultimatum to Acting Governor Thomas Hutchinson: the two British regiments occupying Boston must leave. Hutchinson passed the decision off to the military officer in charge of the troops, William Dalrymple, who agreed to remove one regiment. But this was not good enough for the body of the people, who had moved to the larger hall at Old South Meeting House. The compromise solution was rejected by a vote of 4,000 to 1.

Samuel Adams chaired a committee that responded to Hutchinson and Dalrymple. On behalf of the people gathered at Old South, Adams told Dalrymple "that if he could remove the 29th regiment, he could remove the 14th also, and it was at his peril to refuse it." In the end Hutchinson, his governing Council, and Dalrymple capitulated. Samuel Adams is sometimes credited with having effected the bargain, and he did play his part, but the most powerful men in Massachusetts did not back down because of his say-so. They relented because the body of the people, 4,000 angry souls, could have turned Boston upside down if the soldiers were not withdrawn.

FOUNDER ID

Samuel Adams (1722–1803). Boston tax collector, 1756–1765. Clerk, Massachusetts House of Representatives, 1766–1774. Continental Congress, 1774–1781. President, Massachusetts Senate, 1782–1785, 1787–1788. Massachusetts Ratification Convention, 1788. Massachusetts Lieutenant Governor, 1789–1793. Massachusetts Governor, 1793–1797. Signed the Declaration of Independence and helped draft the Articles of Confederation and Massachusetts Constitution.

Samuel Adams (please, not just "Sam") was dedicated, persuasive, and a savvy politician. Publishing pamphlets and letters in the press, active in Boston town meetings, the Massachusetts Assembly, and committees of all kinds, he seemed to be everywhere at once. His Tory adversaries, fearful of his effectiveness and misconstruing popular protest, believed that rebellious commoners were merely his puppets, but Adams was not the flame-throwing radical they conjured up and we have mythologized. He promoted "piety and virtue," abhorred mob violence, and honored the "compact with our King" before finally pushing for independence. In the Massachusetts Constitution, which he helped write, he supported property qualifications for voters and state-sponsored religion. During the post-war rebellion in Massachusetts (see Chapter 9), he wanted to suspend writs of habeas corpus and hang the rebels. Although he had opposed distant authority with great verve, he did not believe people who enjoyed a representative government had the right to rebel. After independence, serving in Congress and the highest state offices, he worked within the governmental system and resisted all moves against it.

Tossing Tea

After a decade of tussles, things came to a head in the strangest of ways. The climax started on the other side of the globe when the giant East India Company overextended itself with its colonies in India. Soon thereafter, a speculative bubble burst in Europe, and the company found itself deep in the red, and with 18 million pounds of surplus tea. Because Britain considered the company too important to its economy to fail, Parliament offered it a corporate tax break so it could undersell American smugglers and dump some of its surplus on the American market. No new taxes were levied in America, nor were any taxes raised.

Boston merchants, who were smuggling Dutch tea, realized they would be undercut. They gained the support of rank-and-file patriots, who still had issues with British tea since it was the last item being taxed under the Townshend Act.

The story of the Boston Tea Party, a name bestowed more than half a century later, is well known. On the night of December 16, 1773, several dozen men, thinly disguised as Mohawk Indians, chopped open the chests of tea stored in the hulls of three ships and dumped the contents into the Boston Harbor. Less celebrated, but equally important, is the buildup to that event. For almost three weeks, starting with the arrival of the first of the vessels, the body of the people—several thousand strong—held repeated meetings in Old South, showing their displeasure and debating the appropriate response. On the day of the event, the crowd overflowing Old South was estimated at 7,000. Through popular resistance, common people sanctioned the most consequential act of political vandalism in American history. And Boston was not the only scene of popular protest. Tea shipped to New York and Philadelphia was sent back to London before political vandals could get to it, and the following year shipments of tea to Annapolis, Maryland, and Charleston, South Carolina, were destroyed.

From protesting Writs of Assistance to hanging Stamp Tax collectors in effigy to boycotting British goods to intimidating local Tories to hurling snowballs at Redcoats, colonials had taken concrete actions to register their resistance. They had also written their share of petitions and passed resolutions without end, but words alone did little to affect British policies. It was actions that mattered.

This last action, the destruction of property belonging to the most powerful corporation in the British Empire, drove the point home. When King George III and Parliament heard the news, all hell broke loose. Pay for the damage or else, they proclaimed. But nobody paid, so the "or else" clause took effect. Parliament's so-called punishments for the destruction of tea escalated the conflict to a point of no return.

The Least You Need to Know

- In debt from the French and Indian War, and facing new expenses from an expanded empire, Parliament imposed various taxes on their North American colonies.
- Dramatic resistance and the nonimportation agreements caused the repeal of the Stamp Tax and all Townshend Duties, except that on tea.
- Protests ranged from gentle (vowing not to import or consume British imports) to rough (physical intimidation).
- Without massive popular resistance by "the body of the people," there would have been no Revolution.
- In 1773, the destruction of tea in Boston led Parliament to pass repressive measures, opening a new chapter in the resistance movement.

Shall We Go It Alone?

In This Chapter

- The Coercive Acts
- The Massachusetts Revolution of 1774
- The First Continental Congress
- Preparations for a showdown
- The British counter-revolution at Lexington and Concord

The Boston Tea Party excited many patriots, but not George Washington or Benjamin Franklin. Washington chided Bostonians for "their conduct in destroying tea," and Franklin argued the East India Company should be compensated for the ruined merchandise. Opinion was divided, and the event did nothing to unify the populace.

What pulled Americans together were the punishments administered several months later through a series of laws dubbed the *Coercive Acts.* Parliament closed the port of Boston. Beyond that, it unilaterally revised the Massachusetts Charter, denying not only Bostonians but citizens throughout the colony the rights they had enjoyed for a century and a half. The goal of the Coercive Acts was to isolate radicals in Massachusetts, but instead 12 colonies formed a Continental Congress and agreed to mount a general boycott of British goods.

Meanwhile, people throughout the Massachusetts countryside took matters into their own hands and overthrew British rule—more than half a year *before* the dramatic events at Lexington and Concord. Then, 21 months to the day before Congress declared independence from Great Britain, the town meeting of Worcester, Massachusetts, proclaimed that it was time to form a new government.

This chapter tells the story of the critical 16 months between the Boston Tea Party and the outbreak of war, when American colonists turned from resistance to revolution.

The First American Revolution

Back in London, Parliament responded quickly and decisively to the destruction of East India Company tea. Members of Parliament who were sympathetic to America's plight were no match for hardliners, who urged a crackdown on Boston and all of Massachusetts. With little debate, Parliament closed the port of Boston. Only after Bostonians had paid in full for the tea would they be allowed to resume commerce, the lifeblood of their city.

People from all across the colonies came to the aid of Bostonians, most history books tell us, and this act of solidarity somehow led to the outbreak of war the following year. But that's not how revolutions generally start, and it's not how this one did.

The most punitive of the four *Coercive Acts* was not the *Boston Port Act* but the *Massachusetts Government Act*, which revoked key provisions of the Massachusetts Charter, the colony's working constitution. For generations, people in Massachusetts had been coming together freely in their town meetings, where they discussed anything they wished. Now, meetings could be held only once a year and only after the agenda had been approved by the Governor. Formerly, the people's representatives had chosen the powerful Council members and exercised the power to approve or deny all lesser officials. Now, the Crown and Royal Governor filled all offices, top to bottom. The people had been disenfranchised.

Imagine how you would feel if the U.S. Constitution, with its provisions for free elections and guarantees against government abuse, was suddenly declared null and void. You'd rebel in a moment, and so did the people of Massachusetts in the late summer and early fall of 1774.

DEFINITION

The **Coercive Acts** were passed by Parliament to punish colonials for the Boston Tea Party. Americans called them **the Intolerable Acts.** The **Boston Port Act** closed the port of Boston. The **Massachusetts Government Act** revamped the Massachusetts Charter, shut down town meetings, and filled formerly elected offices with royal appointees. Other acts allowed for the quartering of soldiers and the movement of trials to Britain. A fifth measure passed at the same time, the Quebec Act, was not intended to punish Boston or Massachusetts, but it angered colonists by transferring jurisdiction of the trans-Appalachian West to Quebec, while simultaneously recognizing the Catholic Church.

My Constitution Revoked? No Way!

All across Massachusetts, people defied the Massachusetts Government Act. In direct violation of the new law, they held town meetings whenever they wanted, and if that led to arrest, the people only became more bold. When Governor Thomas Gage jailed seven men in Salem for calling a town meeting, 3,000 farmers immediately gathered to free the prisoners. Two companies of British soldiers, on duty to protect the Governor, retreated rather than force a bloody confrontation.

Meetings convened in some 300 towns, and there was no way to stop them. "Not-withstanding all the parade the governor made at Salem on account of their meeting, they had another one directly under his nose at Danvers [a neighboring town], and continued it two or three howers longer than was necessary, to see if he would inter-rupt 'em," one man reported. "He was acquainted with it, but reply'd—'Damn 'em! I won't do any thing about it unless his Majesty sends me more troops.'"

In Cambridge, 4,000 patriots forced the lieutenant-governor of Massachusetts to resign his seat on the Council. When crowds intimidated the other Crown-appointed members of the Council, most resigned their seats and the rest fled to Boston, where they sought protection from the British Army. Boston itself became a garrison town commanded by the Redcoats, but in other towns across the countryside, where 95 percent of the population resided, patriots reigned supreme.

In every shiretown, as a county seat was called, patriot militiamen terminated the quarterly session of the courts. At Springfield, more than 3,000 patriots marched "with staves and musick" to unseat the officials. "Amidst the Crowd in a sandy, sultry place, exposed to the sun," said one observer, judges renounced their posts. In Plymouth, some 4,000 rebels celebrated the unseating of officials by trying to move Plymouth Rock from the shoreline up to the courthouse. They failed. Plymouth Rock proved more difficult to displace than Crown-appointed judges.

Committees of Correspondence

Town meetings convening in 300 towns, 4,000 patriots gathering in one place and then another, courts closing and officials resigning—we are looking at organized, concerted actions by rural people who lived distant from one another. There were no Revolutionary governing bodies at this point, but there *was* a communications network, called the Committees of Correspondence. Without it, such large-scale rebellion could never have succeeded.

The Committees included daring schemers and organizers who met in almost every township to hash out plans and make necessary arrangements. Riders spread news and carried warnings from place to place. Representatives from one town met with those in others, and before long, in more deliberate fashion, all came together at County Conventions. These were not yet governing bodies, but they practiced self-governance. And they planned an overthrow of British authority that rocked the province and started the Revolution.

A Day to Remember in Worcester

On a hot summer day in September 1774, more than seven months before the showdown at Lexington and Concord, militiamen from across the county of Worcester marched into the town of Worcester and gathered on the common. By ten o'clock, as the day grew hotter, 4,622 men from 37 different towns stood at the ready. (We know the numbers because Breck Parkman, one of the participants, counted the men in each militia company.) Approximately half the adult male population of a county that ranged from the Connecticut to the New Hampshire borders had mustered in force to topple British rule at the local level.

When two dozen Crown-appointed court officials showed up to work, they found the courthouse doors had been barricaded. They huddled instead in Daniel Heywood's tavern, halfway between the courthouse and the green. There they waited, knowing they were ridiculously outnumbered and waiting for the throngs to determine their fates.

Across from the courthouse, at the home of blacksmith Timothy Bigelow, the Worcester County Committees of Correspondence tried to coordinate the day's activities, but they soon adjourned "to attend the body of the people" outside. Each of the 37 militia companies had recently elected a new military captain, and now each selected a political representative as well. These men appointed a smaller committee, which visited the court officials to work out the details of their resignations. But the plan they settled on had to make its way back to the 37 representatives, and through them to the "body of the people," who nixed the first draft. The process then began anew. The apparatus was democratic but cumbersome, heavily weighted at the bottom. Things moved slowly. People became impatient.

Finally, by midafternoon, the stage was set. In full company formation, the militiamen lined both sides of Main Street from Heywood's tavern to the courthouse, while the 25 officials, hats in hand, walked the gauntlet between the rows, each one reciting his renunciation more than 30 times so that all the patriots could hear. With this ritualistic act of submission, all British authority disappeared forever from Worcester County, as it did in all of Massachusetts outside of Boston, where British soldiers remained garrisoned. "Government has now devolved upon the people," one despondent Tory grumbled in his diary, "and they seem to be for using it."

The Continental Congress

Would other colonies support the rebellion, or would Massachusetts have to stand alone?

That decision fell into the hands of 50-odd delegates from 12 of the British colonies in British North America, who attended in varying numbers a convention in Philadelphia. The inter-colonial network of Committees of Correspondence and colonial assemblies that organized this gathering also had sent invitations to Quebec, Nova Scotia, St. John's Island, Georgia, East Florida, and West Florida, all of which declined. Still, the vast majority of British colonials in America had representatives in what we call today the First Continental Congress.

"All America waited in anxious hope and expectation the decisions of a continental congress," wrote Mercy Otis Warren in her *History of the Rise, Progress and Termination of the American Revolution*, one of the few early histories authored by actual revolutionaries of the times. One Connecticut politician wrote, "Our whole dependence is in the wisdom, prudence and determination of the Congress, the highest and most respectable Council that ever was (and perhaps ever will be) in America."

Originally, delegates were to meet in Philadelphia's State House, seat of the colonial government and meeting place of the colonial assembly, which opposed the Congress. But how could they resist British authority while gathering in its very home? Instead, they convened in Carpenters' Hall, built recently by and for the city's artisans. There, delegates were literally and physically supported by ordinary men: each chair in the hall had been individually crafted by a Philadelphia artisan.

Taking Sides

At the outset, delegates fell into three groups. Some cautioned moderation. Joseph Galloway of Pennsylvania, for example, wanted to create a new legislative body in America, a "Grand Council" of representatives from the various colonies. The British Parliament would need approval from this body before passing laws or taxes that affected Americans. The plan proposed a working partnership between England and America, not defiance and rebellion.

Others were more rebellious. Leading the radical charge, in addition to Samuel Adams and John Adams of Massachusetts, were Christopher Gadsden of South Carolina and Richard Henry Lee and Patrick Henry of Virginia. We think of Boston's leaders as being the most radical, but in comparison to Virginians like Lee and Henry, Pennsylvania's Joseph Reed wrote, "the Bostonians are mere milksops." And Silas Deane, another delegate, said, "Mr. Gadsden leaves all N England Sons of Liberty far behind, for he is for taking up his firelock, & marching direct to Boston [where British troops were garrisoned]. He affirmed this morning, that were his wife and all his children in Boston, & they were there to perish by the sword, it would not alter his sentiment or proceeding, for American Liberty."

FOUNDER ID

Christopher Gadsden (1724–1805). South Carolina Commons House of Assembly, 1757–1776. Stamp Act Congress, 1765. Continental Congress, 1774–1776. South Carolina Provincial Congress, 1776. Commander, First Carolina Regiment, 1776. Brigadier General, Continental Army, 1776. South Carolina House of Representatives (1776–1783), Vice President (1777–1778), and Lieutenant-Governor (1778–1780), and Ratification Convention (1788).

Gadsden cut his patriotic teeth by opposing British control over Indian policy in the early 1760s. The British were being too soft, he said. Gadsden claimed that colonials should be running the show and fighting the Indians as they pleased. "The only way to fight a Cherokee War is to destroy as many of these people as we can & when an opportunity offers to miss it by no means," he said. After that, he became a vigorous opponent of all imperial policies. When the South Carolina Royal Governor tried to keep him from taking his seat in the Assembly, he fought back and won, forcing the governor to be recalled. In 1765, he wrote a newspaper column under the Latin head, "Aut Mors Aut Libertas," meaning "either death or liberty." Ten years later, he designed the "Gadsden flag," a timber rattlesnake with the words, "DON'T TREAD ON ME." Gadsden never ceded to British authority in any way, shape, or form. He opposed the surrender of Charleston in 1780. He was imprisoned after it fell, and he suffered in solitary confinement rather than accept British parole.

The majority of delegates stood somewhere between these outspoken radicals and the moderates. They favored cautious resistance, whatever that meant. How far should they go?

The decision was more or less made for them. At two in the afternoon on September 6, the second day of proceedings, they received alarming "news" that Boston had been bombarded by British artillery, and six patriots killed. Two days later, Congress learned the rumor was false, but in the interim, the imaginary calamity united the delegates against British rule as never before. (It had also united the people in Massachusetts. Upon hearing the rumor of the assault on Boston, tens of thousands of men and teenage boys marched toward the city, ready to take on the British Regulars.)

Ten days after that, Paul Revere arrived in town with a fresh dispatch from Boston and a copy of the Suffolk Resolves, which justified the rebellion that had enveloped Massachusetts. Drafted by Joseph Warren and educated patriots from Boston, this document differed little in content from resolutions in other Massachusetts counties, but it was better crafted, and this undoubtedly impressed the learned delegates to Congress. Ironically, Suffolk County, which included Boston and its garrison of 3,000 British troops, was the only county in mainland Massachusetts that did *not* overthrow British rule in 1774.

On September 17, Congress endorsed the Suffolk Resolves. The vote was unanimous because no one could risk being branded a traitor to the cause, not even Joseph Galloway, the advocate for colonial-British power sharing. "This was one of the happiest days of my life," John Adams wrote in his diary. "In Congress we had generous, noble sentiments, and manly eloquence. This day convinced me that America will support the Massachusetts or perish with her."

The Continental Association

The greatest achievement of the First Continental Congress was not its aggressive, rhetorical petitioning of the King, featured in many history books. Of more significance was the decision to escalate economic warfare. By implementing, and enforcing, a sweeping nonimportation, nonconsumption, and nonexportation agreement for all the colonies, delegates intended to cripple British trade and cause Parliament, King George III, and the royal ministers to rescind their latest, most offensive measures. This "Continental Association," as it was called, became the voice, and force, of Revolutionary America. The key lay in its implementation, outlined in section eleven:

> That a committee be chosen in every county, city, and town, by those who are qualified to vote for representatives in the legislature, whose business it shall be attentively to observe the conduct of all personals touching this association; and when it shall be made to appear, to the satisfaction of a majority of any such committee, that any person … has violated this association, that such majority do forthwith cause the truth of the case to be published in the gazette; to the end, that all such foes to the rights of British-America may be publicly known, and universally contemned as the enemies of American liberty; and thenceforth we respectively will break off all dealings with him or her.

With this provision, Congress created a new level of quasi-official authority. Each local enforcement committee, called a Committee of Safety or Committee of Inspection, quickly assumed legislative, police, and judicial powers in all matters pertaining to political conduct. And in those days, nearly everything *did* pertain to politics, not only what people said, but what they bought or sold, produced, or consumed. Using the potent weapon of social and commercial ostracism, the committees for each city, town, or village enforced standards of proper revolutionary behavior. These committees functioned as crude local governments, formed in direct opposition to British law. However, they dispensed with such rights of the accused as trial by jury, a concept central to British heritage.

Preparing to Fight

Back in Worcester, the people who had toppled British authority on September 6 braced for a counterattack, which they knew would come sooner or later. The British Crown was not likely to give up Massachusetts without a fight. A county convention of the Committees of Correspondence, meeting on September 21, asked each township to arm for war and enlist one third of its men between the ages of 16 and 60 "to be ready to act at a minute's warning." That's when the Minutemen were born. The convention also recommended that each militia company elect its own officers, who would then choose field officers for their regiments. This was to be a thoroughly democratic army of citizens, from bottom to top.

The Worcester Committees of Correspondence also took the lead in civilian affairs. When patriots cast off British rule throughout Massachusetts, they'd created a vacuum. No one had authority, and that was worrisome. To remedy the situation, the Worcester Committees of Correspondence called for a special Provincial Congress of representatives from all towns in the colony. The Congress would coordinate the rebellion and determine the colony's future actions. Even then, the patriots of Worcester were not done, and their next act was amazing. On October 4, 1774, the town meeting issued instructions to Timothy Bigelow, its representative to the coming Provincial Congress. It was time, the local citizens said, for the people of Massachusetts to form a new government of their own, no matter what the British might say. This is the first recorded declaration of independence by a public body—exactly 21 months *before* the more famous Declaration of Independence.

FOUNDER ID

Timothy Bigelow, (1739–1790). Hogreave, tithing man, surveyor of highways, collector of highway taxes, and fence viewer, Worcester Town Meeting. Organizing member, Worcester Committee of Correspondence (1773–1775) and American Political Society (1774–1775). Massachusetts Provincial Congress, 1774–1775. Captain of Worcester Militia, 1774–1775. Major in Continental Army (1775–1776), then Colonel (1777–1781).

A self-educated blacksmith and workhorse for the Worcester Town Meeting, Bigelow wrote flamboyant resolutions, helped form a radical caucus called the American Political Society, organized resistance through the Committees of Correspondence, and represented his town in the revolutionary Provincial Congress. Patriots used his house for their headquarters and his shop to prepare arms and ammunition. We might call him a leader, but his leadership stemmed from being truly representative of the people. In response to the Lexington alarm, as the elected captain of Worcester's militia, Bigelow marched at the head of his townsmen to face the Regulars. He became a professional soldier and helped command the invasion of Quebec, where he was captured and imprisoned for six months. He fought at Saratoga, Monmouth, and Rhode Island, and he wintered at Valley Forge, but while Bigelow thrived in the democratic political arena of pre-war Worcester, he paid a large personal price for becoming a professional soldier. At war's end, having lost his trade and his health, he did not readjust well to civilian life. He died in debtor's prison in 1790, at the age of 50.

The next day Timothy Bigelow arrived at the Massachusetts Provincial Congress, his instructions very much in mind. Money was the first object, however, for patriots realized that war was on its way and the coffers must be filled. Even though the Provincial Congress wasn't technically a government, it did what governments normally do: collect taxes. It asked citizens to pay their money to its own receiving agent rather than to the British tax collector. With these funds, it purchased weapons and ammunition. It reorganized the provincial militia and called for each company to train according to uniform exercises. By April 1775, Massachusetts militiamen were ready to fight.

Other colonies were preparing as well. In Virginia on March 23, 1775, at a province-wide convention that served much the same function as the Massachusetts Provincial Congress, a hawkish hardliner named Patrick Henry introduced a resolution declaring that "this colony be immediately put into a posture of defence," and that a committee be appointed "to prepare a plan for embodying, arming and disciplining such a number of men as may be sufficient for that purpose." Henry's resolution is known in history not for its content but for the speech he made to support it, which supposedly closed with the dramatic line, "I know not what course others may take; but as for me, give me liberty, or give me death!" Although the speech we know as Henry's was actually written by William Wirt 42 years later (see Chapter 24), Henry did make a thundering appeal, and his motion passed narrowly. Virginia was ready for war.

BY THE NUMBERS

Part of the Massachusetts Provincial Congress's shopping list, six months *before* Lexington and Concord:

- 16 field pieces, with 3-pound balls
- 4 field pieces, with 6-pound balls
- 12 battering cannons
- 4 mortars
- 10 tons bomb shells
- 5 tons lead balls
- 20 tons grape and round shot
- 5,000 arms and bayonets
- 75,000 flints
- 1,000 barrels and power

FOUNDER ID

Patrick Henry (1736–1799). Virginia House of Burgesses, 1765–1776. Continental Congress, 1774–1775. Virginia's Revolutionary Conventions, 1774–1776. Commander, Virginia forces, 1775–1776. Governor of Virginia, 1776–1779, 1784–1786. Virginia House of Delegates, 1780–1784, 1787–1791. Declined appointment to Constitutional Convention (1787) and opposed ratification of the Constitution at the Virginia Convention (1788).

Henry was "all tongue," Thomas Jefferson said. He "read nothing" and "could not write." (Jefferson, by contrast, read and wrote but did not make grand speeches.) Henry's blistering attack on the Stamp Act in 1765, his appeal to arms in 1775, his dramatic opposition to the Constitution in 1788, and countless speeches in between made the legendary "Son of Thunder" a dominant force in Virginia politics throughout the Revolutionary Era. He served two extended terms as governor and exerted great influence in the state legislature. Henry's peers praised him as the most powerful orator of the Revolutionary generation, a giant among giants. His speeches appealed to noble ideals but also to hatred of outsiders and fear of slaves and Indians. "Your passions are no longer your own when he addresses them," said George Mason. Although Henry served in no federal office after 1775 (he was offered several appointments but refused), his prominence in the nation's largest state kept him on the national stage. To oppose Henry was to face a formidable foe.

Blood Flows

We all know what happened next. On the night of April 18, 1775, Paul Revere rode through the night to wake sleepy-eyed farmers along the road from Boston to Lexington. But these men were much better prepared than we have been led to believe. They had already staged a revolution that toppled British authority in all of Massachusetts but Boston. Then, for half a year, they had been arming, training, and developing their intelligence and communications networks.

So when Paul Revere mounted his horse for that now-famous ride, so did scores of others. They rode not just along the road to Lexington, but every which way, spreading the word to every hamlet in Eastern Massachusetts. Church bells rang and guns shot in the air, prearranged signals for militiamen to muster and march and confront the advancing Redcoats.

FOUNDER ID

Paul Revere (1735–1810). Member, Masonic Lodge of St. Andrew, North End Caucus, Long Room Club, and Sons of Liberty (political clubs in Boston). Courier, Committees of Correspondence and Massachusetts Committee of Safety. Lieutenant Colonel, Massachusetts Militia, 1776–1779.

Most of us met Paul Revere when we were kids—"one if by land, two if by sea" and all that. But we would not have known about this silversmith from Boston if Henry Wadsworth Longfellow hadn't written a poem in 1861, 86 years later, about one of his many rides (see Chapter 24). Those famous lines, which directly contradict Revere's own version of what happened, mask his many other important contributions. An activist and patriot, he belonged to nearly all of Boston's revolutionary organizations. In the wake of the Boston Massacre, he used an engraving of that event, copied from Henry Pelham, to propagandize against the military occupation of Boston. In addition to his legendary ride on April 18, 1775, Revere carried critical messages on at least a dozen other occasions. There were others like him, but few who worked so hard for their country's cause. After the Revolution, Revere opened an iron foundry that produced church bells, military wares, and naval hardware. Politically, he became a staunch Federalist.

At Lexington, perhaps by mistake, British Regulars opened fire and killed eight fleeing militiamen on the village green. Near Concord, though, militiamen didn't flee. They stood their ground and fired their first deadly shots. The fight was on. As the British retreated toward Boston on what we call today "Battle Road," militiamen exacted a deadly toll. These were not hick farmers firing pot shots with shoddy muskets, but organized companies engaging in strategic combat. Six different times, disciplined formations of Americans faced off against the invading force.

Blood flowed for the first time, but not for the last. We don't need to retell the story of the Revolutionary War here—the Siege of Boston, the Battle of Bunker (Breed's) Hill, the March on Quebec, and so on. But we do need to realize that at first this was a civil war, pitting British North Americans against British combatants from the British Isles. Check the dates: war starts April 19, 1775. Congress declares independence from Great Britain July 2, 1776 (see Chapter 4). For 441 days, patriot forces aimed their muskets at soldiers who represented their official government, embodied in their British King.

And the conflict was not limited to the North. Two days after the fighting at Lexington and Concord, and weeks before news of that event arrived in the South, patriots in Charleston, South Carolina, and Williamsburg, Virginia, challenged British officials over access to arms. In Charleston, the rebels' "Secret Committee" broke into the colonial armory and seized "eight hundred stands of arms, two hundred cutlasses, beside cartouches, flints, and matches," while their comrades took 1,600 pounds of gunpowder from two nearby magazines.

In Williamsburg the royal governor, Lord Dunmore, struck first by ordering 15 marines to seize the city's supply of gunpowder from the magazine. When local patriots protested, Dunmore claimed he was keeping the powder from slaves who might revolt and try to grab it, but two days later, upon hearing that patriots from the countryside were marching on Williamsburg, Dunmore flipped his argument around. If patriots continued to challenge his authority, he said, he would "declare freedom to the slaves and reduce the city of Williamsburg to ashes." (That fall Dunmore did in fact offer slaves their freedom if they joined British forces, as you will see in Chapter 5.) By the close of 1775, still six months before Congress declared independence, fighting had broken out in several locations along the Virginia coast and the South Carolina interior.

Now What?

At the First Continental Congress in September 1774, delegates were inspired by a false rumor, which claimed that the British had bombarded Boston and killed six Americans. By May 1775, when the Second Continental Congress met, dozens of patriots had in actuality fallen and war was a terrible reality. Though the assembled delegates could not claim powers of government, they certainly weren't eager to take orders from a distant Parliament that had passed tyrannical "Intolerable Acts" and now seemed intent on their destruction. When others turned to this assembly for guidance, it had to function like a government. At the request of the Massachusetts

Provincial Congress, the Continental Congress assumed responsibility for the thousands upon thousands of soldiers who held the British at bay in Boston. It asked other colonies to send soldiers, and these, when combined with the troops already there, became the Continental Army. Congress hired a new commander, Virginia's George Washington, to replace Artemas Ward, who had been in charge since the Lexington Alarm. To pay for all this, the new quasi-government even printed its own money—$2 million in paper currency, pegged to the Spanish dollar rather than the British pound.

So was this a government or not? It fought a war. It issued money. But it *still* claimed allegiance to the King, whom it fought against.

When would the Founders step up to the plate, live up to their future name, and create a nation?

The Least You Need to Know

- As punishment for the destruction of tea, Parliament closed the port of Boston and, worse yet, revised the Massachusetts Charter to take away the colonists' political rights.
- In rural Massachusetts, where 95 percent of the colony's inhabitants lived, people rose up from mid-August to mid-October 1774 and cast off British rule.
- Twenty-one months before the Declaration of Independence, the Worcester town meeting said it was time for the province of Massachusetts to set up a new government and sent its own declaration to the colony's Provincial Congress.
- The First Continental Congress, meeting in Philadelphia in 1774, endorsed the revolution in Massachusetts and called for a continental boycott of British goods.
- While staging a counterattack against the successful rural revolt in Massachusetts, the British faced thousands of militiamen who had been arming and training for more than half a year.
- In 1775, the Second Continental Congress decided to raise an army, appoint George Washington its general, and print money, all the while maintaining its allegiance to the Crown.

Yes, We Can! Independence Declared

In This Chapter

- Thomas Paine's *Common Sense*
- Prohibitory Act, the last straw
- State and local declarations favoring independence
- The Congressional vote for independence
- Jefferson and the official Declaration
- How history distorted the nation's signature moment

Although ordinary people in Massachusetts were ready to declare independence back in 1774, national leaders hesitated. "Independency" and "setting up a new form of government of our own" were ideas that "startle people here," John Adams wrote from Philadelphia, where the Continental Congress was meeting. Even at the close of 1775, eight months after Lexington and Concord, major political figures regarded independence as taboo. Although some, privately, favored a break with Britain, publicly they were all still loyalty addicts.

That all changed early in 1776, with two unprecedented events. First, an outsider named Thomas Paine wrote a defiant, startling pamphlet in favor of independence, which was read by just about everybody. Secondly, Great Britain declared the rebellious colonies to be "open enemies," and placed them beyond her protection. At that point, independence was not a choice, but the only available option.

This chapter follows the dramatic political changes during the first half of 1776, as Americans mustered the courage to go it alone. It concludes by discussing how the newly independent people chose to declare and celebrate their momentous decision.

Common Sense: A Book Club Like No Other

Thomas Paine was a failed 37-year-old dressmaker, sailor, shopkeeper, teacher, and petty government official who left England and arrived in Philadelphia late in 1774. He had little money, strong opinions, and nothing to lose by voicing them. Unlike many prominent figures who were wary of promoting independence for fear of appearing too radical, Paine was openly, even recklessly, in favor of it, and he said so in language that ordinary people not only understood but relished.

FOUNDER ID

Thomas Paine (1739–1808). Editor, *Pennsylvania Magazine,* 1775. Author, *Common Sense* (1776), sixteen articles collectively called "The American Crisis" (1776–1783), *The Rights of Man* (1791–1792), *The Age of Reason* (1794–1795). Continental Army, aide to General Nathanael Greene, 1776. Secretary, Congressional Committee of Foreign Affairs (1777–1779); Clerk, Pennsylvania Assembly (1779–1780).

Paine was a revolutionary without a home. When Ben Franklin said, "Where liberty is, there is my country," Paine retorted, "Where liberty is *not,* there is *my* country." His *Common Sense* won over an American audience. While accompanying Washington's army a year later, in the first of his "American Crisis" essays, he opened with the famous line, "These are the times that try men's souls." Paine became a national hero, but he moved to England after the war, and there, when he praised the French Revolution and called for economic leveling in *The Rights of Man,* British officials promptly exiled him. He then ventured to France to support the Revolution there, but he was jailed during the Reign of Terror. Although he believed in God, Paine claimed in *The Age of Reason* that all organized religions were "set up to enslave mankind, and monopolize power and profit." That turned former fans against him in the United States, where he died in poverty and disrepute. Only six people attended Paine's funeral; Franklin, by contrast, had some 20,000 mourners.

Paine didn't think much of monarchy, and he said so in terms that ordinary people, not just the college-educated elite, could understand and relish. "One of the strongest *natural* proofs of the folly of hereditary right in kings," he wrote, "is that nature disapproved it, otherwise she would not so frequently turn it into ridicule by giving mankind an *ass for a lion.*" No American leader, not even down-home Ben Franklin, could have talked that way and gotten away with it.

In addition to mocking time-honored conventions, Paine condensed complex arguments in a no-nonsense, plain-spoken manner. For example: "There is something very absurd, in supposing a continent to be perpetually governed by an island. To be always running three or four thousand miles with a tale or a petition, waiting four or five months for an answer, which when obtained requires five or six more to explain it, will in a few years be looked upon as folly and childishness."

Common Sense was an immediate hit. In taverns across America, people read it aloud so those who were illiterate could hear. Within three months, 120,000 copies of *Common Sense* had been sold (per capita, that would be over 12 million copies today). By the end of April, it was hard to find someone who *hadn't* read or listened to Paine's words. *Common Sense* was today's equivalent of a book club special, prompting a grand, extensive, and influential discussion. That discussion helped lead Americans, as a collective body, to the biggest decision they would ever have to make: should they, or should they not, form their own nation?

Declarations Before *the* Declaration

Parliament and the King's ministers helped them make up their minds by passing the Prohibitory Act, which amounted to a declaration of war on the colonies. Calling the rebellious colonials "open enemies," the act outlawed American commerce and proclaimed that American vessels belonged to the Crown, whether anchored in harbors or at sea. British armed forces could raid American ports, seize ships and anything else, and even carry off sailors. In short, they could attack port cities at will—and they did. From the harbor in Falmouth, Massachusetts (part of which is now Portland, Maine), the Royal Navy discharged incendiary cannonballs that destroyed buildings and homes; sailors then came ashore and set fire to anything left standing.

The Prohibitory Act did as much to promote a final separation as Paine's *Common Sense*. Calling the new measure "the Act of Independency," John Adams asserted boldly: "King, Lords and Commons have united in sundering this Country and that I think forever." The time for talk was over. People were ready to act.

But how? Following the tradition of New England town meetings, people in communities throughout America met in bodies and issued instructions to representatives, who were duty-bound to do what the people told them to do. Towns instructed counties, and counties instructed provincial congresses or conventions, and those colonial bodies instructed the Continental Congress, which held its meetings in Philadelphia. The chain of command was democratic. The instructions were clear: representatives in lower bodies instructed the representatives in higher bodies to break away from Britain.

Historian Pauline Maier, by examining firsthand documents, has uncovered 90 local "declarations of independence" that preceded the famous document we know so well. These came from 85 different groups, ranging from town meetings to state conventions. (Yes, we can finally start calling them "states," because they no longer wanted to be colonies.)

BY THE NUMBERS

State and local bodies that officially urged independence in the months prior to Congress's famous declaration:

- 85 lesser bodies issued declarations favoring independence before Congress did.
- 57 of these were townships in Massachusetts.
- 9 were state assemblies or conventions, each instructing its delegates to Congress to make the break.
- 8 were county conventions in Virginia and Maryland.
- 5 were militia units and military associations in Pennsylvania.
- 3 were grand juries in South Carolina.
- 3 were from New York—the New York City Mechanics' Union plus two upstate districts.

If you read these documents, you may wonder, "Haven't I seen these words before?" From Virginia: "That all men are by nature equally free and independent, and have certain inherent rights, … namely, the enjoyment of life and liberty, with the means of acquiring and possessing property, and pursuing and obtaining happiness and safety." These words were echoed in the first paragraph of the Declaration of Independence, which would follow shortly.

And from Frederick County, Maryland: "Resolved, unanimously, that all just and legal Government was instituted for the ease and convenience of the People, and that the People have the indubitable right to reform or abolish a Government which may appear to them insufficient for the exigency of their affairs." Compare that with the second paragraph of the Declaration of Independence. Then there's that famous last line of the Continental Congress's Declaration: "We mutually pledge to each other our lives, our fortunes, and our sacred honor." Before those words were written, patriots at more than twenty conventions pledged to support independence with their "lives and fortunes." Sometimes, they added flourish or wit. The people of Malton, Massachusetts, concluded, "Your constituents will support and defend the measure to the last drop of their blood, and the last farthing of their treasure," while Boston delegates pledged "their lives and the remnants of their fortunes."

Crunch Time: The Final Vote

On Friday, June 7, Virginia's Richard Henry Lee presented a resolution in the Continental Congress: "That these United Colonies are, and of right ought to be, free and independent States, that they are absolved from all allegiance to the British Crown, and that all political connection between them and the State of Great Britain is, and ought to be, totally dissolved." Although Lee wanted independence, he was also obeying the instructions of the Virginia Convention, which ordered its congressional delegates to introduce just such a resolution.

FOUNDER ID

Richard Henry Lee (1732–1794). Virginia House of Burgesses, 1758–1776. Virginia's Revolutionary Conventions, 1774–1776. Virginia House of Delegates, 1777–1778, 1780–1785. Delegate (1774–1779, 1787) and President (1784–1785) of the Continental Congress. United States Senator, 1789–1792.

Although Lee, a fourth-generation Virginian, inherited a vast fortune built on tobacco, slaves, and trade, he knew the real wealth of America lay in land. With Washington and others, he hoped to develop the Ohio country. In the buildup to the Revolutionary War, he focused on British imperial policies, which he resisted with great zest. A skilled orator and writer, he drafted many strong resolutions, including the Congressional motion for independence. After the war, although he served one term as president of Congress, he opposed a stronger national government. When the new Constitution was first presented to Congress in 1787, he tried and failed to add a Bill of Rights, leading him to oppose ratification of the Constitution. (Two generations later, in the very different setting of the Civil War, his grand-nephew, General Robert E. Lee, also resisted national authority.) When Congress passed the Bill of Rights two years later, Lee finally warmed to the idea of a central government, and he finished his political career in the United States Senate.

Seven of the thirteen states were in favor of Lee's resolution—New Hampshire, Massachusetts, Connecticut, Rhode Island, Virginia, North Carolina, and Georgia. Technically, by a slim majority, it could have passed then and there, but on a matter of such vital importance, the states would have to be unanimous, or nearly so.

Lee's motion was tabled for three weeks to buy time. Delaware came around quickly. The New Jersey legislature arrested its loyalist Governor, William Franklin, the estranged son of Benjamin Franklin, and instructed its delegates in Congress to vote for independence.

On the morning of June 1, when Congress again took up Lee's motion, independence had nine votes. Then, just as the session began, a courier arrived with a letter for John Adams. The Maryland Convention, responding to specific instructions from four counties, now supported independence, the letter said. "See the glorious effects of county instructions," Maryland's Samuel Chase told Adams. "Our people have fire if not smothered."

The count was up to ten, and the following day, South Carolina signed on, making it eleven. Only New York and Pennsylvania remained. The New York Convention would not meet for two more weeks, so its delegates were stuck with old instructions to oppose independence. But Pennsylvania delegates could choose between opposite instructions from competing bodies, one from the conservative Assembly, the other from a radical convention that claimed authority from "the body of the people."

All eyes were on Pennsylvania. If it continued to oppose independence, New York would probably join it, and the absence of these two giants would leave a gaping hole in the geographic middle of the wannabe nation. The previous day, four Pennsylvania delegates had voted against independence and three in favor. But on June 2, both Robert Morris and John Dickinson, although opposed to a final break with Britain, agreed to abstain, making the vote three to two in favor of independence. The deal was sealed. The final count on Richard Henry Lee's motion: twelve states in favor, none opposed. Behold, the birth of the United States of America, July 2, 1776!

THEIR OWN WORDS

The *second* day of July, 1776, will be the most memorable epocha in the history of America. I am apt to believe that it will be celebrated by succeeding generations as the great anniversary festival. It ought to be commemorated as the day of deliverance, by solemn acts of devotion to God Almighty. It ought to be solemnized with pomp and parade, with shows, games, sports, guns, bells, bonfires, and illumination, from one end of this continent to the other, from this time forward forevermore."

—John Adams to Abigail Adams, July 3, 1776.

Jefferson Expresses the "American Mind"

Having declared independence in chambers, Congress naturally wanted to DECLARE INDEPENDENCE to the world. For years, American patriots had been passing resolutions and making declarations about this and that, and now that they had done something truly momentous, they were eager to make the grandest declaration of all.

Back on June 10, hoping for eventual passage of Richard Henry Lee's motion, Congress had directed a five-man committee to write a declaration as the motion was being debated. The committee asked one member, Thomas Jefferson, to prepare the initial draft. Jefferson's commission, as he saw it, was not to invent anything new but to summarize what he called "the American mind." He would give all that people had been saying and declaring over the previous few months the clearest possible expression.

Jefferson's draft was amended first by members of the committee and then by Congress meeting as a whole. On July 4, two days after the nation-creating vote, delegates accepted the final version, known ever since as the Declaration of Independence, the first of our nation's two founding scriptures. Broadsides announcing the Declaration placed "July 4" on their banners, ignoring the July 2 date, when the nation actually came into existence. And that's why, every year, we have to wait two days longer than we should to set off our fireworks.

THEIR OWN WORDS

"This was the object of the Declaration of Independence. Not to find out new principles, or new arguments, which had never been said before; but to place before mankind the common sense of the subject, in terms so plain and firm as to command their assent, and to justify ourselves in the independent stand we were compelled to take. Neither aiming at originality of principle or sentiment, nor yet copied from any particular and previous writing, it was intended to be an expression of the American mind, and to give to that expression the proper tone and spirit called for by the occasion. All its authority rests on the harmonizing sentiments of the day."

—Thomas Jefferson

FOUNDER ID

Thomas Jefferson (1743–1826). Virginia House of Burgesses, 1769–1775. Continental Congress, 1775–1776 and 1783–1784. Virginia House of Delegates, 1776–1779 and 1782–1783. Virginia Governor, 1779–1781. Minister to France, 1785–1789. Secretary of State, 1790–1793. Vice President, 1797–1801. President, 1801–1809. Primary author of the Declaration of Independence (1776), Ordinance for Western Territories (1784), Virginia Statute for Religious Freedom (1786), Kentucky Resolutions (1798). Founder, University of Virginia, 1819.

Jefferson, a "Renaissance man," was "at once a musician, skilled in drawing, a geometrician, an astronomer, a natural philosopher, legislature, statesman, Senator of America, and Governor of Virginia," a French visitor wrote in the early 1780s. But he was only getting started. At the dawn of the next century, in an election that almost tore the nation apart, the Republican Party carried him into the presidency. Jefferson had strong thoughts about everything. He valued reason above faith, causing his enemies to vilify him as a deist. Some of his views appeared to contradict each other. He believed that small farms were the future of America, yet he owned a huge plantation and built a mansion like no other. He valued liberty above all else, but held hundreds of humans in bondage. He challenged federal power, yet once he became president, he exerted it boldly. To this day, although Jefferson has found a place of honor in American history, he remains one of its most enigmatic and controversial figures. Historian and biographer Joseph Ellis calls him the "American Sphinx."

Celebrating Independence

When Congress approved the Declaration of Independence, John Hancock, Congress's president, dipped his quill in ink and flourished his famous "John Hancock" at the bottom of the document, just as he did with all other bills and resolutions passed by Congress. Then Charles Thomson, the secretary, signed as well. On July 4, 1776, that's all it took. Two men signed, sealed, and delivered the Declaration of Independence. That night John Dunlap, a Philadelphia printer, set the document in type and printed up 200 copies, to be distributed through the colonies-turned-states and read in public.

FOUNDER ID

John Hancock (1737–1793). Massachusetts House of Representatives (1766–1772, 1774) and Council (1772–1774). President, Provincial Congress, 1774–1775. President, Continental Congress, 1775–1777. Massachusetts House of Representatives, 1777–1780. Massachusetts Governor, 1780–1785, 1787–1793. President, Massachusetts Ratification Convention, 1788.

Hancock liked applause, and some said he received more than he deserved. Drawing on a vast fortune inherited from his uncle's shipping business, he earned popular affection by bankrolling protests and patriotic celebrations in pre-war Boston. In 1768, he became a hero by standing up to British authorities who seized his ship, *Liberty.* A delegate to Congress in 1775, Hancock took over the presidency when Virginia's Peyton Randolph had to leave, and when Randolph returned a few months later, Hancock did not step down, as Samuel Adams and others thought he should. Hancock's duties as president were to write official letters and sign congressional actions, including the Declaration of Independence. In 1780, he became Massachusetts' first governor since independence, receiving over 90 percent of the vote. He was reelected annually without serious opposition. He retired briefly in 1786, but after a rebellion unsettled the state he regained the office and remained Governor until his death. Using his popularity, Hancock tipped the balance in favor of the state's ratification of the Constitution in 1788. That was his final impact on national affairs.

On July 9, the Dunlap broadside arrived in New York City, where General George Washington was preparing his troops for a likely British invasion. In his General Orders on that day, Washington commanded that the complete text of the Declaration be read to the troops at 6 P.M. "with an audible voice," so the soldiers would hear and understand "the grounds & reasons" for independence. "The General hopes this important event will serve as a fresh incentive to every officer, and soldier, to act with fidelity and courage, as knowing that now the peace and safety of his Country depends (under God) solely on the success of our arms," the order stated. This was not the first item of the day's General Orders, however. It came after sentencing two deserters to 39 lashes, issuing passes to three city officials, moving a guard post "to the Market House near the Ferry-Stairs," and recruiting army chaplains—"The blessing and protection of Heaven are at all times necessary but especially so in times of public distress and danger."

After the formal reading, a crowd consisting of both soldiers and civilians gathered at Bowling Green and proceeded to yank down the giant gilded statue of King George III and his horse. Once on the ground, the people mutilated their former sovereign, cleaving his head from his body and his nose from his head, then placed the remnants of the skull on a spike.

So much for "God Save the King." Those days were over.

In Worcester, after a reading of the Declaration on the town common, a large crowd cheered "huzzah," fired muskets and cannons, built bonfires, and made as much of a commotion as had ever been heard in that staid New England town. Some tore down and burned the sign on the King's Arms tavern, then went inside and offered 24 toasts. The rounds started with a prosaic "Prosperity and perpetuity to the United States of America," then became increasingly creative: "Perpetual itching without benefit of scratching, to the enemies of America" and "May the freedom and independency of America endure, till the sun grows dim with age, and this earth returns to chaos."

Signing the Declaration: A Staged Non-Event

Still, one state had not come around, but on July 19, the New York Provincial Congress finally voted for independence. Also on July 19, the Continental Congress passed this resolution: "That the Declaration passed on the fourth be fairly engrossed on parchment with the title and stile of 'The Unanimous Declaration of the 13 United States of America' and that the same when engrossed be signed by every member of Congress."

Then Timothy Matlack, an expert scribe, went to work, and on August 2 the congressmen in attendance that day affixed their names to Matlack's handiwork. It was the nation's first staged event, eighteenth-century style, a prelude to the modern photo-op. Over succeeding days and weeks, those not present on August 2 added their names, but it wasn't until the following year that the last of the 56 signers, Thomas McKean, added his. Matlack's copy of the Declaration of Independence, the "official" version, is treated as scripture and preserved in the National Archives.

> **FOUNDER ID**
>
> **Timothy Matlack (1736–1829).** Philadelphia Committees of Safety and Inspection, 1775–1776. Clerk, Continental Congress, 1775–1776. Pennsylvania Constitutional Convention, 1776. Colonel, Philadelphia Fifth Rifle Battalion, 1776–1777. Secretary, Pennsylvania Supreme Executive Council, 1777–1782. Trustee, University of Pennsylvania, 1779–1785. Continental Congress, 1780. Annual oration, American Philosophical Society, 1780. Board of Directors, Bank of North America, 1781–1782. Clerk, Pennsylvania State Senate, 1790–1800.
>
> Matlack, a merchant and brewer, took pleasure in horse racing, gaming, cock fighting, and fighting—unusual activities for a Quaker. In 1765, the pacifistic Society of Friends disowned him, but 16 years later, he and others who fought in the Revolutionary War formed their own offshoot, the Society of Free Quakers. In the summer of 1776, as he prepared the parchment copy of the Declaration of Independence, Matlack served on the committee that drafted Pennsylvania's radically democratic constitution, which placed common people in charge of their government (see Chapter 6). He believed in economic as well as political equality, and he promoted agriculture as "the Star-bespangled genius of America." He was also a fierce advocate for the abolition of slavery. Late in 1776, leading his rifle battalion of volunteer "Associators," he joined Washington's campaign along the Delaware River. Again in 1799 this "fighting Quaker" volunteered for military service, and also in 1812, at the age of 76.

Once the signatures were affixed, Congress inserted a copy of the document into the official journal of its proceedings. For historical purists, this presents problems. On July 4, the date of the entry, only 12 states were onboard, not 13. Also, 14 of the "signers" of the Declaration of Independence were not even present on July 4, 1776, the day they allegedly signed the Declaration of Independence. Eight had not yet been elected to Congress, while six had returned to their home states—three to help defend against the British and three others to organize new state governments. (The absentee signers were Matthew Thornton, William Williams, Charles Carroll, Benjamin Rush, George Ross, James Smith, George Clymer, George Taylor, Oliver Wolcott, Lewis Morris, Philip Livingston, William Hopper, George Wythe, and Samuel Chase.)

To mask these inconsistencies, when Congress printed its official journal the following year, it deleted telltale entries. One redacted entry from the original journal, for July 19, noted that New York had finally voted for independence. The other, for August 2, noted that those in Congress inscribed their names on Timothy Matlack's beautiful copy of the Declaration of Independence. Either of these would have blown the story. This was the nation's first cover-up, undiscovered until 1884, when historian Mellon Chamberlain finally consulted the original Congressional Journal instead of the printed version.

The "signing" of the Declaration of Independence on July 4 is cemented in our national memory, manufactured as the event was. Folklore reinforced the falsehood. Although Samuel Chase, for example, was known to be in Maryland on July 2, he supposedly hopped on his horse and "rode one hundred miles and arrived in Philadelphia just in time to sign the Declaration of Independence." Or so says the authoritative *American National Biography*. Their proof: his signature on the document. In fact, Chase fell ill and did not return to Philadelphia until July 17. Like the others, he did not sign until August 2 at the earliest.

But the larger story, the huge nation-changing and history-changing story, is absolutely true. The United States of America had cast off British rule, with its monarchical and aristocratic traditions. Better yet, Americans were ready to form a new nation "of the people, by the people, and for the people," as Abraham Lincoln would later say. It was a glorious moment.

The Least You Need to Know

- Americans engaged in a national discussion on independence as they debated the ideas set forth in Thomas Paine's *Common Sense*.
- Parliament's Prohibitory Act declared open warfare on the rebellious colonies, making reconciliation virtually impossible.
- At least 85 state and local bodies declared in favor of independence before Congress did.

- Our nation was born on July 2, 1776, when Congress voted for independence, 12 states to none.

- In writing the preliminary draft of the Declaration of Independence, Thomas Jefferson summarized "the American mind," all that Americans had proclaimed before him.

- The physical document enshrined as the Declaration of Independence, pronouncing the unanimous consent of 13 states and boasting 56 signatures, was printed and signed after-the-fact, not on July 4, when 14 of the "signers" were absent.

But *Whose* Independence?

Chapter

5

In This Chapter

- The meaning of "liberty" for the oppressed
- Native Americans on each side
- Slaves who ran to the British or fought for the patriots
- Women and independence
- Poor whites who fought against the patriots

As the king's subjects insisted on "liberty," no one wanted it more than a slave who had been sold at auction. As patriots espoused *sovereignty*—the right to self-government and freedom from outside interference—no one had a better claim to it than native tribes, whose own long-established sovereignty was now endangered. While merchants denounced restrictive regulations, custom and law constrained women, whose plight was rarely discussed. As wealthy landlords complained of not being allowed to vote for representatives in England's Parliament, their tenant farmers could not vote for the men who made the rules right here in America.

These vulnerable populations had few options, and even these were fraught with danger. Whether they became allies of the British or of the patriots, Native Americans lost villages, saw crops destroyed, and faced devastating hardship. As the British entreated them to run away, slaves were kept under increasingly strict guard. Their men off to war, women who defended households were at increased risk of theft, injury, and rape. In increasing numbers, those from the lower social orders were armed and sent into battle. Off the battlefield, the poor were subject to abuse by their so-called "betters."

Yet these people were not simply victims. As active agents, they shaped proud histories, whatever the outcome. They made complex decisions. They fought and died for freedom. They dared to hope that if independence came, new laws, governors, and systems might offer protections they had never known.

Native Americans

Native people, who might have preferred to remain on the sidelines, had to choose sides in this war between contesting white forces. The Revolution would become the largest and most destructive Indian war fought in our entire history. The nations were many—Abenaki, Shawnee, Delaware, Cherokee, Catawba, Chickasaw, Choctaw, Creek, or Seminole. In this war, some of these nations would turn against others. Within each one, there were rifts and divisions as elders and young warriors vied to enforce their wills. As whites advanced and battles raged, all would be drawn in. Happy endings don't exist, but dramatic stories emerge and honor the various native peoples who struggled to retain the lands that supported them.

BY THE NUMBERS

Indian nations east of the Mississippi ceded 240,373 square miles of land in 28 treaties between 1768 and 1798. This is approximately equal to the combined lands in 11 of the 13 original colonies, almost doubling the size of the United States.

Chief White Eyes and the Fourteenth State

After the outbreak of fighting in the summer of 1775, Lord Dunmore, the royal governor of Virginia, tried to turn the Delaware and Shawnee, who inhabited the Ohio Valley, against the rebels. Come fall, the "Big Knives," as Indians called white colonists, tried to turn these same tribes against the British.

Representatives from the Delaware and the Shawnee in the Ohio Valley met with colonists, who claimed to carry a message of peace from "our great United Council of wise men now assembled at Philadelphia." It was well received by Cornstalk, a Shawnee chief, and White Eyes, a chief of the Delaware Indians. White Eyes promised that if any of his "foolish young men should do any harm to your people," they would be punished severely. Further, he was happy "to comply with the dictates of the Christian Religion and commands of our Savior whose hands were nailed to the Cross and sides pierced for our sins."

But in fact, these native leaders could not speak for their "foolish young men," who were eager to wage war on white colonists. In 1777 some of these ardent young fighters joined Mingo warriors in attacks on major colonial towns in Virginia.

If tribal chiefs were unable to speak for all their people, white chiefs did no better. Forbidding attacks on Shawnee or Delaware Indians, Patrick Henry, Virginia's new governor, cautioned whites: "Any injury done them is done to us while they are faithfull." That didn't prevent raids by frontier whites. As hostilities escalated, the Shawnees sent two messengers to Fort Randolph "with strong protestations of friendship," but they were seized as hostages to prevent future attacks by Shawnee warriors. When Cornstalk himself went to protest, he too was taken, and when his son came to inquire about Cornstalk, he became a prisoner as well. Then, while these Shawnees were held hostage, a white hunting party was killed by Mingos warriors, and angry whites took out their anger by butchering all four Shawnee captives.

In 1778 White Eyes and others ventured to Fort Pitt for yet another council. Hoping to end conflict, they once again pledged their loyalty and said they would act as guides when Americans fought hostile tribes to their west. Then White Eyes insisted on a remarkable treaty clause. A new state would be formed "whereof the Delaware nation shall be the head, and have a representative in Congress." White negotiators at Fort Pitt signed on to this promise, knowing full well that Congress, which had to approve all treaties, was not about to create a fourteenth state just for Indians.

Less than two months later, White Eyes, like Cornstalk, was murdered. While visiting Fort Pitt, he was "treacherously put to death, at the moment of his greatest exertions to serve the United States, in whose service he held the commission of colonel," as United States Indian Agent George Morgan later admitted. At the time, officials covered up the deed by telling Delaware Indians that White Eyes had died of smallpox.

Dragging Canoe Leads a New Nation

Other Native Americans charted a very different course through the troubled waters of the Revolutionary War.

In the spring of 1776, at a Cherokee gathering in the village of Chote, 14 warriors arrived from nations to the north, their faces painted black. Henry Stuart, a British agent, was there, and in a letter to his brother, also a British Indian agent, he reported the scene in great detail. The visiting warriors—Shawnees, Delawares, Mohawks, Nanticokes, and Ottawas—urged the Cherokees to "drop all their former quarrels and to join in one common cause" against the intruding white Americans.

One warrior, presenting "a war belt about 9 feet long and six inches wide, of purple whampum, strewed with vermillion," argued that it was "better to die like men than to dwindle away by inches."

How could any self-respecting youth resist talk like this? Few did. One year earlier, Cherokee chiefs had been hoodwinked into signing away almost 30,000 square miles of land, the heart of present-day Kentucky and some of Tennessee. Young warriors like Dragging Canoe had refused to sign that document. Now, they were ready to collaborate with other nations and fight back. They joined in singing a war song, while the old chiefs who had signed the earlier treaty, including Dragging Canoe's father, "sat down silent and dejected."

"After that day," Stuart reported, "every young fellow's face appeared black and nothing was talked of but war." They pledged to fight and did so. Led by Dragging Canoe, and using gunpowder provided by the British, they spread terror among white outposts.

The young warriors' timing could not have been worse. American patriots had just repelled a British attack on Charleston. Trained and mobilized for war, but with no other enemy to fight, 6,000 militiamen from Virginia and the Carolinas turned on the Cherokee raiding parties, drove them back, and then proceeded to wreak havoc among civilians in Cherokee villages. "I have now burnt down every town, and destroyed all the corn, from the Cherokee line to the middle settlements," wrote Colonel Andrew Williamson, one of the commanders.

THEIR OWN WORDS

"It is expected you make smooth work as you go—that is, you cut up every Indian corn-field, and burn every Indian town—and that every Indian taken shall be the slave and property of the taker; that the nation be extirpated [exterminated], and the lands become property of the public."

—William H. Drayton, giving instructions to the militiamen on behalf of the South Carolina Assembly

Cherokees suffered severe losses, and the following year, the chiefs were forced to cede even more land. But Dragging Canoe and other militants refused to accept defeat. Calling themselves "Ani-Yunwiya"—the real people—they withdrew and rebuilt settlements near Chickamauga Creek, to the south and west of their old homes. There, they started life anew, and for the next seventeen years these "Chickamaugas" continued to resist white intrusions. To a group of Shawnee who visited his new home, Dragging Canoe said of his white enemies: "They were numerous, and their hatchets were sharp. After we had lost some of our best warriors, we were forced to leave our towns and corn to be burned by them, and now we live in the grass as you see us. But we are not conquered."

Dragging Canoe was a "founder" in his own right, helping his people create a new, although not permanent, home. But the Chickamaugas were now separated from their original tribe. As the white nation united in victory, the Cherokee nation was split asunder.

FOUNDER ID

Dragging Canoe, or Tsi'yu-gunsini (1730s–1792). Cherokee warrior and leader against white Americans, 1776–1792. Founder of independent Chickamauga towns, 1777–1792. Organizer of pan-Indian resistance, 1782–1792.

As a youngster, Dragging Canoe wanted to join a Cherokee war party leaving the village, it is said. His father, Little Carpenter, told him he couldn't. Defiant, Dragging Canoe slipped through the forest to reach a portage point before the warriors did. Finding him there, his father said he could come, but only if he portaged his own canoe, a seemingly impossible challenge. Though the boy couldn't hoist it as the men did, he dragged his canoe, demonstrating his prowess and earning his name. In manhood Dragging Canoe again defied his father and other tribal elders, who negotiated with whites and who forfeited millions of acres of Cherokee land. Throughout the Revolutionary period Dragging Canoe led Cherokee warriors in attacks on encroaching whites. He even established autonomous Indian towns in Tennessee, where separatist Cherokees were known as Chickamaugas. A diplomat, he helped form a confederacy that included Shawnees, Delawares, Ottawas, and Iroquois and attempted to establish international trade that could ensure Indian survival. Two years after his death, the separatist Chickamaugas were defeated at their new villages, but they continued to pursue an independent existence west of the Mississippi well into the nineteenth century.

Slaves and Free Blacks

On May 25, 1774, several African Americans held in bondage appealed to the governor and council of Massachusetts: "The Petition of a Grate Number of Blackes of this Province who by divine permission are held in a state of Slavery with [within] the bowels of a free and Christian Country, Humbly Shewing, That your Petitioners apprehend we have in common with all other men a naturel right to our freedoms."

Here was John Locke's Enlightenment argument, and slaves were bringing it into play. Enslaved Americans had long rebelled against their situation, but now they used the lofty words of Whig philosophy to explain their drive for freedom to a white audience.

If Locke's argument was used to attack the institution of slavery in the North, in the South Locke appeared to defend it. He had also claimed that people should be able to turn to their government for aid in defending property, and for a slaveholder, *slaves* were property.

In both North and South, the Revolutionary War was catastrophic. But enslaved men and women, taking enormous risks, tried to turn catastrophe to their advantage. In the North, male slaves of fighting age (yes, there were still slaves in the North) offered to serve in the Continental Army as substitutes for whites who had been drafted but did not want to fight. These brave men, with promises of freedom in return for military service, placed their lives on the line. Sometimes the promises were honored, other times not. Free blacks also enlisted, whether for patriotism, economic desperation, or some combination of the two. Most were poor, and with soldiers in short supply, and substitutes in high demand, they too could wager a deal for their services (see Chapter 8).

In the South, slaves seeking freedom saw a different way out. They could flee to the enemy, fight against their patriot masters, and hopefully, if the British won, never be enslaved again.

"Liberty to Slaves"

As early as 1774, rumors were spreading throughout the South. The British were "tampering with our Negroes." Slaves "entertained ideas," ideas concerning liberty, of course. Beyond rumor, there was real cause for worry. Why *wouldn't* slaves rebel or run if wartime conditions gave them that chance? Slave patrols were doubled in places, and men came armed to church. Nervous and frightened, whites talked of planned slave insurrections. Sometimes there were such plans, sometimes not. In either case, suspicion brought trials and reprisals—even sentences of death by hanging.

Then on November 15, 1775 (the document was dated November 7 but issued eight days later), Lord Dunmore, the royal governor of Virginia, put his official stamp on the widespread, unspeakable fears of slaveholders: he promised freedom to all slaves who would flee rebel masters and fight on the side of the British. Here was the world turned upside down. If Dunmore terrified slaveholders, he inspired men and women who had spent most or all of their lives enslaved. They fled their plantations to British ships in great numbers, taking Dunmore up on his offer. (British authorities had lost control of the land in Virginia and were conducting the war from the rivers and Chesapeake Bay.)

THEIR OWN WORDS

"And I do hereby further declare all indented Servants, Negroes, or others, (appertaining to Rebels,) free, that are able and willing to bear Arms, they joining HIS MAJESTY'S Troops as soon as may be, for the more speedily reducing this Colony to a proper Sense of their Duty, to HIS MAJESTY'S Crown and Dignity."

—Lord Dunmore's famous or infamous (depending on one's viewpoint) proclamation

THEIR OWN WORDS

Since Lord Dunmore's proclamation made its appearance here, it is said he has recruited his army, in the counties of Princess Ann and Norfolk, to the amount of about 2000 men, including his black regiment, which is thought to be a considerable part, with this inscription on their breasts: "Liberty to slaves."

—a newspaper dispatch from Williamsburg, December 2, 1775

By war's end, tens of thousands would flee their owners, a mass exodus that preceded the fabled Underground Railroad by several decades. George Washington had once complained that habitual bowing to British control "will make us as tame, and abject slaves, as the blacks we rule over." Now, slaves themselves, no longer "tame" or "abject," were defying their own rulers.

Slaves even fled from our Founders. On January 5, 1781, after Thomas Jefferson, Governor of Virginia at the time, left Richmond, which was under British assault, troops marched off with one of his slaves. This was 5-year-old Isaac, who could already play the drums, a valuable skill. When Isaac's mother set to "cryin' and hollerin'" over losing him, they took her and five others, too.

BY THE NUMBERS

Enslaved people who escaped from Thomas Jefferson and George Washington during the Revolutionary War:

- 23 slaves from Jefferson's Elk Hill plantation fled with the British in June, 1781.

- 16 men and women enslaved to George Washington boarded a British boat near Mount Vernon in April, 1781. At first, Washington claimed the plantations along the Potomac, including his, had been "stripped of their Negroes," but he soon admitted his slaves had "deserted."

- 27 slaves, more than half the workforce, left the Great Dismal Swamp, which the British raided in July, 1781. Washington owned an interest in the Great Dismal Swamp Company, which he had helped organize back in 1763 to drain the swamp and make it productive.

To Run or Not to Run

Any escape required a decision. It might be taken following whispered interchanges in slave cabins in the dark of night. It might be made abruptly, after a severe lashing. Danger had to be balanced against the possibility of success, departure from the known world against the potential difficulties in an unknown one, love of those one was leaving against the hope they might become free.

What happened to the slaves who fled? Not all wound up where they thought they would. Some were recaptured, or even returned by a British commander who ceded to a slaveholder's ardent petitions. One slave who was recaptured, a 15-year-old girl, was given 80 lashes and had embers pressed against her wounds. Unable to cope with the overwhelming number of arrivals, British officers were known simply to refuse blacks. These took refuge wherever they could but were subject to attack and reprisals by Southern masters.

Others crossed safely to the British side. Some served officers. Others, familiar with the waterways, piloted boats. Often, blacks performed labor that was considered too hard, hazardous, or demeaning for whites. In effect, they exchanged one master for another. Those who actually became soldiers served under the watchful supervision of white officers. At war's end they were asked to release their rifles. Some defied the order, making off in bands to form maroon communities in deep woods or swamps.

On crowded ships or in crowded camps, blacks were exposed to dysentery, typhus, typhoid fever, or smallpox. Thousands upon thousands died. When there were severe shortages of food, blacks might be fed "putrid ship's meat and wormy biscuits." At

Yorktown, when food ran out in the weeks before the famous British surrender, diminishing rations were saved for white soldiers, and blacks who had joined with the British were sent out into a no-man's land between enemy lines. Many died there.

But during the years of warfare, some did escape to Philadelphia or New York or, at war's end, to Canada, evacuated on British ships. Having paid a terrific price, having subjected themselves to incredible risks, they reached freedom's shore.

FOUNDER ID

Harry Washington (Born about 1740–Death not recorded). Enslaved to George Washington, 1763–1776. Served in Lord Dunmore's "Ethiopian Regiment," 1776; served under other British officers, 1776–1783. Lived in a free black community in Nova Scotia, 1783–1789. A settler in Sierra Leone's Free Town, 1792–1800. Exiled in 1800.

Harry Washington did not attempt to found a nation on this continent, but he carried that dream to another. When young, he traveled to America from Gambia on a slave ship, imported by George Mason's brother. Eventually Mason's good friend George Washington purchased him. He escaped from Mount Vernon, was recaptured, and fled to the British in 1776, establishing his independence as the nation did. One of 3,000 free blacks under British charge at war's end, he sailed from New York to Nova Scotia, where he acquired 40 acres of unproductive land in a community of free blacks, who were poor to the point of starvation, some forced to eat their dogs and cats. Propelled by a founder's hope, he continued to seek a new land for his people and a new beginning. Alongside 1,192 black colonists, he worked to establish an independent black community in Sierra Leone. There, once more, he rebelled against injustice and was exiled. He ended his life in Africa, not far from the spot where he was born.

"Remember the Ladies"

With British goods forbidden by nonimportation agreements, Temperance Smith, a parson's wife, reported that "all had to be raised and manufactured at home, from bread stuffs, sugar and rum to the linen and woolen for our clothes and bedding." With men off to war, women planted fields and hoed corn. They added men's work to their own. When states set production quotas in order to clothe soldiers, the women of Hartford were told to produce 1,000 coats and vests and 1,600 shirts. The war was woman's work.

And war posed dangers. Near the battlefield, "camp followers" were ever-present, nursing the sick, fetching water, cooking, and laundering. They were exposed to the same diseases that felled about half the men who perished in the Revolution. At times they were equally exposed to gunshot or cannonballs.

As soldiers foraged for food, clothing, and sometimes possessions of value, women in households were endangered, too. Custom protected upper-class ladies from any affront, but not those from a lower social rank. Illiterate women and girls, signing their names only with an X, registered official complaints of rape by British soldiers. These legal records are both credible and dismayingly numerous. One woman, made desperate by warfare, asked, "Where God can we fly?" She spoke for many.

If Native Americans fought to protect sovereignty and slaves risked their all in order to be free, what reward could women expect from their overwhelming efforts? What could they want?

The family household was the very center of any community. A man was the patriarch. In all legal and civic matters he represented other household members, including his wife. She was constrained by legal precedents, cultural expectations and customs, religious doctrine, and limited education. Economic dependency made her especially vulnerable. If she had property at all— whether cash or cattle, a house or pots—she lost all control over it when marriage made her a *feme couvert*, a "covered woman." The renowned English jurist William Blackstone defined that expression in reassuring terms; a wife would be taken under her husband's "wing, protection and cover." Abigail Adams, the spouse of future President John Adams, defined it in a somewhat less complacent tone when she said that a woman's property was "subject to the controul and disposal of our partners, to whom the laws have given a sovereign authority." The only way a married woman could own property legally was for her husband to die.

BY THE NUMBERS

Of 218 people on the 1779 voters' list for Worcester, Massachusetts, 8 were women. So did women have the right to vote? Yes and no. Worcester's eight female voters were property-owning widows, so in a sense it was their property that voted. Lest we get over-excited about women voting during the Revolution, note that 11 dead people in Worcester could also vote, via the executors of their unsettled estates.

A married woman was less likely to assert personal rights because, economically, she was not her own person. The "sovereign authority" in a wife's life was not a king but her husband. In many marriages, no doubt, women were protected by a husband's affection and respect. Certainly Abigail Adams was. But a woman couldn't depend on custom or on law, and that wouldn't change within her lifetime.

And yet, through the Revolutionary years, women engaged in politics in their own ways and proved their valor. They participated in boycotts, rioted in the marketplace over soaring food prices, and sewed shirts for soldiers. Bolstered by these experiences, some women were ready to question the order of things. More soon would (see Chapter 24).

THEIR OWN WORDS

"I long to hear that you have declared an independency. And, by the way, in the new code of laws which I suppose it will be necessary for you to make, I desire you would remember the ladies and be more generous and favorable to them than your ancestors. Do not put such unlimited power into the hands of their husbands. Remember, all men would be tyrants if they could. If particular care and attention is not paid to the ladies, we are determined to foment a rebellion, and will not hold ourselves bound by any laws in which we have no voice or representation."

—Abigail Adams to John Adams (then a delegate to Congress), March 31, 1776, three months and three days before Congress voted in favor of independence.

Tenant Farmers: Tories or Freedom Fighters?

In both the South and in the North, from the first, those who had little influence or money were often rebels, opposing King George III and Parliament (see Chapter 2). Yet others of the "lesser sort," as they said back then, pledged loyalty to the Crown. Why would a bunch of poor people turn into King's men?

Here's the back story. Robert Livingston Jr., one of a large clan that vied for power within the state's ruling elite, owned a 160,000-acre manor in New York's Hudson Valley. To work the land, he engaged hundreds of tenant farmers. Like rural tenants on other manors or in other states or in past decades, these hardworking folk complained of rising rents, short leases, paltry pay, frequent evictions, and other abuses. They were primed to be rebels, but whom should they rebel against?

To answer that, we need to look at the Livingston clan's political affiliation. Their upper-crust adversaries in New York, the DeLanceys, were all Tories, while the Livingstons declared themselves patriot Whigs. Because the Livingstons were Whigs, many of Robert's tenants signed the "King's Book," promising to fight on behalf of the Crown. If the Livingstons were defeated by King George III, tenants could potentially divide up his mighty acreage, creating farms of their very own.

In siding with a distant King, tenants were simply opposing local elites. In Delaware's Sussex County, so-called Loyalists rebelled against rich men who could buy their way out of the draft (see Chapter 8). In Maryland's Baltimore County, debtors rebelled against their creditors, who happened to be Whigs. By default, that turned these poor people into Tories. One told an official to "kiss his arse and be damned, pulling his coat apart behind." This reflected personal and class rage, not political philosophy.

Indians, slaves, women, poor people—they might have been outsiders, but they listened carefully to talk of liberty and sovereignty, and to the words of the Declaration of Independence. Each group, and each individual, engaged fully in the sweeping drama of the times, and the nation that emerged bears their stamp. We understand that now, even if some people at the time denied it. Freedom and equality, once set in motion, have a trajectory all their own.

The Least You Need to Know

- In a war fought for the freedom and independence of a nation, personal freedom was the goal of the nation's most vulnerable people.
- Native Americans, caught up in a white man's war, tried to protect their own sovereignty.
- Blacks fought on the patriot side or fled to the British, hoping for their freedom.
- Women met wartime hardship and danger with great courage, growing more confident, but not more independent.
- Many poor people rebelled against a monarch, but some rebelled against well-to-do patriots who ruled their everyday lives.

First Drafts

The new nation, in its infancy, faced troubled times. It was fighting a war with the world's strongest power, yet it didn't even have a government. Only the states, at that moment, possessed the power to levy taxes and pass laws, but the states needed new constitutions, now that they were free of colonial rule. In drafting these codes, the people of Virginia, Pennsylvania, Massachusetts, and all the rest had to figure the proper balance between liberty and authority, always a touchy business, and particularly so in wartime.

Some Americans wanted to form a national government, but others preferred to continue the current arrangement, in which Congress was more of a coordinating body. They settled on a loose-knit set of rules called the Articles of Confederation. But the whole messy business—thirteen state governments and a weak Congress—made a difficult war even more difficult. This flimsy edifice nearly fell apart, and near war's end, the nation almost went bankrupt.

One man saved it, though. He is not a household name, but you will learn about him here. You will also learn that the solution was not permanent. As long as Congress had no way to raise its own funds, and states bickered over who should shoulder the burden, the so-called United States would not be so united after all.

State Constitutions

In This Chapter

- Republic vs. democracy, as understood in those times
- The meaning and implications of popular sovereignty
- Virginia's first government, with a bill of rights
- Pennsylvania's experiment with democracy
- John Adams and the Massachusetts Constitution of 1780

So you think you're a nation, just because you declared your independence? Not so fast.

First off, you have to figure out a way of defending your Revolution against the British, who are amassing a terrifying military force—23,000 Regulars, 9,000 Hessian mercenaries, a few thousand seamen, and 427 seaworthy vessels (both transports and warships), armed with some 1,200 cannons. They are the Goliath in the coming fight and are about to invade New York and cut the United States in two. How, pray tell, do you intend to stop them?

An army would help, but there is no national government that can simply call one up. Congress must beg the states for money, men, and patriotic sacrifice. But states don't have governments yet either, having just deactivated the British colonial structures. Unless each state quickly forms a viable government and joins with other states to defend America, all will be lost.

The emerging governments need to be strong enough to pursue a war, but not so strong as to threaten people's liberties. They need to gain the allegiance of the people, who expect to be involved. The body of the people, not just elite leaders, has already been directing affairs for Committees of Correspondence, Committees of

Safety, and state provincial congresses and conventions. Will this continue in the more permanent structures? How will money be raised, but liberty preserved? Each state will answer these questions in its own unique way.

A Republic or a Democracy?

Revolutionaries were not starting from scratch. Under British rule, each colony had experienced at least partial self-rule. Even if they were hindered by Crown-appointed governors and their councils, citizens did elect representatives to the lower house of the legislature, which held the power of the purse. Reflecting Britain's House of Commons, House of Lords, and King or Queen, the colonies contained democratic, aristocratic, and monarchical elements that functioned side-by-side. Now, with Britain out of the picture and monarchy discredited, states would decide on what components, if any, to carry over into their new governments, and what new ideas they would try.

For starters, Americans who wished to gain a seat at the political table needed to embrace the basic concept of *popular sovereignty:* governmental authority stems from the people. They also had to favor a *republican* form of government, where citizens freely chose their governmental representatives. All Revolutionaries subscribed to these notions.

People held differing views, however, on the relationship between the people and their representatives. Those who believed in *democracy* thought all leaders must be directly elected by the people and do the people's bidding. In their view, governmental bodies, such as the British House of Lords, that represented propertied interests were a threat to the people's authority. Further, they favored few if any restrictions on who should be allowed to vote.

Others thought people should select a handful of wise and virtuous leaders, and these men should make the decisions. Such statesmen should be well educated and have a sufficient level of property, so supposedly they would not use their public positions to gain more, as a less affluent person would be tempted to do. The voters, too, should be property holders because the business of government was to protect property as well as people. Those who subscribed to this view still considered themselves republicans because people elected their leaders, but they decried direct democracy, in which the uneducated masses could wield political power. (A cautionary note: The terms "democrat" and "republican," as used in Revolutionary times, do not translate directly to the political parties we have today.)

Sovereignty means the right to self-government. A **sovereign** nation is one that governs itself.

In a state or nation based on **popular sovereignty,** the people are the only legitimate source of political authority. Even if they designate authority to their chosen leaders for certain periods of time, they can take that authority away if they wish. Under popular sovereignty, people themselves have the ultimate say.

Democracy is the form of government in which the people rule directly or tell their representatives what to do.

A **republican** form of government has two meanings. In a broad sense, any government in which people elect their representatives is republican. In a narrower sense, a republican government is run by wise and virtuous leaders, elected by the people but not beholden to them in their decision making.

People who hold the **franchise** or enjoy **suffrage** have the right to vote. Groups who can vote are **enfranchised,** while those who can't are **disenfranchised.**

When it came to practical decisions, those who preferred a democracy wanted a single branch of government, directly beholden to the people, with the exclusive authority to make laws and select officials who would execute its policies. They also wanted to extend the *franchise*, meaning the right to vote, to all citizens, regardless of personal wealth.

Those who favored a pure republic, on the other hand, wanted two legislative bodies, one representing people and the other property, as well as separate and distinct executive and judicial branches, each capable of exercising checks on the others. They also wished to limit the franchise to those who possessed property, differing only on how much property a voter needed to own.

Property requirements for voting and office holding in three colonies:

- To vote in South Carolina, a person needed 50 acres or a town lot, but to serve in the legislature, he needed land worth £1,000 if he lived in the district or £3,500 if outside the district. For the Senate, it was £2,000 for residents, £7,000 for outsiders. To be governor required a "settled plantation" worth £10,000 "clear of debt."

- In Georgia, £10 or "being of any mechanic trade" earned the right to vote, but to serve in the lower house of the legislature required 25 times that amount, £250.

- In Maryland, a voter needed 50 acres or £30, but his representative had to possess £500 and be among "the most wise, sensible, and discrete of the people." In most states, but not all, only the wealthy were supposed to rule.

Virginia Sets the Pace

So which kind of governments should the states adopt, democratic or republican ones? The men who framed the various state governments were influenced by both philosophies, but republican views proved more dominant.

In May 1776, in a specially elected convention, the most populous state in America not only declared its readiness for independence, but also called for a new constitution. The state was Virginia, and its convention handed the task of constitution-drafting to George Mason, Washington's close neighbor, good friend, and political mentor. (Thomas Jefferson wanted to come home from Philadelphia to work on the Constitution, but his peers didn't let him. He had to settle for second best and pen the Declaration of Independence instead.)

Mason's draft opened with a long declaration of rights that still resonates today: freedom of religion and the press, trial by jury, the right to remain silent and to confront one's accusers, and so on. To these guarantees, the committee that reworked his draft added another important protection: "That excessive bail ought not to be required, nor excessive fines imposed, nor cruel and unusual punishments inflicted." The full Convention then added the right to a "well-regulated militia" and the subordination of standing armies to "civil power." This Declaration of Rights served as a preamble to Virginia's new constitution, and several states copied parts verbatim (see Chapter 16).

The body of the work started with a basic premise that became a model for other states: "The legislative, executive, and judiciary departments shall be separate and distinct, so that neither exercises the powers properly belonging to the other."

All branches of government were not equal, however. In annual elections the people could choose new members of the lower branch of the legislature, called the House of Delegates, or of course dismiss ones who didn't perform as expected. All acts and laws originated in a body that was responsive to the will of the people. Moreover, the lower body chose members of the upper body, called the Senate. The Senate, for its part, could accept or reject any acts and laws proposed by the House of Delegates, but it was specifically forbidden from amending money bills. Further, while Mason's draft had set high property requirements for office holders—£1,000 for House members, £2,000 for Senators—the convention declared that any person owning his own land could vote and be eligible to serve in the government. Was Virginia's constitution, adopted three days before Congress voted for independence, democratic or republican? It did create an upper house and a governor, both of which could check the will of the people, as expressed in the lower house. Those were republican features. But even though these men were usually rich, they did not *have* to be. Also, given the opportunity to vote for powerful House of Delegates, the people had the largest say in legislative and in money matters. These were democratic features. Call it a draw.

Power to the People: Pennsylvania

Pennsylvania created a constitution on an entirely different model, one strongly influenced by its unique history. At the outbreak of war, workingmen around Philadelphia formed into military associations that elected their own officers, and these groups coalesced into the "Committee of Privates," a powerful force for democracy. When the old Assembly withered because it refused to support independence (see Chapter 4), the Privates and their allies called for a constitutional convention and created a founding document like no other in the land.

Pennsylvania's constitution contained a strong Declaration of Rights, copied in large part from Virginia's, and then went Virginia one better in granting people unparalleled power. A single Assembly, chosen by the people and directly responsible to them, would make the laws; no upper body, representing men of property, could check its actions. The new code included the following vigorously democratic features:

- All free, tax-paying males were allowed to vote and hold office.

- Assemblymen, elected every year, could serve only four years in any seven-year period. They called this rotation in office; today, we call provisions like this term limits.

- Instead of a single man at the head of the government, there would be a 12-man executive council, with each member elected directly by the people of local districts. The council and the assembly, by joint ballot, would annually elect a president from among the council members, but the president had no separate powers.

- Members of the executive council, including the president, who served three consecutive years would have to sit out the next four.

- Pennsylvania delegates to the United States Congress, elected annually, could not serve more than two terms in a row.

- The state was required to print weekly reports on roll-call votes, and the chambers were to "remain open for the admission of all persons who behave decently." The people could therefore monitor their representatives.

- Most significantly, "all bills of public nature" had to be "printed for the consideration of the people" before coming to a vote, and no bill could be passed until the session after it was introduced. If people disagreed with the views of their legislators, they could vote them out of office *before* new laws were passed. This gave ordinary citizens unparalleled control over their governance.

THEIR OWN WORDS

"That an enormous proportion of property vested in a few individuals is danger-ous to the rights, and destructive to the common happiness, of mankind; and therefore every free state hath a right by its laws to discourage the possession of such property."

—First draft of the Pennsylvania Constitution of 1776, deleted from the final document. The convention favored political democracy but stopped short of economic leveling.

The 1776 Constitution was a blueprint for direct government and was acclaimed by common people, particularly those who had been politically excluded in the years building up to the Revolution. That included Scotch-Irish Presbyterians, primarily from the western districts, and Germans, who made up more than one third of Pennsylvania's population. Not surprisingly, well-to-do merchants in Philadelphia, the largest center of commerce in the nation, opposed the constitution. Relentlessly they tried to overturn it, but failed to do so until 1790 after the new Constitution of the United States took effect. The new state constitution introduced a Senate and a Governor, who checked the Assembly, and it gutted many democratic features. But Pennsylvania's Declaration of Rights survived, along with the expanded franchise. Once people acquired the right to vote, there was no taking it away.

John Adams Gets His Chance: Massachusetts

John Adams thought the Pennsylvania Constitution of 1776 made a mistake when it traded the unchecked tyranny of a monarch for unchecked tyranny by the people. No unicameral body should have such absolute control as Pennsylvania's did; distinct branches of government must curb the power of one another. In this, Adams followed the French philosopher Montesquieu, who influenced many of the founders. At the time, in a pamphlet called *Thoughts on Government*, Adams set out his ideas, and three years later, in 1779, he would try to implement them while drafting a constitution for the state of Massachusetts. As it turned out, this would be his only chance to create a government. When the framers drafted the federal Constitution in 1787, Adams would be representing his nation in England.

FOUNDER ID

John Adams (1735–1826). Continental Congress, 1774–1777. Board of War, 1776–1777. Minister to France, (1778–1779), Great Britain (1779), and the United Provinces (1780). Peace Commissioner, 1779–1783. Ambassador to the United Provinces (1782–1788) and Great Britain (1785–1788). Vice President, 1789–1797. President, 1797–1801. Primary author, Massachusetts Constitution, 1779. Author, *Thoughts on Government* (1776) and *Defence of the Constitutions of the United States* (1787–1788).

Adams loved to write, and much of our nation's early history comes to us filtered through his lens. A lawyer by trade, Adams defended British soldiers after the Boston Massacre, wrote treatises on government, pushed hard for independence in Congress, and penned the Massachusetts Constitution. He left for Europe in 1778 and spent the next decade there, returning home only once, briefly, in 1779. In France, the Netherlands, and finally Britain he procured loans, negotiated commercial agreements, and helped conclude the Treaty of Paris, which ended the Revolutionary War. While abroad, he warmed to European ways, more so than many Americans thought fit. He succeeded Washington in the presidency, but his single term was mired in factional politics and marked by the Alien and Sedition acts, intended to stifle dissent. After losing the election of 1800 to Jefferson, Adams spent the next quarter-century writing about events of the Revolutionary and Founding Era. Both Adams and Jefferson, having buried their political differences in their waning years, died on July 4, 1826, the fiftieth anniversary of the Declaration of Independence (see Chapter 24).

In the new code Adams drafted, the upper branch of the legislature was apportioned by the amount of taxes each district paid, not by population. By design, it represented property but was counterbalanced by a lower house that represented people. Unlike Virginia or Pennsylvania, Massachusetts had property requirements for assemblyman, senator, and governor. While these were not as steep as in some southern states, the restrictions ensured that men of means would fill these offices. The franchise was less inclusive than it had been before the Revolution, so, ironically, many soldiers who were still fighting for the nation's independence lost the right to vote, while almost all were rendered ineligible for high public offices.

The Massachusetts Constitution had one distinctive and very democratic feature, but this had nothing to do with John Adams. Back in 1775, when war first broke out, Massachusetts had decided to adopt the basic form of its colonial government, minus the royal governor and all the appointments he made. But that did not satisfy many residents in the western part of the state, who thought the people themselves should have a say in creating their own government. For years they pushed and pushed, and they even shut down courts to show how serious they were. Finally, in 1779, they managed to get a special convention to draw up a new constitution. Further, before that constitution could take effect, it was sent back to the town meetings for final approval. No other state required the people themselves to sign off on their new constitutions. (The town meetings were even allowed to suggest amendments, and many did, but because there was no way for the rest of the state to act on these amendments, this extreme nod to democracy came to a dead end.)

Sorry, Not You: A Limited Franchise

By 1780, the new rules in all states were set—but they were not set in stone. If they had been rigid, women and people of color would not be voting today. In some states, people who did not own their own homes, or an equivalent amount of property, would also be denied the right to vote. Let's say that the old rules still reigned and you are a professional woman with three kids—sorry, citizenship is not for you. A responsible black business owner, a 27-year-old male college graduate with a student loan to pay back, and a 20-year-old soldier serving overseas would also be forbidden to vote.

Luckily, in the nineteenth century, states began expanding the franchise to include all white males who had reached their majority, even those without property. It took the Civil War to grant blacks the *legal* right to vote, and blacks in many states did not get the *actual* right to vote until the 1960s. Women did not obtain the vote for a century and a half, in 1920. Males between 18 and 21, although old enough to die for their country, could not vote until 1971.

There has been a significant tilt toward democracy in the nation's philosophy of governance. Today, few would say that our leaders *must* be wealthy, and that these rich men should make decisions for the masses. Back then, some did think that way, particularly men of the upper classes, but common folk thought otherwise and expected representatives to do the bidding of the people. There was a genuine split.

So when you hear people say, "This nation was formed as a republic," they are correct, and when you hear people say, "This nation was formed as a democracy," they are also correct. The founders gave us both strains, and what we have done with these since is our business.

The Least You Need to Know

- Following independence, each sovereign state needed to create a new set of governing rules that were efficient but not oppressive.
- People who preferred a republic thought that wise and virtuous leaders, once elected, should make the decisions. Those who wanted democracy thought representatives should obey the will of the people.
- Republicans favored distinct branches of government, including an upper house of the legislature to check the popularly elected lower house, and property qualification for voters and office holders. Democrats preferred a single-house legislature, unchecked by men of property, and a broad franchise.
- Virginia, leading the way, included a Declaration of Rights, which influenced similar guarantees of rights in other states.
- Pennsylvania's Constitution, the most democratic, included many safeguards to ensure that people had a strong voice in their government.
- The Massachusetts Constitution, drafted by John Adams, included an upper house that represented property, but it was the only one that required final approval by the people.

The Articles of Confederation

In This Chapter

- The Iroquois, Dutch, and New England confederacies
- Benjamin Franklin's schemas, from 1750 to 1775
- John Dickinson's draft of the Articles of Confederation
- Congressional passage of a weakened version, 1777
- Final passage by the states, 1781

Although the states were sovereign, they also needed to live up to their new name, "The *United* States." What, exactly, did "united" mean? Would the states actually cede authority to Congress, the only body that represented the interests of the nation as a whole?

The states, still in their infancy, were reluctant to do that. Americans were not ready to form a central government, with the power to levy taxes and pass laws. Instead, they agreed on a loosely knit group (a "confederation") of state governments. The agreement that shaped this amorphous entity they called the Articles of Confederation.

Congress started working on this set of rules at the same time it declared independence. Each draft was progressively weaker than the last, and 16 months later, Congress finally sent the Articles of Confederation out to the states. All 13 would have to sign on before the Articles took affect, and that didn't happen until 1781, almost five years after independence.

In the meantime, Congress operated under no formal authority. People talk with some pride about the rag-tag soldiers who won the Revolutionary War. But in this chapter we will see that the whole so-called nation was just as rag-tag. It was not even an official confederacy until the Revolutionary War was almost over, and that confederacy was never a real government.

Precedents and False Starts

If delegates to Congress had wanted to form an actual, full-fledged *government*, they could have looked to the British system, which they had grown up with, and taken what they wanted while discarding the rest. They also could have sought guidance from a host of Enlightenment philosophers, who, in volume after volume, offered advice on grand models for governance. Unfortunately, these men had less to say about a mere *confederacy*, which was no more than a bunch of states agreeing to help each other out.

DEFINITION

A **government** has a direct relationship to the people governed. It makes laws, which the people must obey. In Western culture, starting with the Enlightenment, free governments have legitimized their authority only by gaining the consent of the people they govern. A **confederacy,** on the other hand, has no direct relationship with the people. It is an agreement between separate governments to join together for their mutual benefit, but only in specified and limited ways.

If one wasn't interested in a full-on government, where could one find recommendations or designs for a confederacy? Our very well-read founders knew all about the confederacies of Greece and Rome, but these ancient civilizations were like museum pieces, admired from a distance. They could not be carted out for everyday, practical use two millennia later.

There was, on the other hand, a current, operating Iroquois Confederacy, whose council fires burned brightly close at hand, some 200 miles from Philadelphia. Some people have claimed that the Founding Fathers, and in particular Benjamin Franklin, looked to the Iroquois for inspiration. But if so, they were strangely silent about it. In the countless debates and discussions, the Iroquois Confederacy was never mentioned. Nor did anyone propose Iroquois practices that might have been worthy of consideration, like granting governing powers to women or keeping the council fires burning at all times.

The Founders did talk about The Republic of the Seven United Netherlands, a.k.a. the United Provinces. These people, the Dutch, were Britain's chief commercial rivals, and they had operated as a confederacy for almost two centuries. But the Founders did not wish to imitate the on-again, off-again relationship with monarchy that characterized the United Provinces. Dutch history was too scattered; Americans wanted something better.

There was one direct precedent. Back in 1643, the colonies of Massachusetts Bay, Plymouth, Connecticut, and Hartford entered "into a firm and perpetual league of friendship and amity for offense and defence, … and for their mutual safety and welfare." Their collective purpose was simple—to fight Indians—and they formed an alliance called "The United Colonies of New England." Does that name sound almost familiar? When the First Continental Congress met in 1774, it echoed this name by calling itself "The United Colonies of *America*." Two years later, when colonies turned to states, the name became "The United *States* of America." At least in name, it all started with that New England confederacy.

Could we go to our own history and find building blocks? After all, the United Colonies of New England had made rules. They had decided, for example, that no colony could enter into a war on its own and that each must contribute soldiers in proportion to the number of male inhabitants over 16 years old in a colony. Commissioners from each colony came together to make policy, and they even elected a leader, though he did little beyond presiding, and was therefore called a *president*. The New England Confederacy lasted for a quarter-century. It broke up after King Philip's War (1675–1676), when the largest colony, Massachusetts Bay, balked at picking up the lion's share of the bill.

If there were lessons in this history, they were simple and meager. A confederation shouldn't collapse; it must have staying power. And a confederation should serve its member states in times of peace as well as war.

Ben Franklin's Bright Ideas

Over the next century, at various times, colonists proposed plans for confederations that were essentially military alliances against native inhabitants, like our very first alliance. None of these came to pass. But one man would keep the dream of an alliance alive. That was Benjamin Franklin, a godfather to the Articles of Confederation.

Benjamin Franklin (1706–1790). Pennsylvania Assembly clerk (1736–1750) and representative (1751–1757). Postmaster General for British North America (1753–1774) and the United Colonies/United States (1775–1776). Albany Congress, 1754. Agent for Pennsylvania in Britain, 1757–1762 and 1764–1774. Continental Congress, 1775–1776. Commissioner/Minister to France, 1776–1785. President, Pennsylvania Executive Council, 1785–1788. Constitutional Convention, 1787. Author/printer/editor, *Pennsylvania Gazette* (1729–1748) and *Poor Richard's Almanack* (1732–1757). Author, *Experiments and Observations of Electricity*, 1751. Copley Medal of the Royal Society, highest scientific prize in the world, 1753. Founder, Library Company of Philadelphia (1731), Union Fire Company (1736), Academy and College of Philadelphia, later University of Pennsylvania (1743), American Philosophical Society (1745), Pennsylvania Hospital (1751).

The scientific and cultural accomplishments of Benjamin Franklin, America's first iconic celebrity, would fill an almanac, which he himself could set in print. His experiments with lightning and electricity brought him world renown. He invented a host of useful objects (lightning rod, bifocal glasses, Franklin stove, paper money that was hard to counterfeit), gadgets (a soup bowl that stands upright on a rocking ship in stormy weather), and clever sayings ("He that lieth down with dogs, shall rise up with fleas"). He was versatile politically as well. Before the Revolution, he represented the interests of Pennsylvania and three other colonies in England. During the war, he represented the struggling nation in France, seeking and getting financial aid. After the war, he helped negotiate the Treaty of Paris. He also helped draft rules for two confederations (the Albany Plan, which was never adopted, and the Articles of Confederation) and finally, at the age of 82, the United States Constitution. A generation or two older than other Founding Fathers, Franklin was America's original elder statesman, but always, as biographer Walter Isaacson observes, with a wink in his eye.

As early as 1750, in a private letter, Franklin outlined his ideas for "a general council formed by all the colonies." The meeting place would rotate from colony to colony. A colony's representation would depend on its contributions to the common treasury, and Franklin suggested colonies raise the necessary money by placing an "*excise tax* on strong liquors" or "a *duty* on liquor imported" or a *fee* "on each license of a public house." It didn't really matter how liquor was taxed; Franklin was certain that any tax on liquor would keep the coffers full. Imagine: the confederated colonies, and later the nation, bankrolled by a tax on booze! What if people stopped drinking? Franklin did not worry about that. He knew this was America.

An **excise tax** is placed on the sale of a specified item. A **duty** is collected on imported goods. A **fee** is charged by the government for issuing a license or providing a service. **Luxury taxes** place the burden on the well-to-do, the only ones who can afford the items being taxed.

The Albany Plan of 1754

Four years later, nine colonies responded to a call by the Crown for a conference in Albany, and they came from Maryland northward. (Virginia declined and the Carolinas and Georgia weren't invited.) Britain was waging war against France and various Indian nations and wanted the colonies to present a common front. Here, at Britain's urging, was Franklin's chance to put forward ideas for confederation, and his broad outline was included in the final version that all the delegates agreed on—known as the Albany Plan. Lost, however, was Franklin's tax on liquor. Other delegates preferred a *luxury tax* on high-priced goods, one that could "be collected with the least inconvenience to the people."

The "Albany Plan" would have created a pan-colonial, quasi-governmental council. That was more than the British authorities had bargained for and they recoiled at the thought it might challenge government policies. The colonial assemblies, meanwhile, did not want to hand over the power of taxation to some "Grand Council," even if it was based in America. In his newspaper, Franklin tried to bring the public to his side by depicting a snake cut into pieces, accompanied by the words "Join or Die," but the public wasn't buying it. That image means more to us now than it did back then. The plan never received serious attention.

Albany Redux, 1775

Twenty-one years later, America and Britain were at war, and Benjamin Franklin dusted off his scheme and presented an expanded version to the Second Continental Congress. This time he had actual government in mind and even talked of Congress's receiving ambassadors, entering alliances with other nations, settling inter-colonial disputes, regulating commerce and currency, and making "general ordinances" for the "general welfare."

Once again, the sage was ahead of his time. Colonies were looking to their own interests, and those with claims in the West were not about to cede them to Congress. Southern colonies worried that their northern neighbors, citing the "general welfare" clause, might put an end to slavery. Small colonies could not accept representation according to population, a key component of the plan. Finally, most Americans were not so hospitable as Franklin, who wanted to invite Ireland, Quebec, St. Johns, Nova Scotia, Bermuda, the West Indies, and East and West Florida to join the confederation if they so desired.

But Congress let Franklin down gently. Five days later, it adopted his idea for "establishment of posts" and appointed him to serve as Postmaster General.

Writing the Articles

But if Franklin's notions seemed excessive, the idea of an alliance was not, particularly when colonies were at war and when independence was in sight. The Connecticut delegation came up with an alternate plan that denied Congress the power to settle the west, regulate commerce, or impose taxes on the states. This schema might create less resistance than Franklin's, but could it do the job? Would a weak confederation suffice?

Independence brought the issue of confederation to a head. On June 7, 1776, as part of his resolution to separate from Great Britain, Richard Henry Lee included two other proposals. First, "That it is expedient forthwith to take the most effectual measures to form alliances." And then: "That a plan of confederation be prepared and transmitted to the respective colonies for their consideration and approbation." These two were connected. If the United States was to attract foreign allies, it must first be a nation, with definite rules. The time for definition had arrived.

"The Farmer" Sows his Seeds

Five days later, Congress assigned one delegate from each colony to a committee that would "prepare and digest the form of a confederation." That committee, in turn, tapped the talents of the nation's number one pre-war writer, popularly known as "The Farmer." Back in 1767, John Dickinson had authored *Letters from a Farmer in Pennsylvania*, which derided taxation without representation and became the bible of patriotic tracts. Now, he was to produce new rules for a new nation.

> **FOUNDER ID**
>
> **John Dickinson (1732–1808).** Speaker of Delaware Assembly, 1760–1761. Pennsylvania Assembly, 1762–1765, 1770–1771, 1774–1778. Stamp Act Congress, 1765. Delegate to Continental Congress from Pennsylvania (1774–1776) and Delaware (1779–1781). Chairman, Committee to draft Articles of Confederation, 1776. President of Delaware (1781–1782) and Pennsylvania Executive Council (1782–1785). President, Annapolis Convention, 1786. Constitutional Convention, 1787. Author, *Letters from a Farmer in Pennsylvania*, 1767–1768.
>
> The "farms" belonging to the author of *Letters from a Farmer in Pennsylvania* were in Delaware and Maryland, worked by slaves and laborers. Dickinson was a successful lawyer and politician in both Pennsylvania and Delaware. Regarded as a hero for his writings in the 1760s, he opposed independence, which lessened his popularity. In Congress, the day before the final vote, he spoke for hours against independence, but the next day he abstained so the decision would be

unanimous (see Chapter 4). During the war, he fought the British, first as a colonel with the First Philadelphia Battalion, and then as a private in the Delaware militia, having declined an appointment as Brigadier General. Dickinson prepared the first draft of the Articles of Confederation. In 1786 he presided over the Annapolis Convention, which was called to revise the Articles, and in 1787 he helped replace the Articles with the Constitution, which more closely resembled the British system of government he admired. To this day, historians have difficulty placing this middle-of-the-road statesman, so fond of parsing words.

Dickinson copied passages from Franklin's plan verbatim. He, too, favored a strong confederation. He wanted "one body politic" that could determine western settlement, regulate commerce, and provide for the "common defence" and "mutual & general welfare" of "the said colonies and all the inhabitants, for their posterity." He delineated a long list of Congress's "exclusive" powers in considerable detail, and he suggested some additional restraints on the states–most notably, they could not secede or raise standing armies in times of peace. (The Connecticut plan, by contrast, had prohibited *Congress* from maintaining a standing army.) But Dickinson did place one major constraint on Congress: it should never interfere with the "internal police" of any state.

Once on the floor, Dickinson's draft provoked heated debates. According to the plan, each state should contribute to the common treasury according to its population, excluding Indians but including slaves. This infuriated the delegates from southern states, who maintained that slaves must legally be construed as property, not people. Eleven years later, in 1787, these same states would insist that slaves *should* be counted as people when determining representation in Congress–but not in apportioning the tax burden (see Chapter 13). From the start, special interests in Congress trumped logic.

Meanwhile, delegates from the more populous states complained just as loudly about Article XVII: "In determining questions in Congress, each colony shall have one vote." Was it really fair that the large states pay the bulk of bills, while the small states have an equal say in making decisions?

Also, states with western claims wanted to keep them, while states without claims to the West wanted Congress to take charge of expansion. States like Virginia, whose charter gave it access to land extending clear to the "South Sea" (Pacific Ocean), managed to strike out provisions that would have given Congress power over the West. Naturally this infuriated states like Maryland, which were counting on Congress to open the land to everybody.

Late in 1776, while delegates bickered, the British Army approached Philadelphia. Congress, suddenly in survival mode, fled to Baltimore. Temporarily, the bickering stopped—but nothing got done. The young nation still had no rules to go by. Congress could not govern. It could only improvise.

A Diminished Harvest

By the fall of 1777, inaction was no longer an option. France seemed ready to form an alliance, but would only ally itself with a real nation. Also, the continental currency was losing its value, and it could not be salvaged unless the body that issued it showed more signs of permanence.

Debates had to end. Whether delegates liked the Articles of Confederation or not, the rules were set. Each state, whether large or small, would receive only one vote. Expenses would be proportioned among the states according to the value of landed property, including improvements. This pleased southern delegates because slaves would not be taxed, while it displeased delegates from New England, where land was the most "improved." Although outvoted only five-to-four, with the other delegations split, the losers let it be.

The most enduring controversy centered on western lands. This was a deal-breaker for Virginia, which wouldn't sign on if Congress usurped its claims. Disgruntled delegates from Maryland, defeated by Virginia's unwillingness to compromise, finally allowed the Articles to be sent out for approval by the states, but that didn't mean their own state was ready to ratify them.

On November 15, 1777, Congress approved the Articles of Confederation, which were considerably weaker than Dickinson's original version. Henry Laurens, Congress's new president, and Charles Thomson, its longtime secretary, then sent the Articles out to each of the sovereign states. The official rules would not take effect until ratified by all 13 state legislatures.

FOUNDER ID

Henry Laurens (1724–1792). South Carolina Commons House of Assembly, 1757–1770. Lieutenant Colonel, Provincial Regiment in Cherokee War, 1760–1761. President of South Carolina Provincial Congress, Executive Committee, and Council of Safety, 1775–1776. South Carolina Vice President, 1776–1777. Delegate (1777–1780) and President (1777–1778) of the Continental Congress. Commissioner to the Netherlands, 1780. Prisoner in Tower of London, 1780–1781; exchanged for Lord Cornwallis, 1782. Peace Commissioner for Treaty of Paris, 1782. Appointed to Constitutional Convention, 1787, but claiming poor health from his captivity, he declined to serve.

Laurens was among America's least likely Revolutionaries. A merchant who traded everything from deerskins to human beings, he was among South Carolina's richest and most conservative figures in late colonial times, always supporting the Crown. During the Stamp Act crisis, a mob scoured his house for government stamps and terrified his pregnant wife. But in 1767, when a customs inspector unfairly seized two of his ships, he tweaked the inspector's nose and instantaneously became a patriot celebrity. Although Laurens headed all of South Carolina's Revolutionary organizations, he opposed independence and cried when it was declared. During the war, as president of Congress, he covered Washington's back when the General's command was challenged at Valley Forge. Laurens resigned after a year because of personal squabbles, and Congress then sent him to Holland in search of a loan. He was captured at sea and imprisoned in the Tower of London, the highest-ranking political prisoner in American history. Philosophically, Laurens came to oppose slavery and supported his son John, who wanted to free slaves in return for military service, but at the Treaty of Paris, he helped ensure slavery's survival by insisting that the British return all former slaves.

A Tough Sell

Back in the states, the Articles received a less-than-overwhelming welcome. Weak as the confederation was, many felt that it still took too much power away from the states. Almost all the state legislatures offered amendments. South Carolina alone wanted to make 21 changes. Maryland offered up this little piece of self-protection: "That one State shall not be burthened with the maintenance of the poor who may remove into it from any of the others in this union."

If Congress agreed to add Maryland's provision or any others, the whole measure would have to be sent back out to the states. This could go on forever. So Congress just turned down all new ideas, however good they might be. Ten states accepted the Articles as-is, but New Jersey, Delaware, and Maryland refused. Requiring unanimity of passage, the Articles of Confederation remained on hold.

New Jersey signed on late in 1778, then Delaware early the next year, but Maryland held firm until Virginia ceded most of its western land to the confederacy. It took a bit of foreign intervention to bring this last state into the fold. British ships commanded the Chesapeake Bay, and the French minister hinted that his government would not lend military assistance unless the Articles were adopted. So finally, on March 1, 1781, under dire threat of attack, Maryland relented. Nearly five years after it declared independence, the United States finally had some rules to live by.

The Least You Need to Know

- After independence, the United States was only a confederacy, not a government, so it could not pass laws or levy taxes.

- A century earlier, four New England colonies had formed a confederacy for military purposes, the first attempt at union of any kind.

- The first draft of the Articles of Confederation, modeled on Benjamin Franklin's ideas and penned by John Dickinson, gave Congress more power than states were willing to concede.

- The competing interests of states—small vs. large, south vs. north, those with western claims vs. those without—delayed agreement.

- The final draft of the Articles treated the states as sovereign governments, and all 13 needed to agree before the confederation took effect.

- Maryland did not sign on until 1781, so in the meantime, through most of the Revolutionary War, the nation was under interim management.

The Nation Goes Belly-Up

In This Chapter

- Supporting, and not supporting, an army
- The continuing struggles of hungry soldiers
- The collapse of continental currency
- The nation's first official financier, Robert Morris
- A debt unpaid and a nation still splintered

In those dangerous and demanding times, through most of the Revolutionary War, Congress was just a coordinating body, not a viable government. The states, on the other hand, did have governments, and they were expected to support Congress and its Continental Army. As this chapter reveals, they did not always come through. Soldiers received no pay and little food, and they understandably complained. Congress complained, too, but it could only beg the states to pony up, and beg again and again when they didn't.

To fill a worrisome financial chasm, Congress printed "Continental" currency. These bills were backed only by the promise that Congress would redeem them, and when people realized that wasn't likely to happen, the bills lost nearly all their value. Flat broke, Congress recruited the services of the richest man in the nation, Robert Morris, whom you will meet here. Amazingly, this single individual offered to back up the nation's currency with his own credit, and citizens who didn't think Congress's word was any good did think they could trust Morris.

Morris gave the country a quick way out of a crisis, but no one man could buttress the nation forever. State governments simply had to come through, yet they were so strapped they began printing their *own* paper money. Individuals were strapped, too, and when disgruntled farmers in Massachusetts rose up to challenge legal authority, Congress could not raise troops to restore order. Such was the state of affairs in 1787, when a few dozen delegates from 12 states met in Philadelphia to beef up the Articles of Confederation.

Who Will Fight? Who Will Pay?

George Washington wanted a well-trained and experienced professional army, but many patriots did not. Recalling their pre-war encounters with British Redcoats, they believed standing armies were part of the problem, not the solution. So at first, Washington found himself relying on citizen-soldiers from state militias and recent recruits. These volunteers might be fueled with patriotic fervor but were not, in Washington's mind, a reliable military cohort, not by a long shot. He wrote Congress: "Men accustomed to unbounded freedom, and no controul, cannot brooke the restraint which is indispensably necessary to the good order and government of an army, without which licentiousness & every kind of disorder triumphantly reign." He groused, "To place any dependence upon militia, is assuredly resting upon a broken staff. If I was called upon to declare upon oath, whether the militia have been most serviceable or hurtful, upon the whole I should subscribe to the latter."

The situation grew worse when large numbers of the volunteers Washington was complaining about left for home late in 1775, urgently needed on their farms or in their places of business or by the families they had temporarily deserted. Only then, with the nation undefended, did Congress admit that a more stable military force was required. With Washington's view now prevailing, Congress ordered each state to come up with a given number of soldiers, plus money to support those men. In turn, the states tried to raise an army the old-fashioned way, luring soldiers with bounties and promises. When even that failed to attract enough men, they resorted to the option of last resort: the draft.

Uncle Sam Wants *You!*

A draft in those times was not what it is today. If you were drafted, that didn't mean you had to march off to war and incur hardship and danger. It meant you had to provide a body, either yours or someone else's. If you had enough money, you could hire a raring-to-go teenage boy or some hard-pressed fellow desperate for cash to go in your stead.

THEIR OWN WORDS

"To Dea. John Sail, SIR:

This is to inform you are this evening drafted as one of the Continental men to go to General Washington's headquarters, and you must go or find an able bodied man in your room, or pay a fine of twenty pounds in law, money in twenty-four hours.

[Signed] Samuel Clark, Capt."

Soldiers who were "poorer, more marginal, and less anchored in society than average colonial Americans" filled the ranks of the Continental Army, says military historian John Shy. Poor or not, they did expect to be fed, clothed, sheltered, armed, and paid, as they'd been promised. Unfortunately these recruits weren't seen as Revolutionary War heroes in their own time (that would not come until the nineteenth century), and contemporary civilians sometimes balked at paying for the upkeep of men they considered riff-raff.

If state governments failed to supply soldiers, they were left to fend for themselves. Joseph Plumb Martin, a private who fought two wars, one against the British and the other against hunger, reported on the sad state of affairs. "We [18 privates and 3 officers] understood that our destiny was to go into the country on a foraging expedition, which was nothing more nor less than to procure provisions from the inhabitants for the men in the army … at the point of the bayonet." This did not help soldier-civilian relationships, as Martin reported once more. "And if I stepped into a house to warm me, when passing, wet to the skin and almost dead with cold, hunger, and fatigue, what scornful looks and hard words have I experienced."

A Tale of Two Winters

For good reason Joseph Plumb Martin grumbled, yet one Revolutionary story celebrates those who supposedly never complained. In grade school we learned that Revolutionary troops suffered stoically during a terrible winter at Valley Forge. Tested under the harshest of conditions, they remained stalwart and unfailingly loyal to their commander-in-chief. The tale is something of a yardstick by which school children measure heroism.

Most still believe that winter was the most severe and Valley Forge a turning point, after which hardened troops fought valiantly, and things got better. In fact, conditions continued to deteriorate throughout the war, and as they did, no-nonsense, everyday soldiers became the protagonists in less-heroic tales. To their credit they survived, an admirable feat in its own right.

Two years after Valley Forge, in 1779–1780, the Northeast seaboard experienced the coldest winter on record. The New York harbor froze solid. Horses and cannons and firewood and deserters traveled over the slick ice from New Jersey to Manhattan to Staten Island to Long Island, any which way they wished. The upper Chesapeake Bay froze, too, and even saltwater inlets in Virginia and North Carolina. By contrast, the winter spent at Valley Forge was actually milder than the historical average.

BY THE NUMBERS

Weather record keeping was spotty in those days, but we do know from people who took readings and recorded them in their journals that the winter of 1780 was a whole lot colder than the one the Continental Army spent at Valley Forge, as indicated by these records:

- In January 1778, when soldiers were camped at Valley Forge, the *low* temperature in nearby Philadelphia fell below freezing on 15 of the 31 days.

- On average, historically, it freezes in Philadelphia on 25 days in January.

- In January 1780, when soldiers were camped some 70 miles to the north near Morristown, the *high* temperature in Philadelphia rose *above* freezing on only one day. "The ink now freezes in my pen within five feet of the fire in my parlour, at 4 o'clock in the afternoon," wrote Timothy Matlack, the scribe of the Declaration of Independence. Inland, at Morristown, it was colder yet.

At Morristown, it wasn't just the cold but the snow. On January 3, the soldiers' camp was engulfed by "one of the most tremendous snowstorms ever remembered," army surgeon James Thacher wrote in his journal. When tents blew off, men were "buried like sheep under the snow, almost smothered in the storm." The snow cut off all supplies. "For a fortnight past the troops both officers and men, have been almost perishing for want," George Washington wrote to civilian officials. Soldiers were reduced to eating sticks, old shoes, and the officers' dogs.

The troops endured the worst Mother Nature could muster, but what they couldn't bear was the inefficiency of civilian governments, both state and federal, and what they perceived as a lack of support from their countrymen. Soldiers stewed and almost mutinied in May because even at that late point, inexcusably, they *still* had no food.

Rebel Soldiers Rebel

There was "no alternative but to starve to death, or break up the army, give all up and go home," Martin recalled years later. The soldiers "were truly patriotic, they loved their country, and they had already suffered everything short of death in its cause.

Now, after such extreme hardships, to give up all was too much, but to starve to death was too much also."

Finally, on May 21, 1780, Martin and his cohorts in the Connecticut Line refused to obey officers' orders. But that's as far as they went. After pointing bayonets at the officer's chests and "growling like soreheaded dogs," they backed off. Their protest did accomplish some good. Washington understood their plight and made sure some food was sent their way.

FOUNDER ID

Joseph Plumb Martin (1760–1850). Private, Connecticut Militia, 1776. Private (1777–1780) and sergeant (1780–1783), Continental Army.

Martin is the Revolutionary War's "everyman." In 1776, at age 15, he and the Connecticut State Troops, under Washington, got routed in the Battle of New York. The next year he entered the Continental Army, in which he served until war's end. He fought at Monmouth and Yorktown, wintered at Valley Forge and Morristown, and rarely got paid. After the war he settled in Maine, but was evicted from his farm by general-turned-land-baron Henry Knox. In 1830, still poor, Martin published a witty and irreverent account of his "adventures, dangers and sufferings" during the war, which, according to historian Phil Mead, corresponds perfectly to what we know about the events Martin describes. Martin wanted to depict the war from the perspective of common soldiers. "Great men get great praise; little men, nothing," Martin protested, but today, because of his superb narrative, this private gets more attention in chronicles of the Revolutionary War than most generals.

Seven months later, soldiers of the Pennsylvania Line decided they had had enough as well. They had enlisted for "three years *or* the duration of the war." Three years had passed and they were ready to go home, but officers reminded them of that word "duration" and pointed out that the war was still going on. On New Year's Day, 1781, intent on having it go their way, upward of a thousand men from the Pennsylvania Line marched from Morristown toward Philadelphia, where Congress was meeting. Pennsylvania authorities quickly ceded to their demands.

Three weeks later, when soldiers of the New Jersey Line tried to follow suit, Washington clamped down. "I prefer any extremity to a compromise," he told Congress. "Unless this dangerous spirit can be suppressed by force, there is an end to all subordination in the Army, and indeed to the Army itself." Loyal troops rounded up the mutineers and shot two ringleaders.

Washington knew repression was no answer. The answer lay elsewhere. "More certain and permanent funds must be found for the support of the war, than have existed," he wrote to Congress in January of 1781. "Without them, our opposition must soon cease."

Not Worth a Continental

Where would the funds that Washington wanted be found? Could Congress just *print* some money and hope people would accept it?

In June of 1775, at the outset of armed confrontation, Congress had issued $2 million in paper currency. The following month it added $1 million more, and then another $3 million that year and $19 million more in 1776. Back then, at the beginning of the war, printing money worked. When the commissary department of the army offered *continental dollars* to a farmer in return for some cattle to feed the troops, the farmer agreed to the deal. Perhaps he accepted this *continental currency* because he had no other way of making the exchange and knew he wasn't going to receive coins of gold and silver. So-called *hard money* or *specie* was scarce as hen's teeth. Perhaps, too, that farmer was swayed by patriotic allegiance or assumed that the states would come through in the end and meet their respective quotas, giving Congress required funds and ensuring the value of dollars he had just been paid.

DEFINITION

Specie, also referred to as **hard money,** is money, usually gold or silver, which cannot be printed or issued at will. Because Congress possessed no specie, it printed **continental currency,** which it pegged to the Spanish dollar rather than the British pound. A **continental dollar** could be turned in for one Spanish dollar or "the value thereof in gold or silver."

Down the line, though, the farmer found he was in trouble. In this war, as in most wars, essential items became scarce, so prices rose. He had to ask more for his cattle if he were to buy needed supplies himself. Meanwhile, Congress kept issuing more money, which lessened the value of his. If this was a problem during the early years of the war, in the later years it created a national emergency—not only for that farmer, but also for everyone else. Prices doubled, tripled, quadrupled, and worse. In April 1778, it took $6 in continental currency to purchase $1 in specie. Two years later that had risen to $60, and by April 1781 to $167.50. A continental buck couldn't buy a penny's worth of goods. Few suppliers would accept money that was losing its value daily. Even now, more than two centuries later, if something is "not worth a continental," it's not worth anything at all.

BY THE NUMBERS

Congress also tried to raise money through a lottery. Here's how it worked:

- On November 18, 1776, Congress decided to sell 100,000 $10 tickets and an equal number of $20, $30, and $40 tickets.
- Total sales would come to $10,000,000.
- Prizes amounted to $8,500,000, with $3,100,000 coming in small cash prizes.
- The other $5,400,000, including a grand prize of $50,000, would be bank treasury notes that bore 4 percent interest. "Adventurers" (as Congress called lottery customers) were essentially lending the government money.
- The lottery was not terribly popular. The first drawing of $10 tickets, scheduled for March 1, 1777, was postponed 14 months until May 1, 1778, but even then, only 20,433 of 100,000 tickets had been sold.
- To attract more adventurers, Congress raised the interest on prize bank notes to 6 percent.
- The final drawing for $40 tickets did not start until April 2, 1781. Because of depreciation, Congress had to readjust the value of the prizes or the "fortunate adventurers" (winners) would have won far less then they put into it.

THE Financier, America's First Bailout Czar

Enter Robert Morris, the nation's most prosperous merchant. Early in 1781, Congress created a special new office—Superintendent of Finance—and asked Morris to take charge of the government's affairs. He agreed, but only if he were allowed to run the show entirely. He wanted to handle all money without oversight, dismiss any government worker at will, import and export on the nation's tab, negotiate with and borrow money from foreign governments on his own accord, run the Navy, and simultaneously continue to build his private fortune.

FOUNDER ID

Robert Morris (1734–1806). Continental Congress (chair of Executive Committee, Committee of Secret Correspondence, Secret Committee of Commerce, Marine Committee), 1775–1778. Pennsylvania Assembly, 1776, 1778, 1780, 1785–1786. United States Superintendent of Finance, 1781–1784. Founder, Bank of North America, 1781. Constitutional Convention, 1787. Senator from Pennsylvania, 1789–1795.

The merchant Robert Morris made a fortune in the French and Indian War by selling scarce goods to consumers, supplying the army, and sending his ships to prey on enemy commercial vessels ("privateering"). In the early years of the Revolutionary War, serving on every committee in Congress that procured military wares, he issued many contracts to his own firm but did deliver the goods. "He has vast designs in the mercantile way," John Adams wrote, "and no doubt pursues mercantile ends, which are always gain, but he is an excellent member of our body [Congress]." Washington would not have had an army without him. In the winter of 1776–1777, when the rest of Congress fled from Philadelphia, Morris stayed behind to conduct the affairs of the nation by himself. The most powerful civilian in Revolutionary America, he was called on to rescue the nation near war's end. In the 1790s, Morris invested in 6 million acres of land across seven states, but when his scheme went belly-up, he landed in debtor's prison. America's richest man became the poorest, $2,948,711.11 in the hole.

Desperate, Congress agreed to Morris's demands. It had nothing left to lose, and Morris was the only person with the resources, contacts, and experience to bail them out. Most important of all, his credit, unlike the nation's, was still good. People wouldn't accept continental currency, but they would take "Morris Notes." If the government couldn't make good on its notes, Morris himself promised he would.

That was only a stopgap measure. "THE Financier," as people called him, had a two-part master plan. First, a national bank, capitalized by private investors, would extend credit to the government. With this bank, wealthy men would assume public debt, and once they did, they would make sure the government did not fail. The bank would operate without any restraints. There would be no limitations on the type of investments, no restrictions or regulations, and no time limit for the charter. To keep operations secret from "national enemies," the books would be closed. One person alone would provide oversight: "the officer who is appointed to manage the monied interests of America," which is to say Robert Morris. Although the very notion of such an institution flew in the face of prevailing republican ideology, it took a mere nine days for Congress to approve Morris's Bank of North America.

By issuing Morris notes, establishing a national bank, and improving the nation's credit abroad, THE Financier managed to avert the immediate crisis, but these measures only bought some time. Ultimately, Morris wanted the federal government to assume all public debt, which would be paid off by national revenues. He wanted Congress to levy taxes independently of the states, and he even listed these in full detail.

BY THE NUMBERS

Robert Morris's proposal for national taxation:

- Import duties on 24 items, ranging from 50¢ per pound for brown sugar or empty black glass bottles to $36 per pound for bottled wine.
- Export duties on eight items, from 6¢ per pound for salted beef to $180 per head for horses.
- An excise tax of $6 per gallon for "all distilled liquors to be collected at the still."
- A sharply graduated tax on houses, based on the number of glazed windows. No tax for the first 5, 50¢ for fewer than 10, and then increasing steadily, peaking at $100 for a 70-window mansion.

The Perils of Peace

As powerful as he was, THE Financier could not place the United States on a firm financial footing without federal taxation, but people at the close of the Revolutionary War were in no mood to pay taxes on anything. Ordinary Americans had sacrificed greatly and did not want to sacrifice more. They did not consider the country's war debt of $42 million as their problem. So the end of the war was actually a setback to those, like Morris, who wanted a stronger central government. Morris's assistant Superintendent of Finance, Gouverneur Morris (no relation to Robert), believed that peace was "not much for the interest of America." Only a "continuance of the war" would "convince people of the necessity of obedience to common counsel for general purposes." On November 1, 1784, Robert Morris and Congress terminated their relationship by mutual consent.

After THE Financier's three-year "reign," as people called his term in office, it was back to the drawing boards. Congress wanted to divide payment of the war debt among the states, apportioning it by land values, but because methods of appraisal varied, this proved impossible. It then switched to population as the key indicator, but delegates squabbled about whether to include enslaved African Americans in their calculations. Southern states, hoping to lessen their tax burden, said slaves should not count because they were property and not citizens. Northern states, not wanting to pick up more than their fair share, said slaves should count because their labor provided wealth. In what would become a grand tradition of irrational compromise, Congress agreed in the end that each slave would count as three fifths of a person.

Does that fraction sound familiar? If it doesn't, you will read about it soon (see Chapter 13). A quick preview: When debating the issue of representation by population during the Constitutional Convention, each side would reverse its position. The South suddenly decided that slaves were people after all, while the North said their numbers should not be counted. To settle the matter, the same magic fraction would come to the rescue once again.

How long would states continue to bicker about who should pay? And would they ever come through with their respective shares?

The Least You Need to Know

- When fewer men volunteered for the army, men were drafted, but a draftee could buy his way out by hiring a substitute.
- Soldiers were rarely paid and often suffered long periods of cold and hunger, not just at Valley Forge but also at Morristown and throughout the war.
- To pay its bills, Congress issued continental currency, but by the end of the war this money had lost nearly all its value.
- When Congress gave Robert Morris unprecedented powers to bail out the nation, he created a national bank and offered his private credit to back Congress's debt.
- Still, because Congress lacked the power to raise money through taxes, it had to rely exclusively on the states.
- With the end of the Revolutionary War, Americans were exhausted and less interested in sacrificing for the national cause.

A New Plan

After the Revolutionary War, the "United States" were not very united. The states had different and competing interests, while class and regional divisions within each state produced great tensions. When protestors in Massachusetts closed courts and took up arms, men with property to protect panicked. In 1787, seizing the political moment, those favoring a stronger national government called for a convention to overhaul the Articles of Confederation. At the outset of that meeting, delegates scrapped the Articles and started working out a brand-new plan.

Under the Articles, Congress was the only branch of the confederated government. There was neither a separate executive authority nor a national judiciary, and Congress itself had only one chamber. Under the plan devised by the "Framers" (as we now call delegates to the Constitutional Convention), the central government would take on more powers, but these would be distributed among separate and distinct branches, which would check and balance each other. There would be two houses in the legislature. One man, called a president, would head the executive department, while a Supreme Court would anchor a national judiciary system.

But who should get what powers? How should the various offices be filled, and how long should the officers serve? There was much room for debate and no shortage of men with bright ideas and strong opinions to conduct that debate. In this part, we will travel back in time to that momentous summer of 1787, when 55 delegates from 12 states developed the basic rules we live by today.

A Revolution in Favor of Government

In This Chapter

- Overburdened taxpayers and the war debt
- Bondholders who want to be paid back
- Civil unrest and the misnamed "Shays' Rebellion"
- An historic convention in Philadelphia
- Tossing off the Articles of Confederation and starting anew

Because states had the ability to raise their own money and pay off war debts, it might seem they would fare better than Congress. But raise money from whom? In this chapter, we will see how people resisted taxation throughout the nation, especially when taxes produced profits for speculators who had preyed on them.

In Massachusetts in the fall of 1786, things came to a head. Angry farmers shut down the courts and took up arms, and no government could stop them—not the state and not Congress. Private parties had to do the job. The uprising alarmed prominent leaders like George Washington. These men felt the national government must be strong enough to suppress rebellions like this and resist the pressure commoners were placing on legislatures in all the states.

The next spring, in May, delegates from 12 states met in Philadelphia to broaden the Articles of Confederation. We will follow them as they take a vow of secrecy and then set to work. Their first surprising move is to abolish the Articles, in complete disregard of their instructions. They prefer to start from scratch.

Passing the Buck: Taxpayers and Speculators

If you think taxes are a big issue now, imagine yourself in Revolutionary times. Your state government has to pay off a huge war debt, and on top of that it must shell out money to pay the federal war debt, because Congress can't raise its own funds. State officials want you and your neighbors to foot the bill. Not only that, they say you must pay mostly in specie—those gold and silver coins that you haven't seen lately because everyone has been using government-issued paper money instead. Upset? Had enough? Could it get any worse?

It does get worse. Imagine that you are a farmer who supplied the army with beef and other goods during the war and only received an IOU, because the government couldn't pay at the time. Now it will pay off that IOU, but only with a bond, a certificate that you can cash in at a specified later date, at a fixed rate of interest. But you are hard pressed for cash and really can't wait for your money, and you learn that a merchant is buying up bonds from other poor farmers. He isn't paying full price—perhaps only 20¢ on the dollar, but you are desperate. You sell that piece of government paper to him, taking a big loss, not happy about it.

Here's the rub: when the bonds actually come due, the merchant who bought from you at fire sale prices will receive the full price, plus the interest that has accrued. Your loss is his gain. Not only that, *you*—the taxpayer—are the one who will be paying him the full price when your government redeems the merchant's bond. He bought it from you for 20¢, and now you and your fellow taxpayers are buying it back from him at a dollar plus interest.

BY THE NUMBERS

Clever investors could leverage their money, but at taxpayer expense. Here are two examples:

- In Massachusetts, Abigail Adams purchased a "consolidated note" at a third of its face value. The interest the Adamses collected was 6 percent of face value, and that meant they received an 18 percent return (3 times 6 percent) on their investment.

- In Virginia, speculators could find an even better deal. There, "military certificates" sold for a fifth of their face values. These, too, yielded 6 percent interest, so people who brought them at the discount rate pocketed 30 percent profit per year (5 times 6 percent)—if the taxpayers came through!

Okay, farmer, will you stand for this? The farmer who had sold bonds to merchants didn't want to stand for it. He insisted that state legislatures prevent speculators from getting a free ride at the taxpayers' expense. First, bond speculators must not be paid in specie. Give them paper money only. Next, pay speculators only what the bonds had cost them, plus interest on that reduced amount, rather than full face value of the notes. That seemed fair enough. Current bondholders would be paid off but denied any super-profits.

So said the farmer, but switch hats and imagine for a moment that you are the merchant. If the farmer gets his way, you will be receiving only modest interest on your investment, and if the state pays you with money it prints, that will soon lose value and you'll be even worse off than before you purchased the bond. Your investment will have produced a net loss. "It's not just me," you declare. "If the state won't honor its commitments to people who have lent money, nobody will lend money again. Without good credit, the state will collapse, and there goes our experiment in independent government!"

Welcome to post-Revolutionary America in the mid-1780s. Tension everywhere. Something will have to give. Stay tuned to see how this plays out.

A Rebellion in Massachusetts

In a deteriorating economy, money was hard to come by. Farmers in Western Massachusetts were both disgruntled and indebted, with creditors harrying them and bringing suits for collection of money owing. (Between 1784 and 1786, roughly one third of the adult males in Worcester and Hampshire Counties were either suing or being sued.) By the summer of 1786, stressed-out farmers had had enough. Following a script written 12 years earlier, when many of these very same people had toppled British rule (see Chapter 3), they gathered in taverns, called for county conventions, and forcefully resisted those who seemed to be oppressing them. This time, though, their opponents were neither Tory officials nor a distant Parliament but merchants in the eastern seaboard towns who were prospering while they themselves were hurting. Furthermore, those eastern towns paid a disproportionately small share of levied taxes because those were based more on land and less on commerce. According to the farmers, Massachusetts had become a two-tiered society, with the well-heeled and favored Easterners occupying the top tier.

At their conventions, protestors determined that if they closed the courts, they could not be sued for debts. So they went on the offensive. In the five westernmost counties, which covered two-thirds of the state, angry farmers marched on their county seats and shut down the machinery of government.

Merchants and moneyed men attempted to raise a countervailing force. First, they called out the local militias, only to discover that many militiamen identified with the protestors and wouldn't go up against them.

Next, they went to Congress, which commissioned loans for half a million dollars to support an army that could suppress the "dangerous insurrection" in Massachusetts. But the loans were to be paid back by the states, which were hopelessly strapped and far behind with prior obligations to Congress. Only one state, Virginia, agreed to raise money for a federal army.

That left Massachusetts on its own. Flat broke, all it could do was pass repressive laws, including a riot act that forbade 12 or more people from gathering with arms and a sedition act that made it illegal to spread "false reports to the prejudice of government." Local sheriffs could shoot and kill protesters, confiscate land, and apply "thirty-nine stripes on the naked back" of any who resisted. Joining the vindictive charge was Samuel Adams, of all people, who had championed American rebels when they resisted British tyranny but had no sympathy for these farmers, who were resisting an elected, constitutional government.

Finally, in January 1787, 129 merchants and professionals from Boston and other eastern cities paid to raise a private army. Led by Benjamin Lincoln, a Revolutionary general, this army had the personal sanction of Governor James Bowdoin, himself a wholesale merchant. On January 25, 1787, when rebels tried to take over an armory in Springfield with a three-pronged attack, they had a lapse of communication that proved lethal. After being routed, the rebels fled. Pockets of resistance continued, but by March the rebellion had been entirely squashed. Most rebels escaped punishment. A few were jailed, and two were hanged, but the rest were pardoned the following year.

Today, we call the revolt of these farmers *Shays' Rebellion*, after Captain Daniel Shays, a veteran of the Revolutionary War. But Shays was not even present for many of the early protests, and he later rose to a leadership position only to make military decisions for rebels from one of several counties, not to command or even represent the entire movement. Like its predecessor, the Massachusetts Revolution of 1774, the movement was highly democratic, with neither Shays nor any of the other leaders calling all the shots. But the rebels' opponents found it convenient to name the uprising after a single man. They wanted people to think that the protestors were blindly following the orders of a rabble-rousing director and had no legitimate grievances of their own.

> **DEFINITION**
>
> **Shays' Rebellion** refers to the 1786–1787 farmers' rebellion in Massachusetts. Although this name appears in our history textbooks the rebels themselves never used that term. They sometimes referred to their movement as a Regulation, meaning they were taking the regulation of government into their own hands. This term had been used by pre-war protestors in North and South Carolina, who called themselves Regulators, and it would be used again by protesters in Pennsylvania in the 1790s (see Chapter 19). But this name has been largely forgotten. Winners often spin history's story, while losers are left speechless, and here's a case in point.

Protests were not limited to Massachusetts. In nearby Connecticut, New Hampshire, and Vermont, hard-pressed farmers toyed with rebellion. In Rhode Island, debtors and taxpayers gained control of the legislature and forced the state to issue paper money. Governmental leaders in New York, North Carolina, and Georgia debated whether to circulate paper money in their own states in order to escape the wrath of indebted farmers, and then did so in all three states. In York, Pennsylvania, 200 men armed with guns and clubs took back cattle that had been seized by the government in lieu of taxes. Farmers closed a court in Maryland. After a court closure in South Carolina, Judge Aedanus Burke said that not even "5,000 troops, the best in America or Europe, could enforce obedience to the [Court of] Common Pleas." The struggling nation was on the verge of going to war with itself.

The Call for a Federal Convention

After the "reign" of THE Financier (see Chapter 8), those who favored a stronger central government had lost power. But the financial crisis gave them a new opportunity. As state governments caved to farmer unrest by issuing paper money and passing debt relief measures, those with property to protect, IOUs to call in, or bonds to redeem went into a panic. Seizing on these fears, *nationalists* argued that only through centralization could property be secured and the country saved.

> **DEFINITION**
>
> A **nationalist,** in the Founding Era, was someone who believed in a stronger central government.

In September 1786, just as the rebellion in Massachusetts was beginning, a group of nationalists led by Alexander Hamilton, James Madison, Edmund Randolph, and John Dickinson met in Annapolis, Maryland, to consider amending the Articles of Confederation and strengthening the federal government. Had they succeeded in their mission, perhaps Annapolis today would be filled with history-loving tourists, hoping to catch a brief glimpse of the place that marked a coming together of the states. But states from the Lower South sent no delegates, and New England states boycotted the meeting. It was a flop. The twelve men from five middle states who did attend could do no more than issue a call for a wider convention, to be held the following spring in Philadelphia.

The second convention, held in the spring, might have fared no better than the first, if not for the winter's unrest in Massachusetts. Washington, among others, was horrified by the "disorders." "Good God! Who, besides a Tory, could have foreseen, or a Briton predicted them?" he exclaimed, writing to General Henry Knox. The dangers of protest were immediate and physical. Men of property recognized that without quick and assertive action, local rebellions could spring up everywhere.

In February 1787, Congress sanctioned the second convention "for the sole and express purpose of revising the Articles of Confederation." A special convention was "the most probable means of establishing in these states a firm national government," it said. Such wording would not have been approved a few months earlier.

This time, the state legislatures from twelve states sent delegates. (The Rhode Island legislature, suspicious of the convention's intent, refused to participate.) Although the upcoming convention aroused considerable interest in political circles, it attracted only spotty attention on the local levels, where people were grappling with their own immediate issues. For more than two decades, since the Stamp Act Congress in 1765, Americans had been staging conventions and passing resolutions to suit every purpose, and in the minds of many, the Philadelphia convention appeared like more of the same. This grassroots inattention provided fertile ground for men who wished to plant some unexpected seeds.

By May 14, the appointed day, delegates from a grand total of two states were in Philadelphia. It was a poor initial showing, but over the next 11 days delegates straggled in from hither and yon, and finally, on Friday, May 25, the convention achieved a quorum of seven states. (The number seven was borrowed from the Continental Congress, which was having difficulty fielding a quorum for its own meetings in New York.) On that day, 29 men took their seats in Windsor chairs, each at a writing desk, in the East Room of the Pennsylvania State House, which we now call Independence Hall. Eventually, 55 delegates would take part in some or all of the proceedings of the "Federal Convention," as people at the time called it. Although many had been in the room before as members of Congress, only Robert Morris, Benjamin Franklin, and Connecticut's Roger Sherman had signed or helped to write both great documents that emanated from that location: the Declaration of Independence and the young nation's working constitution, the Articles of Confederation.

No dirt farmers had been selected as delegates, although there were plenty of gentleman planters. Also present were numerous lawyers and a healthy share of graduates from Princeton, Yale, and Harvard, the nation's preeminent colleges. Most had actively opposed independence during the grand debate in the early months of 1776. Now, many of these cautious patriots were the foremost advocates of a nationalist agenda.

Significantly absent from the Federal Convention were the following key historical figures:

- John Adams, future president, who was then in London serving as Ambassador to Great Britain

- Thomas Jefferson, future president, who was representing the United States in France

- Richard Henry Lee and Patrick Henry, powerful political figures from Virginia, who decided not to attend because they opposed greater centralization of government

- Samuel Adams, also suspicious of greater centralization

- John Hancock, who was deeply engaged in the messy politics of Massachusetts

America's three greatest superstars were in attendance. Eighty-one-year-old Benjamin Franklin dutifully attended every session. As usual, Franklin had some very wise words to say, but he sometimes wrote them out first and asked others to read them. Some writers have stated that Franklin was so weak during the Convention that he had to be transported to and from the proceedings in his Parisian-made sedan chair, but this seems unlikely. Although Franklin did own such a chair, his own words suggest that he did not rely on it during the stimulating summer of 1787. Three days after the Convention adjourned, he wrote to his sister, Mrs. Jane Mecom: "I attended the business of it 5 hours in every day from the beginning, which is something more than four months. You may judge from thence that my health continues; some tell me I look better, and they suppose the daily exercise of going & returning from the State-house has done me good."

THE Financier, Robert Morris, showed up along with his lawyer, James Wilson, and his former Assistant Superintendent of Finance, Gouverneur Morris. All three men were vigorous proponents of a stronger national government. Although Robert Morris said hardly a word, Gouverneur Morris and Wilson were, with Madison, the most talkative men at the convention.

Finally, and most significantly, George Washington left retirement to attend this gathering. His impact on the convention cannot be measured by the number of times he expressed his personal views, which happened to be one. It lay merely in his presence, for he lent the gathering an air of authority and legitimacy it might otherwise have lacked. With characteristic precision, "The General," as people still called him, arrived in Philadelphia on the evening of May 13, one of only five out-of-state delegates who showed up on time.

This Meeting Will Now Come to Order

Outside, on a rainy day in Philadelphia, no public fanfare marked the convention's commencement. Inside, to add a bit of a flourish, the illustrious elder statesman Benjamin Franklin was supposed to nominate George Washington for President. But Franklin did stay in from the rain on opening day, so Robert Morris nominated Washington instead. To affirm solidarity across regional lines, John Rutledge of South Carolina seconded the nomination, which was approved by unanimous consent. Morris and Rutledge accompanied Washington to an armchair with a tall back topped by a carved image of the rising sun. From there Washington would preside, although when delegates turned the meeting into a "committee of the whole," Nathaniel Gorham of Massachusetts took the chair instead.

Can You Keep a Secret? Madison's Notes

The first item of business was to establish some rules on procedure. One in particular stands out: "That nothing spoken in the house be printed, or otherwise published, or communicated, without leave." Delegates did not wish their deliberations to be influenced by public opinion, and unfortunately for them, that meant they had to shut all windows and doors in a muggy Philadelphia summer so no passersby could hear. Wanting to speak freely, they pledged their honor, gentlemen to gentlemen, that they would keep all deliberations to themselves.

But if everything was supposed to be such a secret, how do we know so much about the momentous deliberations through the hot summer of 1787?

Ask James Madison, unofficial and self-appointed court recorder of the Constitutional Convention. Actually, the meeting did have an official secretary, an army major and former member of Washington's staff named William Jackson, but he only recorded the motions and votes, not who said what. For that we must turn to Madison, whose "notes" extend to over 225,000 words, about 600 printed pages. Other delegates jotted notes now and then, but nobody else covered the entire proceedings in detail. In honor of the vow of secrecy he had taken, Madison did prohibit publication of his notes until all participants were dead, half a century later.

How did Madison carry off his 600-page transcribing feat? Here's how he described his method: "I chose a seat in front of the presiding member, with the other members on my right & left hands. In this favorable position for hearing all that passed, I noted in terms legible & in abreviations & marks intelligible to myself what was read from the chair or spoken by the members, and losing not a moment unnecessarily between adjournment & reassembling of the Convention I was enabled to write out my daily notes during the session or within a few finishing days after its close. It happened also that I was not absent a single day, nor more than a casual fraction of an hour in any day, so that I could not have lost a single speech, unless a very short one."

FOUNDER ID

James Madison (1751–1836). Virginia Convention, 1776. Virginia House of Delegates, 1776–1777, 1784–1787, 1799–1800. Virginia Executive Council, 1778. Continental Congress, 1780–1783, 1787–1788. Annapolis Convention, 1786. Constitutional Convention, 1787. United States House of Representatives, 1789–1797. Secretary of State, 1801–1809. President, 1809–1817.

Today, Madison is known more as an architect of the Constitution than for his two terms as president. This is partly due to the exact notes he took at the Federal Convention, partly to ideas he presented there, and partly to his arguments in *The Federalist* favoring ratification (see Chapter 14). In 1787, he argued for "a due supremacy of the national authority," but a decade later, when his political opponents (ironically called Federalists) tried to stifle dissent, he said states had the right to nullify an unconstitutional federal law. Originally opposed to adding a list of rights to the Constitution, Madison changed his mind after ratification and introduced 19 amendments in Congress. Ten of these passed, our Bill of Rights (see Chapter 16). With Madison, everything was a balancing act. Federal and state power must be finely tuned; theory and practice blended. This was not always easy, and only a serious and committed statesman like Madison would make the attempt. He sought the middle ground but was not always able to locate it. Sometimes, as with his fierce commitment to religious liberty, he allowed his principles to dictate his stand, come what may.

A Government, Not a Confederacy

On Tuesday, May 29, immediately after the convention settled on the rules, Edmund Randolph, Governor of Virginia, "opened the main business," as Madison put it in his notes. The Articles of Confederation, he said, were no longer adequate to the job at hand. That document had been drafted in a different time, "when the inefficiency of requisitions was unknown—no commercial discord had arisen among any states—no rebellion had appeared as in Massachusetts—foreign debts had not become urgent—the havoc of paper money had not been foreseen." To "remedy" these various ills, the Articles of Confederation needed to be "corrected and enlarged."

Having laid out the need, Randolph presented a 15-point proposal, commonly called "the Virginia Plan," which closely resembled many existing state governments. This plan, and its evolution into our Constitution, will be discussed in the following four chapters.

The next morning, before delegates had a chance to discuss the Virginia Plan, Randolph made a surprise announcement: on the suggestion of Gouverneur Morris, "he was willing to drop his weak preamble, which said merely that the Articles of Confederation should be "corrected & enlarged," in favor of something much stronger: "A *national* government ought to be established consisting of a *supreme* legislative, executive & judiciary." (Madison's notes emphasized "national" and "supreme.") A federation of any sort would no longer suffice. Only a real government would do.

FOUNDER ID

Edmund Randolph (1753–1813). Virginia Attorney General, 1776–1786. Continental Congress, 1779–1782. Governor of Virginia, 1786–1788. Annapolis Convention, 1786. Constitutional Convention, 1787. United States Attorney General, 1789–1794. Secretary of State, 1794–1795.

Randolph's grandfather, Sir John Randolph, was Virginia's only knight. His father, a loyalist, emigrated to England, but his uncle, Peyton Randolph, was first president of the Continental Congress. When Peyton died in 1775, Edmund administered his estate and inherited some of his political clout. He served ten years as Virginia's first attorney general before becoming its governor in 1786. Politically, he was a fence-sitter. At the Federal Convention, he presented the initial plan for a national government, but then refused to sign the final document; by the following year, he supported it. As United States Attorney General and confidant to President Washington (he had been one of Washington's aides during the war), Randolph mediated between Hamilton and Jefferson (see Chapter 19). In 1794, he became Secretary of State, but he left office the following year after being framed by political opponents. Having lost both his office and the trust of Washington, whom he had served loyally, Randolph retreated from national politics and turned to writing. In his *History of Virginia,* he portrayed Virginia's Revolutionary elite as disinterested leaders, far superior to the general population they governed.

Randolph's declaration set off a short but spirited discussion "on the force and extent of the particular terms *national & supreme.*" This radical idea would be overstepping their bounds, some delegates protested. The states had not authorized delegates to abolish the Articles of Confederation, only to build on them.

But Gouverneur Morris, who had suggested the idea to begin with, bullied on: a "federal" government was no more than "a mere compact resting on the good faith of the parties," while a "national, supreme" government implied "a compleat and compulsive operation." Because "federal" had proved too weak, it was time to try the tougher brand. "In all communities, there must be one supreme power, and one only," he said boldly.

Morris, Randolph, and the nationalists carried the day. Of the eight states that voted, six approved the revolutionary and unconstitutional move to create a single national government with supreme authority. In one daring stroke, the Articles of Confederation—a contract amongst sovereign states, each "supreme"—had been scrapped.

No wonder the delegates agreed to work in secret. Imagine the uproar back in the states if people knew that their existing constitutions were being eclipsed! If American citizens had been asked at that very moment whether they would submit to the supreme authority of a distant national government vested with sweeping powers that superseded those of their own states, the nays would have dwarfed the ayes.

But the die was cast, and delegates committed to a truly revolutionary act. This revolution did not take place in the streets, but behind closed doors. It was not bathed in blood, and it was not uproarious, but silent. Not until mid-September would people out-of-doors hear about the momentous decision made on the morning of May 30, 1787, by a group of men willfully defying their instructions.

The Least You Need to Know

- Strapped by a shortage of specie, common people pressured state legislatures for paper money and other relief from their debts and taxes.
- Speculators who had purchased bonds at bargain prices wanted to get paid back at full value, but farmers didn't want to pay taxes to make speculators rich.
- The Massachusetts Regulation, misnamed Shays' Rebellion, focused the farmers' anger and scared those with property to lose.
- Before the rebellion, a convention in Annapolis produced a feeble turnout, but after, delegates from 12 states met in Philadelphia to strengthen the Articles of Confederation.
- Instead of amending the Articles, the "Federal Convention" ditched them and started anew.

Special Interests in Congress?

In This Chapter

- State and regional interests at the Federal Convention
- The small state/large state dispute over representation
- Virginia Plan, New Jersey Plan, and Connecticut Compromise
- Congress's new power of taxation
- Congressional powers: strictly limited or loosely implied?

"In all cases of public service, the less the profit the greater the honor," Benjamin Franklin told his fellow delegates at the Federal Convention. He wanted officers in the new government to seek the good of the public, not line their own pockets. Few would disagree with Franklin here. But should government officials look after the specific interests of their class, their state, or their region? That would be selfish, too, Franklin believed—yet that's exactly what was happening during the Convention. However patriotic any delegate appeared, his concept of the "public good" seemed to coincide with the particular interests of constituencies he represented. Defending those interests, delegates clashed, particularly when it came to setting ground rules for Congress.

Should each state have an equal representation in Congress, or were large states entitled to more representatives? If the latter, should slaves count as people, even though they were treated as property and of course had no say in the government?

The battles didn't stop there. Should there be one house of Congress, as in the Articles of Confederation, or two? Who should select the congressmen? How long should they serve? And most critically, how far should their powers extend? There were no easy answers, but the form they settled on is still with us today. Let's see how, and why, delegates to the Federal Convention set up Congress the way they did.

First Try: The Virginia Plan

After voting to replace the Articles of Confederation with a "national, supreme" government, delegates addressed the plan Edmund Randolph and the Virginia delegation had placed before them, which was dramatically different than the Articles of Confederation (see Chapter 9). Key details of the plan are as follows:

- It suggested there would be two houses of Congress, not just the single chamber established by the Articles. Members of the second house would be elected by the first.

- Both houses would have *proportional representation*. (Under the Articles, each state, whether large or small, had exactly one vote.)

- There would be a national executive department, although it didn't specify whether one man or several men would lead it. (Under the Articles, there was no separate executive department.)

- Special new courts—"one or more supreme tribunals"—would deal with national laws. (No such courts existed under the Articles.)

- New states could be admitted to the union.

- The new plan would not require the approval of the state legislatures, which might object to a central government seizing some of their powers. Instead, it would be considered by special conventions of the people in each state.

DEFINITION

Under **proportional representation,** the number of representatives each state could have in Congress would be determined according to (a) its population, or (b) the amount of money it contributed to the national treasury. In this way, large states would have more of a say than small.

The Virginia Plan served as the working draft for a new Constitution. It would be discussed and modified over and over, but it gave delegates somewhere to start. Point-by-point, they debated its suggestions.

Starting from the top, all delegates agreed there should be a Congress. Since independence and even before, starting with the First Continental Congress in 1774, Congress was the only body that "united" the United States. Congress must continue, in one form or another.

But from there, the questions began. What, exactly, *was* Congress? What should it do? Who should select its members—state legislators, as under the Articles of Confederation, or the people themselves?

Filtering Democracy

In this day and age we elect our Congressmen, but we wouldn't be doing it if Roger Sherman had had his way. Sounding more like a pre-war Tory than a Revolutionary, this Connecticut delegate thought "the people should have as little to do as may be about the government. They want information and are constantly liable to be misled." Another Yankee, Elbridge Gerry from Massachusetts, quickly supported Sherman's notion. "The evils we experience flow from the excess of democracy," he cautioned. The rebellion in his home state had taught him "the danger of the levelling spirit."

Then two unlikely candidates came to democracy's rescue. George Mason, Washington's friend, whose large plantation was not far from Mount Vernon, thought Sherman and Gerry were retreating from the founding ideals of the nation. At least the "larger branch" of Congress should be elected by the people because "it was to be the grand depository of the democratic principle of the government."

James Wilson, who once had fired into a crowd of commoners attacking his home, went farther than Mason and farther than any other delegate ever would. This wealthy Pennsylvania lawyer asserted that a government based on popular sovereignty must allow the people to choose not only their representatives in the lower house of Congress, but also their Senators and the President.

FOUNDER ID

James Wilson (1742–1798). Continental Congress, 1775–1777, 1782–1783, 1785–1786. Constitutional Convention, 1787. Pennsylvania Ratification Convention, 1788. Associate Justice of the United States Supreme Court, 1789–1798.

Wilson was an unlikely proponent of direct elections by the people. He was lawyer to the richest and most powerful civilian in America, Robert Morris. In 1779, when hundreds of angry citizens came after Morris, Wilson, and others they accused of war profiteering, the men retreated to Wilson's house, later dubbed "Fort Wilson." From there the wealthy men fired into the crowd of protestors, killing five. Wilson also had worked tirelessly to overturn the democratic Pennsylvania Constitution of 1776. But he believed that a government of the people must feature popular elections for representatives, senators, and the president—a view that was not shared by most of his Convention colleagues. Wilson figured prominently in the creation of the presidency, making the motion for a single executive and suggesting the Electoral College. A vigorous supporter of the Constitution during the ratification debates (see Chapter 14), he applied to Washington for the position of Chief Justice, but Washington made him instead an Associate Justice on the first Supreme Court. Like Robert Morris, Wilson overextended his investments and died deeply in debt.

James Madison, like so many others, feared true democracy, yet maintained that people needed to vote somehow. If not, they "would be lost sight of altogether." So Madison suggested they vote for representatives to the lower house in Congress. These representatives would then choose the Senate, and Senators would choose judges and make other appointments. Congress as a whole would choose the president. In this "great fabric" of "successive filtrations," people would have *some* say, but a limited one.

This compromise won out. For more than a century, American citizens only voted for representatives in the House. Not until 1913, with the ratification of the seventeenth amendment, did they choose their senators, and to this day, the people do not directly select their president. (For more on the strangest of all constitutional anomalies, the Electoral College, see Chapter 11.)

Large States vs. Small

In the past, each state had been given an equal say. When Virginia, the largest state, suggested that representation should instead be proportional to size, it's no wonder that the smallest state, Delaware, strenuously objected. One of its delegates, George Read, even said he was under strict instructions from his state legislature and would pack up and go home if the Convention changed the one-state, one-vote rule.

Virginia's James Madison tried to talk Read out of it. A national government, he explained, had to be responsible directly to the people, "without the intervention of the state legislatures." The citizens, not the states, should have equal representation. But Read was not swayed. He had his marching orders.

Rhode Island was already boycotting the Convention. Fearing Delaware's departure and afraid that other states might take off if they did not get their way, the Convention temporarily tabled the matter. Better to move on and get some agreement on other issues first.

BY THE NUMBERS

Delaware, the smallest state, and Virginia, the largest, had the most to lose or gain from proportional representation. Here is what was at stake:

- 59,094—the population of Delaware in the first federal census, 1790. This included 8,887 slaves.
- 747,610—the population of Virginia in 1790. This included 292,627 slaves.

- Under proportional representation, without counting slaves, Virginia would get 9 times as many congressmen as Delaware. Counting slaves, it would get 12 times as many.
- If each state retained an equal vote in Congress, a citizen in Delaware would have 9 to 12 times more of a say in federal matters than a citizen in Virginia.

Alternatives: The New Jersey Plan and Connecticut Compromise

Delegates wouldn't return to the representation dilemma for another two weeks, when a caucus of small states came forward with a plan of their own. On June 15, their spokesman, New Jersey's William Paterson, challenged Randolph and the Virginians. The Articles of Confederation merely needed to be strengthened, not overhauled. Yes, Congress should acquire the power to tax, but there was no need to make it into two bodies, both with proportional representation. The old rule—one state, one vote—would suffice.

FOUNDER ID

William Paterson (1745–1806). Secretary, New Jersey Provincial Congress, 1775–1776. New Jersey Attorney General, 1776–1783. Constitutional Convention, 1787. United States Senator from New Jersey, 1789–1790. Governor of New Jersey, 1790–1793. Associate Justice United States Supreme Court, 1793–1806.

Educated at Princeton, Paterson had his state's interests at heart. During the Revolutionary years, he served in the New Jersey Provincial Congress, Council of Safety, Legislative Council, and militia. As the state's first Attorney General, he tried to keep the Revolution pure by prosecuting cases of fornication. Later, as Governor, he went after billiards and taverns. In 1780 Paterson was elected to Congress, but he preferred to keep his Attorney General job back home. At the Constitutional Convention, after gaining equal representation for New Jersey in the Senate, he threw his support behind the Constitution. He then became a Federalist, and in 1793 Washington nominated Paterson for the Supreme Court. This time, he left the New Jersey governorship to accept the position. On the high court, Paterson supported judicial review (see Chapter 12) and upheld the supremacy of federal treaties over state laws. In the trials following the so-called Whiskey Rebellion (see Chapter 19), he ruled that opposition to federal law enforcement amounted to treason.

Delegates debated the relative merits of the Virginia and New Jersey plans for two days before taking a vote. Seven states favored the Virginia Plan, three favored New Jersey's, and one state was divided. That decision left the dissenting states dissatisfied. Unless they could get the majority to make some concessions, the minority might simply pack up and go home, as Delaware had threatened.

Three delegates from Connecticut—Roger Sherman, Oliver Ellsworth, and Doctor William Samuel Johnson—tried to bridge the perilous gap that divided large and small states. Their solution, called the Connecticut Compromise, seems obvious now since our system reflects it. Why not let proportional representation determine membership in one house of Congress, they asked, while continuing the one-state, one-vote rule in the other? This was not enough for some delegates, though. Driven by local concerns, they defeated the proposal by a narrow margin. The Convention then did what conventions do best: it created a committee and told it to find an answer.

FOUNDER ID

Roger Sherman (1721–1793). Connecticut House of Representatives, 1755–1756, 1758–1761, 1764–1766. Connecticut Council (Senate), 1766–1785. Judge of Connecticut Superior Court, 1766–1767, 1773–1788. Continental Congress, 1774–1781, 1783–1784. New Haven Mayor, 1784–1793. Constitutional Convention, 1787. United States House of Representatives (1789–1791) and Senate (1791–1793).

Today, Sherman would be considered a "Beltway insider," having spent more time in Congress than any other man of his times. He was blessed with neither social standing nor charisma. "He is awkward, un-meaning, and unaccountably strange in his manner," wrote William Pierce. But Sherman did possess ambition. At first a farmer and shoemaker, he became in rapid succession a surveyor, shopkeeper, and almanac publisher—in the Ben Franklin mold, but without the flash. Upwardly mobile, he passed the bar in 1754 and entered public office. From 1755 to his death in 1793, he served in public capacities continually, several offices at a time, without much of a professional or business life in the private sphere. At the Constitutional Convention, he argued that executive power should always be subservient to Congress and the state legislatures. Although he promoted states' rights at the Convention, afterward he embraced a strong federal government and helped secure ratification. Sherman and Benjamin Franklin were the only founders who helped draft the Declaration of Independence, Articles of Confederation, and Constitution.

Franklin's Middle Way

Benjamin Franklin sat on that committee. At age 81, Franklin struggled just to attend the proceedings and on some days was too weak to read his own speeches, but he sacrificed his own well-being, determined to find a way out.

Each side would have to give a little, Franklin told his stubborn peers. "When a broad table is to be made, and the edges of planks do not fit, the artist takes a little from both, and makes a good joint," he explained. "In like manner here both sides must part with some of their demands."

Preaching aside, Franklin had a very specific idea for breaking the impasse. The Connecticut Compromise had failed to attract the support of delegates from large states, who feared that if small states were represented equally in the Senate, they might levy taxes that placed undue burdens on large states, which had more taxpayers. So he added a third item to the Connecticut Compromise. All money bills would originate in the House of Representatives, where large states had greater control. The Senate, where small states wielded more power, could not amend these bills in any way. After round upon round of further debating, the Convention finally endorsed Franklin's solution on July 16.

What Should Congress *Do?*

By the end of July, after meeting for a full two months, delegates had outlined in broad strokes the structure of Congress. There would be two chambers, referred to at that time as simply the "first branch" and the "second branch." Representation in the first branch would be proportional to the amount of taxes each state contributed to the national treasury. Representatives would be elected directly by the people every two years.

People did not elect representatives to the second branch. State legislatures did, and they could send as many people as they wanted to the second branch. The number didn't matter because each state had only one vote. Members would serve for six years, and they could repeat in office. Other suggestions for term length included four, five, and nine years. Alexander Hamilton favored life terms "during good behaviour."

The Convention had also decided that Congress could legislate "in all cases for the general interests of the union." But what did that *mean?* If the Articles of Confederation were too weak, what new powers should Congress have?

On July 26, delegates appointed a Committee of Detail. Composed of one member from each state, it was supposed to fill in the blanks. Ten days later, this committee presented a vast array of Congressional powers. Congress could now collect taxes, regulate commerce, negotiate and enforce treaties, coin money, emit bills of credit, establish courts, raise armies, call forth militias, build fleets, make war, suppress insurrections, and "make all laws necessary and proper" to accomplish these and other tasks. The Committee of Detail report resembled the Constitution we have today.

Taxes and the Constitution

Without the power to tax, other powers had little meaning. That's why all delegates agreed to a straightforward passage that read: "The Legislature of the United States shall have the power to levy and collect taxes, duties, imposts, and excises." After all, the main reason delegates had gathered in Philadelphia was that the Articles of Confederation denied Congress the power to raise its own money. Repeatedly, Congress had tried to amend this rule, but each time at least one state stifled the plan. (Remember, any changes to the Articles of Confederation required unanimous consent of the 13 states.) The nation would have to move past this no-tax bottleneck in order to survive, delegates knew. It was that dramatic and that clear. To taxes we owe our Constitution.

Even so, taxation was a politically sensitive topic. Pushed beyond endurance in paying for the war, people feared more of the same. As Gouverneur Morris explained, "Seize and sell their effects and you push them into revolts."

Taxes, yes, but who should carry the burden? Should Congress tax a person or his property, or only goods that he bought or sold? Since people could freely decide not to buy or sell a taxed item, this indirect tax on goods seemed the least burdensome. But the line between direct taxes on people or property, and indirect taxes on goods bought and sold, was blurry. What if a farmer needed to export his crop to survive? Was that a direct or indirect tax?

In the end, delegates decided that exports wouldn't be taxed, but all other indirect taxes were fair game. It also decided that direct taxes on people or property were permitted, but only if they were apportioned according to the population of each state. (This would change with the sixteenth amendment in 1913, which permitted Congress to tax people without considering state populations.) Finally, the Convention added broader wording to the taxation clause. Taxes, it said, would be used "to pay the debts and provide for the common defence and general welfare of the United States." Pretty open-ended. Delegates preferred it that way.

Paper Money and Other "Wicked" Projects

When states were the only governments, states made money—literally. They could print it if they wanted, and some did. To many at the Convention this now seemed a bad idea because a glut of state currencies would weaken the value of all money. A ban was in order, all agreed, but two camps emerged. Some thought an outright ban "would rouse the most desperate opposition," while others were in favor of simply "crushing paper money"—no holds barred. Crushing paper money won by a vote of eight to one, with one state divided.

The Convention next declared that states could pass no law "impairing the obligation of contracts," coming down firmly on the side of creditors. Debts would be honored, including the payment of government bonds. Debtor relief by state legislatures would come to an end. With these measures, both contained in Article l, Section 10, Clause l, Congress reigned supreme in monetary affairs.

The ban on paper money and debtor relief played well among the delegates. "The soul of the Constitution," Charles Pinckney called this clause. "One of my favorites," Edmund Randolph added. If this were the only clause in the Constitution, Wilson proclaimed, "I think it would be worth our adoption." But how would this play out-of-doors, when so many citizens were in the red?

THEIR OWN WORDS

"A rage for paper money, for the abolition of debts, for an equal distribution of property, or for any other improper or wicked project, will be less apt to pervade the whole body of the Union than a particular member of it."

—James Madison, arguing for the new Constitution in *The Federalist,* #10

The House or the Senate?

By early September, Congress had assumed roughly the shape it has today. Some changes had been made since July, when Franklin and the delegates from Connecticut had determined the broad outlines of the two houses of Congress. The first branch was named the House of Representatives, and membership would be proportioned according to state population, not contributions to the national treasury. The second branch, called the Senate, would consist of two members from each state, each with a vote. Franklin's idea of keeping the Senate away from money matters had been modified. The House now had to *originate* all money bills, but the Senate could amend them.

The basic structure of Congress, though, remained the same. All bills of any sort needed the approval of both houses before becoming law. But some powers, as Franklin had observed, seemed more appropriate to one chamber or the other. The House, composed of the people's direct representatives, should take the lead in taxation. This followed from the idea of "no taxation without representation," so pivotal in the nation's break from Britain.

Meanwhile, the Senate exercised significant powers of its own, unrelated to legislation. It could try impeachments, ratify or not ratify treaties, and approve or turn down presidential appointments for Supreme Court judges, ambassadors, and other officials. The fact that these weighty matters were entrusted to the upper body, which the people themselves did not elect, rather than the lower body, which the people did elect, would cause much consternation once the doors of the Pennsylvania State House were opened and the Constitution was presented to the public.

The Powers of Congress: A Debate Without End

Under the Articles of Confederation, Congress had not passed any laws, which meant it had no direct authority over ordinary citizens. In contrast, the newly constituted Congress was a law-making body, and it would reach *directly* into people's lives.

Soon enough, that raised questions. Was Congressional power strictly limited by the provisions itemized in the Constitution? (These are listed in Article 1, Section 8.) Or did the final clause of this section, which empowered Congress to "make all laws which shall be necessary and proper" for executing the Constitution, give it broader authority? That question would be contested hotly in the Early Republic (see Chapters 19–22), and it is still debated today.

The Least You Need to Know

- Delegates to the Federal Convention represented the interests of their states.
- The Virginia Plan called for proportional representation in Congress, but in the New Jersey Plan, each state would have an equal say.
- According to a compromise arranged by Franklin and delegates from Connecticut, representation in the House would be by size, in the Senate each state would be represented equally, and all money bills had to originate in the House.
- Delegates were worried about an "excess of democracy," so only representatives to the House would be elected directly by the people.
- The Convention achieved its economic goals: Congress could raise its own revenues, while states were restricted from issuing paper money and passing debtor relief.
- The "necessary and proper" clause left room for debate on how tightly or broadly to interpret Congress's powers.

A King Who Is Not a King

In This Chapter

- One executive or several? Who chooses? For how long?
- Alexander Hamilton's preference for monarchy
- James Wilson, Gouverneur Morris, and the Electoral College
- The last-minute addition of a vice president
- Powers granted to the president

Congress was weak under the Articles of Confederation, but the president was even weaker. In fact, the office barely existed. There was no separate executive department, just a nominal head of Congress. Each year, when representatives gathered, they would choose one member to preside over their meetings and to write and receive official correspondences. Those were the sole responsibilities of President Peyton Randolph (the first man chosen by the Continental Congress back in 1774), President John Hancock (in office when Congress declared independence in 1776), and eleven other men who are little known today. Ever hear of President Elias Boudinot? Perhaps not, but why should you? He enjoyed no special powers and exerted little influence over the course of history.

Most delegates to the Federal Convention believed the president's role should change. A distinct executive department would bring "vigor" and "energy" into government. Without forceful execution of the laws and policies that Congress passed, Congress would remain ineffectual.

A robust executive, something akin to a king? Really? Revolutionary Americans had had their fill of kingly rule. The office had to be strong enough to make government work, but with no hint of monarchy.

What would such an office look like? Should it have one man at the head, or several? Who would choose him or them? How long would he/they serve? What powers would he/they command? How might these powers be held in check? These are the questions the framers faced.

Starting from Scratch: Basic Questions

As they invented the American presidency, the most influential office in the nation and perhaps the world, delegates had no precedents to draw upon. In their new constitutions, states had retreated from monarchy and limited executive power. In the Articles of Confederation, Congress had purposely omitted a separate executive branch. The office delegates were about to invent, whatever it might be, was up for grabs.

Edmund Randolph, in the Virginia Plan, made the first move: "Resolved, that a National Executive be instituted; to be chosen by the National Legislature for the term of ___ years." The executive would receive fixed compensation and possess "a general authority to execute the National laws."

How would you react to that, if you were there? Would you be okay with Congress selecting the executive? Would you care to fill in the blank, stipulating exactly how long the term should be? You might note, by the way, that the resolution says nothing about a "president." In fact, the authors were deliberately silent on whether the executive department should have a single leader. Might you prefer two, three, or more? Wouldn't that be more democratic, and less monarchical?

One Chief Executive, or Several?

On June 1, when this part of the Virginia plan came up for debate, Pennsylvania's James Wilson moved "that the executive consist of a single person." Charles Pinckney of South Carolina seconded the motion, indicating approval across regional lines.

Replying to Wilson's motion, John Rutledge, also of South Carolina, "was for vesting the Executive power in a single person, tho' he was not for giving him the power of war and peace," Madison wrote in his notes. "A single man would feel the greatest responsibility and administer the public affairs best." Rutledge had had some experience in this matter, having headed his state's government two different times.

John Rutledge (1739–1800). South Carolina Commons House of Assembly, 1761–1776. Stamp Act Congress, 1765. Continental Congress, 1774–1775, 1782–1784. President, Provincial Congress, 1775. President of South Carolina, 1776–1778. South Carolina Governor, 1779–1782. Senior Judge, South Carolina Court of Chancery, 1784–1790. Constitutional Convention, 1787. United States Supreme Court Justice, 1789–1791. Chief Justice United States Supreme Court (nominated but not confirmed), 1795.

Like other wealthy young men of South Carolina, Rutledge was sent to England for a formal education. He returned an adept lawyer and entered politics, siding with Christopher Gadsden in the Assembly's challenge to Royal control. Representing South Carolina's interests in the Continental Congress, Rutledge managed to exempt rice growers from the export ban in the Continental Association. In 1776, he headed his state's new government, but he resigned two years later to protest changes in the state constitution that took away his veto authority. He returned to the governorship in 1779, and the following year he was granted extraordinary powers when the state faced a British invasion. People dubbed him "dictator." As a plantation owner, governor, and civilian commander of the state's military forces, Rutledge was comfortable with top-down command. "Democratic power," he said, was "arbitrary, severe and destructive." In 1795, Washington nominated him for Chief Justice of the Supreme Court, but he fell out politically with the Senate, which rejected his appointment because he publicly opposed a treaty most senators favored.

Connecticut's Roger Sherman thought differently. The executive department was "nothing more than an institution for carrying the will of the Legislature into effect," he maintained, so Congress should be left to determine "the person or persons" to lead it. One year they might want one, the next year three—it should be their call.

Then Edmund Randolph, the man who introduced the Virginia Plan, weighed in. He "strenuously opposed a unity in the Executive magistracy," which he regarded "as the foetus of monarchy." As a sitting governor, Randolph favored a *strong* executive but not a *single* executive. "The fixt genius of the people of America," he observed, was set against any imitation of the British monarchy. In other words, people wouldn't go for a single executive.

Unable to agree, delegates placed the issue on hold. As yet, one-man rule was still too hot to handle.

How Long Will He/They Serve?

After this tentative start, delegates moved on to the blank left in Randolph's opening outline: "for the term of ___ years." Wilson opened the bidding with three years, and Charles Pinkney countered with seven. Sherman, for a change, agreed with Wilson. George Mason argued "for seven years at least" with one term only, but Gunning Bedford of Delaware warned against seven because the nation might be "saddled" with a first magistrate who was not up to the job. Three and seven were the only numbers presented. The day was wearing on. Debate was limited. On a hasty vote, the longer term prevailed by five states to four, with one divided. They did not address the question of whether the executive(s) could serve more than one term.

Who Will Choose Him/Them?

The same day, late in the afternoon, delegates turned their attention to the manner of choosing the executive(s). The Virginia Plan assumed this would be Congress, which traditionally had selected its own presiding officer. That was fine with Roger Sherman, a political insider, but not so fine with James Wilson, that unlikely fan of popular elections (see Chapter 10). Wilson thought the executive should be chosen directly by the people, cutting out the middlemen. This shocked most other delegates. They could handle popular elections of Congressional representatives, but not of one, two, or three executive leaders. They assumed people would vote only for their own local heroes, thus tearing the country apart. Or perhaps the people would blindly follow some demagogue.

But if the people were not to be trusted with such a momentous decision, who *should* make the choice? The original plan—selection by Congress—had its own problems. Supposedly, the executive was to be an independent branch, but how could it remain independent if Congress chose who served?

Could the state legislatures make the choice? That, too, would highlight regional jealousies and inhibit national allegiances. It would also open the new government to the same sorts of allegedly pernicious schemes currently under consideration in several states, things like paper money and debtor relief.

So what was to be done? The opening day of deliberations ended with the Convention at an impasse.

First thing the next morning, June 2, James Wilson announced he had solved the puzzle. The executive(s) should be elected by special electors, chosen by the people for this purpose only. Wilson left several blanks in his plan. He expected the

Convention to decide how many electors there would be, how districts would be determined, where electors should meet, and so on. But the outline was there, and what we know today as the Electoral College was born.

Not surprisingly, the concept was just too new and strange for other delegates to embrace. Elbridge Gerry of Massachusetts doubted "that the people ought to act directly even in the choice of electors, being too little informed of personal characters in large districts, and liable to deceptions." Others didn't see the point of creating a third group of representatives because people already had their state legislators and congressmen. Wilson's motion suffered a resounding defeat. Only his own state of Pennsylvania, along with neighboring Maryland, voted for it.

So it was back to the start. Immediately following the defeat of Wilson's elector scheme, delegates voted that the executive(s) should be chosen by Congress and serve a seven-year term. The tally was a decisive eight states to two. Issue settled. That's why Congress, to this day, elects our executive officer(s), who serve(s) for seven years, right?

The President of the United States

Now that the executive office was beginning to take shape, delegates figured it was time to rein it in. If not, opponents of their plan were sure to play the monarchy card for all it was worth. "Vote against this new Constitution," they would say, "or you'll wind up with another king."

First off, the delegates empowered Congress to impeach the executive(s) for "mal-practice or neglect of duty." Then, they disallowed a second term. This passed seven states to two, with Pennsylvania divided.

By limiting the likelihood of high-handed rule, delegates alleviated fears of a sole chief executive. At midday on June 4, they finally voted in favor of a single executive, seven states to three. Virginia voted with the majority, but its delegation was split, with Edmund Randolph still adamantly opposed to the idea. George Washington, the sitting president of the Convention and odds-on favorite to become the nation's first chief executive, cast the deciding vote within his state's delegation. Should the job ever be offered to him, and should he accept, he would exercise executive authority alone, not with others.

Delegates did not use the word *president* until the early days of August, two months later. The Committee of Detail, charged with transforming an outline into a genuine Constitution, produced three drafts. The first, in the hand of Edmund Randolph, referred simply to the "executive." John Rutledge added "*Governor* of the united People & States of America" in the second draft, and James Wilson, in the third and final draft of the committee report, produced this: "The Executive Power of the United States shall be vested in a single person. His style shall be 'The President of the United States of America,' and his title shall be, '*His Excellency.*'" "President" stuck, and so did "His Excellency," at least until Andrew Jackson, the alleged man-of-the-people, assumed the office.

DEFINITION

In colonial and Revolutionary times, a **president** was one who presided over a congress, convention, or almost any meeting. Today, we might call such a person a moderator. The term **governor** was stronger, implying the officer possessed actual powers. In opting for "president" over "governor," delegates to the Federal Convention chose to de-emphasize the power of the individual who held the office. They wanted the office to appear less intimidating. Still, they wished people to show the president respect. Hence the title **His Excellency,** a deferential term normally applied to governors at that time.

Check and Balance: The Presidential Veto

Delegates had to figure out the relationship of the executive office and other branches of government. The most critical issue was the presidential veto, as we call it today, or "negative," in the parlance of the times. Could the president overrule acts of Congress?

James Wilson and Alexander Hamilton thought the president should have "an absolute negative." If he didn't like a bill, the president, on behalf of all the people of the nation, could just say no.

Roger Sherman, a devotee of legislative power, argued "against enabling any one man to stop the will of the whole. No one man could be found so far above all the rest in wisdom," he said.

Most other delegates found themselves in between these two positions. They wanted the president to check ill-conceived notions of Congress but not offset an entire branch of government. They settled on a compromise: the president could negative a bill, but with a two-thirds vote of each house, Congress could then override his veto.

Thinking Outside the Box

Some of this resembles the office as we know it today: the name, the possibility of impeachment, the qualified veto. But not the single seven-year term, much less the president's selection by Congress.

If Congress' choosing the president sounds strange to us now, it worried people then as well. True, it was the custom. Congress had been the sole governing branch of the federal government up to that time. But how could the president be independent of Congress if it placed him in office and could remove him at any time? Over and over, delegates revisited this problem, but the alternatives—popular election or Wilson's crazy elector scheme—seemed worse.

Two forceful men tried to break new ground. One ventured so far from the mainstream that nobody dared follow him. The other turned the Convention around, creating the American presidency we have lived with since.

Alexander Hamilton's Wild Ideas

On June 18, Alexander Hamilton, Washington's protégé during the Revolutionary War and now a delegate from New York, took the floor and didn't relinquish it for almost six hours. He spoke nonstop, telling his fellow delegates exactly what form of government he thought best. Only because they had all taken a vow of secrecy could Hamilton say the things he did.

We know the gist of what Hamilton said because Madison and two other delegates took notes that were published long after, and because Hamilton himself wrote an outline for his preferred plan of government and jotted down notes in preparation for his speech. All these survive, and they are shocking indeed.

According to Madison, Hamilton stated "he had no scruple in declaring that the British Government was the best in the world; and that he doubted much whether any thing short of it would do in America." When forming the American presidency, "the English model was the only good one." In his written plan, he called the American executive a "governor," a stronger word than "president." In his speech and his notes, he unabashedly used the M-word, which nobody else at the Convention dared to do.

THEIR OWN WORDS

"The monarch must have proportional strength. He ought to be hereditary, and to have so much power, that it will not be in his interests to risk much to acquire more. The advantage of a monarch is this—he is above corruption—he must always intend, in respect to foreign nations, the true interest and glory of the people."

—Alexander Hamilton at the Federal Convention, June 18, 1787

Because men are naturally ambitious, Hamilton said, a governor nearing the end of his time in office would naturally do what he could to "prolong his power," even if that meant undermining the Constitution. Better to let him serve for life, rather than just seven years. This would also free him from popular influence, always a threat to stable government.

No delegates dared agree with Hamilton's notions, at least not publicly. Frustrated by this lack of support and outvoted at every turn by his fellow delegates from New York, Hamilton left the Convention. (He would return toward the end, resigned to the new plan and even ready to help polish the final draft.)

Gouverneur Morris Takes Charge

Like Hamilton, Gouverneur Morris thought the executive office was too weak, a mere stepchild to Congress. But Morris's alternative was more saleable than Hamilton's. His main object: remove the executive from the control of Congress.

FOUNDER ID

Gouverneur Morris (1752–1816). Estate owner, merchant, and investor from New York and Pennsylvania. New York Provincial Congress 1775–1777. Delegate to New York's first State Assembly, 1777. Delegate to Continental Congress from New York, 1778–1779. Assistant Superintendent of Finance, 1781–1784. Pennsylvania delegate to Constitutional Convention, 1787. Minister to France, 1792–1794. United States Senator from New York, 1800–1803. Chairman, Erie Canal Commission, 1810–1813.

Morris was accustomed to having his way. The youngest son of the Lord of Morrisania (present-day Bronx), he had the lineage and demeanor of an aristocrat. Known for his wit and debating talents, Morris "charms, captivates, and leads away the senses of all who hear him," in the words of William Pierce. He charmed in romance, too, not slowed down by the loss of one leg in a carriage accident. After drafting New York's Constitution of 1777, he fell out with New York politicians and moved to Philadelphia. There, he became Robert Morris's Assistant Superintendent of Finance and business partner. At the Constitutional Convention he spoke more often and offered more motions than any other delegate. He dramatically altered the shape of the presidency and penned the final draft, making several stylistic changes that conformed to his nationalist views. Afterward, he represented Robert Morris and then the United States in France. There, he bore witness to the Reign of Terror, the worst fear of upper-class Americans who wanted to hold *their* revolution in check.

On July 19, a month and a day after Hamilton's speech, Morris argued that under the plan as it stood, Congress was too powerful. It needed to be checked by a strong chief executive, a "guardian of the people." But if the president was to represent the people against Congress, "let him be appointed by the people." The people could choose him either directly or through special electors, as James Wilson had suggested. Just so long as he was free of Congress, either method would do.

Who, then, would hold the president accountable? The people themselves, by holding elections every two years—a far shorter term than any other delegate had suggested. Given his term's short duration, a president must be able to repeat in office, should the people want him to. Here, then, was an entirely new vision for the executive. The president would answer to the people, not Congress.

Morris, who spoke more often than any other delegate despite missing three weeks of the Convention, must have been extremely convincing. On the very same day as his speech, the Convention reversed its prior positions. Electors, not Congress, would choose the president. He could repeat in office. Delegates also shortened his term, but just to six years instead of Morris's two.

Five days later, Congress recovered from its infatuation with Morris's scheme and scratched it entirely. But Morris would not give up. Again and again he forced the issue, always getting outvoted. Finally, on August 31, as the Convention was drawing to a close, Morris got himself appointed to a committee that was to deal with "unsettled matters." Through devious means, he placed the issue of executive selection on the committee's agenda even though the Convention had actually voted on the matter several times and decided against Morris.

On September 4, less than two weeks before the weary delegates would pack up and go home, the committee unveiled a surprise. Lo and behold, electors would select a president, who would serve as many four-year terms as those electors wanted.

Delegates were stunned. Edmund Randolph and Charles Pinckney "wished for a particular explanation & discussion of the reasons for changing the mode of electing the Executive." Point-by-point, Morris explained the whys and the wherefores of the Electoral College. Get ready; it's complicated.

The Electoral College, Final Draft

A state's number of electors equaled the total of its congressman, in both the House and Senate. (This gave small states extra representation.) Once chosen, the electors would vote for *two* men apiece, including at least one from another state. (This prevented the election from turning into a contest among native sons.) The president of the Senate would tabulate the results. If no candidate appeared on a majority of ballots, the Senate would choose from among the top five vote-getters, thus selecting a winner who had at least been vetted by the electors.

Sound a bit convoluted? Even a bit whacky? Maybe so, but it shows how badly delegates wanted to keep the selection of the president out of the hands of the people. It also shows how tired the delegates were at this late stage of the Convention, for the last-minute adoption of the Electoral College scheme (a later term, not used in the Constitution itself) aroused little opposition. They made only one change to the committee's plan, giving the final say to the House rather than the Senate, with each state delegation receiving one vote.

It would not take long for Americans to game the system of presidential electors, undermining its intent (see Chapters 15, 20, and 21). To this day, we wonder at its strangeness and pledge to change it somehow. It's unlikely we will ever amend the Constitution, which would require ratification by three quarters of the states. Between small states, which each gain two extra electors under this system, and contested "battleground" states, which essentially determine the presidency, at least one quarter of the states will always have a vested interest in keeping things the way they are.

BY THE NUMBERS

The elector system of choosing the president was the framers' most innovative creation. Here are some of its features and historical effects:

- 2—The number of names each elector would place on his ballot for president. There was no separate vote for vice president.
- 3—The fewest number of electors one state could have. Large states would get more.
- 3—The number of presidents who have attained office under this scheme despite being outpolled by their opponents (John Quincy Adams in 1824, Benjamin Harrison in 1888, George W. Bush in 2000).
- 69—The number of electors in the first presidential election.
- 538—The number of electors we have today.

Presto! A Vice President

The new scheme required electors to cast two votes, but how can you vote twice for only one office? The obvious solution was to conjure a new position. North Carolina's Hugh Williamson, a committee member, explained the decision to the Convention: "Such an officer as vice-president was not wanted. He was introduced only for the sake of a valuable mode of election which required two to be chosen at the same time." Purposely, the plan did not require electors to specify which vote was for president and which for vice president. That would have contradicted their goal, which was to keep electors from favoring men from their own states. Confused? So was the entire nation in 1800, when this strange feature almost destroyed the union (see Chapter 21).

Earlier, when Congress was to choose the president, succession had not been an issue. If a president was killed, incapacitated, or impeached and convicted, Congress would simply select another. But the elector scheme would take time, so somebody had to be standing by just in case. This would be the vice president, the man who came in second in the presidential balloting.

But what would the vice president *do?* The best the committee came up with was "ex-officio President of the Senate," with the power to break a tie vote. Not much of a job description. The rest of the vice president's duties would evolve over time.

What we regard today as the second highest office in the land was a fluke of circumstance, an inadvertent last-minute addition to make the elector scheme work. Had delegates not felt so rushed, they might have taken more care and assigned the office definite and appropriate tasks, but they were worn out, and they just let the matter be. The vice president was the bastard son of the Federal Convention.

The President Gets Some Powers

Throughout most of the Convention, delegates were so concerned over who should choose the president, how long and how often he could serve, and how he could check and be checked by other branches of government that they paid little attention to his actual powers. Until the beginning of August, all he could do was "carry into execution the national laws" and make appointments "in cases not otherwise provided for." Big deal. This officer would have done Congress's bidding, and nothing more.

Then, a five-man Committee of Detail (James Wilson, John Rutledge, Edmund Randolph, Nathaniel Gorham, and Oliver Ellsworth) gave the president a few more powers, but he was still reined in. He could "recommend" legislation, but not vote on it. He could commission officers and receive ambassadors, but not appoint them—that lay with the Senate, as did the power to make treaties with foreign nations and appoint Supreme Court justices. He could command military forces but not raise them. He could neither declare war nor negotiate peace.

At the last minute, in early September, executive power was expanded yet again, at Gouverneur Morris's urging. With the "advise and consent" of the Senate, the president could appoint ambassadors, Supreme Court justices, and "other public ministers." He could also negotiate treaties, pending approval of two thirds of the Senate.

The last-minute additions gave the president, not the Senate, leadership in foreign affairs. Even so, the "power of war" remained, as always, with Congress. Not even Gouverneur Morris dared challenge Congress's unique prerogative to send men to war and tax the rest of the nation to support them.

The Least You Need to Know

- The Articles of Confederation had no separate executive department, so the framers were starting from scratch when creating the presidency.
- Several delegates favored a plural executive, while Alexander Hamilton wanted a president similar to the British monarch.
- During most of the convention, the framers favored a president who would be selected by Congress and serve a single seven-year term.
- Gouverneur Morris's persistent maneuverings gave rise to presidential electors (first introduced by James Wilson) and to repeatable four-year terms.
- The vice presidency was an afterthought, introduced only to make the Electoral College system work.
- Only in the final days did the president gain authority to appoint Supreme Court justices and negotiate treaties, but Congress still kept most powers, including raising an army and declaring war.

Should Judges Judge Laws?

In This Chapter

- The role of judges before the Federal Convention
- Advent of "judicial review" in the 1780s
- Judicial review at the Federal Convention
- "Original intent," "original meaning," and "living Constitution" theories
- Popular constitutionalism

"We the people" weren't actually the ones who dreamed up three distinct branches of government and the balance of powers. In his *Spirit of the Laws*, published in 1748, French philosopher Montesquieu had divided the administrative function of government into three spheres: legislative, executive, and judicial. Governments would be more stable, and people better served, if these three functions were lodged in separate bodies, each checking the other's powers, he asserted. Statesmen here had read Montesquieu, and men like John Adams wanted to apply his governing structure. Adams did just that when he wrote a state constitution for Massachusetts in 1780 (see Chapter 6). At the Federal Convention, when it was their turn to create a Constitution for the nation, delegates were committed to creating three distinct branches of government as well.

The legislative branch would make the laws (see Chapter 10). The executive branch would execute them (see Chapter 11). That left the judicial branch with the job of judging the laws. Really? Could they do that? Or should they only judge *people* charged with breaking laws? Maybe they should just let the laws be, even if they seemed unjust or appeared to contradict the Constitution.

The question of whether judges should pass judgment over laws perplexed the Founders from the start. They had to come to grips with a fundamental problem they created when they wrote a Constitution: who, if anybody, should determine whether that hallowed document was being violated? In this chapter, we explore that question and review the history of judicial function in Revolutionary America.

Judges in Revolutionary Times

Before 1776, Americans did not look fondly upon the superior court judges in each colony, who were appointed by the Crown and beholden to it. Administration of justice was not separated from the executive authority; it was just the reverse, with judges directly influenced by a king or his appointed colonial governors. Revolutionaries changed that when they wrote new state constitutions and established separate judicial branches, making judges responsible to the people.

States were now free of Britain and on their own, and state legislatures busily attempted to pass laws that would cover any and every circumstance that might arise. In this new order, judges were to follow these precise new codes and not exercise individual discretion. A judge should be "a mere machine," Thomas Jefferson pronounced in 1776.

But by the 1780s, some people began to worry that the legislatures were going too far in their law making. Upper-class people in particular feared that legislatures, influenced by debtors and poor folks, would pass laws for debtor relief and the issuing of paper money (see Chapter 9). Who, then, would prevent "legislative tyranny"?

There were competing ideas on that score, but one possible solution was for judges to step in and impose certain limits on the legislatures, based on written state constitutions. "Here is the limit of your authority, and hither, shall you go, but no further," Judge George Wythe instructed the Virginia legislature in 1782. The state's Attorney General, Edmund Randolph, who would figure prominently at the Federal Convention (see Chapters 9–11), initially opposed Wythe's view but then came to agree with him. "Every law against the constitution may be declared void," he said. Still another judge, Edmund Pendleton, admitted he had no answer to this predicament but knew the question of whether a judge could invalidate a law presented "a deep, important, and I will add, a tremendous question."

The Problem of "Judicial Review"

A "tremendous question" indeed, and definitely with huge consequences. Broadly speaking, there were three responses to the notion of *judicial nullification*, as it was called at the time, or *judicial review*, as we call it today.

> **DEFINITION**
>
> **Judicial review** is a policy allowing courts to void or cancel bills of Congress or actions of the federal executive department and state and local government if they violate the Constitution. The term "judicial review" was not used at the time. The Founding generation called the policy many names, including **judicial nullification.**

Response Number One: Judicial review was absurd. How could judges, who were generally not elected but appointed, and who weren't supposed to make laws, overrule legislatures, which *had* been elected and were *told* to make laws? Judicial review suggested that the people could not be trusted with their own government. For many, that was an insult to popular sovereignty. There was a much better way to check a tyrannical legislature: the people themselves could throw the bums out at the next election.

Response Number Two: Judicial review was both beneficial and necessary. This process, and this process alone, protected the Constitution, the document that had been written by and for the people. If a law passed by a legislature contradicted a state's constitution, and the matter came before a judge, how could he ignore the constitution? It was the "fundamental law" or the "superior law," the very basis of the people's government. Never should legislators overrule it. Judges were there to make sure they didn't. They had taken a vow to uphold a constitution and thereby *protect* popular sovereignty.

This view was just beginning to take hold when the Federal Convention met in Philadelphia in 1787. North Carolina Supreme Court Justice James Iredell, one of the first and most eloquent proponents of judicial review, wrote to a delegate who was attending the Convention. A constitution, he said, is not "a mere imaginary thing, about which ten thousand different opinions may be formed, but a written document to which all may have recourse."

Iredell argued that if all had "recourse" to one federal constitution, and if its stipulations and rules superseded any others, judges could cite that document in order to toss out unjust laws. They could use it as a reference point when some wanted a law that others resisted. Without the clarity that a constitution provided, civil unrest would ensue, Iredell cautioned—and that was a dangerous prospect. He valued constitutional guarantees that protected minorities and minority opinions, too. Without those, people would join the majority just to be safe. They would be forced to "sacrifice reason, conscience, and duty, to the preservation of temporary popular favor."

"An act of Assembly, inconsistent with the constitution, is *void*, and cannot be obeyed, without disobeying the superior law to which we were previously and irrevocably bound. The judges, therefore, must take care at their peril, that every act of Assembly they presume to enforce is warranted by the Constitution."

—James Iredell, 1786. This is among the first arguments in favor of what we now call "judicial review."

FOUNDER ID

James Iredell (1751–1799). Comptroller of Customs (1768–1774) and Collector of Customs (1774–1776) for Port Roanoke. Deputy King's Attorney for North Carolina, 1774–1776. North Carolina Provincial Congress, 1776. North Carolina Superior Court Judge, 1777–1778. North Carolina Attorney General, 1779–1781. North Carolina Ratifying Convention, 1788. Associate Justice United States Supreme Court, 1790–1799. Compiler, *Laws of the State of North Carolina*, 1787–1791.

After Iredell's father suffered a paralytic stroke, a relative secured young James, age 17, a government position as a collector of customs. Iredell served well and was promoted in 1774, just as tensions between American patriots and British authorities were reaching a fever pitch. He tried to avoid a direct break with Britain, but when that proved impossible, he sided with the Americans. After the war, concerned about radical measures taken by state legislatures (see Chapter 9), he argued that the judicial branch of government could be used to check legislative overreach. In 1788 he was North Carolina's most influential supporter of ratification. Washington appointed Iredell to the first Supreme Court, in part because he hailed from North Carolina, which had no other prominent Federalist. On the court, Iredell paved the way for judicial review, writing in *Calder v. Bull* (1798) that the court could not invalidate a law because it appeared to violate "the abstract principles of natural justice," but only because it violated the Constitution.

Response Number Three: Madison and Jefferson, among others, thought that judges should treat the Constitution as the prevailing standard. But so should other arms of government, which had "a concurrent right to expound the Constitution," Madison said. No arm, in this view, had the final word when deciding what was constitutional and what was not, and no arm could intrude into the sphere of the other. If branches disagreed, then "an appeal to the people themselves can alone declare its true meaning, and enforce its observance," Madison wrote.

Madison's argument, though attractive, was of little help to judges. If they were charged with upholding a law that appeared to contradict the Constitution, which rule should they uphold? They needed to rule on the case before them, not wait around for "the people themselves" to settle the matter.

This hands-off approach faced another problem as well. If neither the courts nor any other body had the final word on enforcing the Constitution, the separate branches of government, and the people themselves, were left to duke it out, without any guidelines to govern their fight. The consequences of that, like the consequences of judicial review, would be "tremendous."

Judicial Review at the Federal Convention

At the Constitutional Convention in 1787, delegates differed on the role of judges. Vested interests played no role in this matter; these were genuine intellectual differences. A case could be made for each of the three perspectives outlined above, but none was immune to criticism.

Before determining if judges should, or should not, hold the power to nullify bills of Congress or actions of the executive, delegates had to deal with an underlying question: *what* judges? There had been no federal judiciary under the Articles of Confederation, so delegates were starting from scratch.

Their Constitutional draft said little about the new federal courts, just that there would be "one Supreme Court" and "such inferior courts as the Congress may from time to time ordain and establish." Federal courts would deal with matters affecting foreign policy (ambassadors, treaties, etc.) and issues involving differences between states. They would not directly enforce state laws. The Supreme Court would be an appeals court for "such regulations as the Congress shall make."

Was that all that need be said about the judicial branch of government? What if a defendant was accused of breaking a Congressional law that appeared to contradict the Constitution? Federal judges would have to know: should they judge the law, or just the person?

I would love to say at this point, "On July ___, upon a motion by delegate ___, the convention addressed the pros and cons of judicial review, and concluded, by a vote of ___ to ___, that the Supreme Court possessed (or did not possess) the power to nullify acts of Congress and lesser governing bodies." But it didn't happen that way. Not once did the Federal Convention address the issue head-on. This left a huge blank in the final document, much larger than the little blanks in this paragraph.

Ever since then, people have wondered why delegates didn't address judicial review straight out. Some say it was an outrageous idea that nobody wanted. Others maintain that the framers simply *assumed* judges would have to rule on the constitutionality of laws, because they could perform their jobs in no other way. Still others point to the political risk the framers would run if they made unelected judges the final arbiters. The people out-of-doors would never buy it.

These varied speculations all contained a kernel of truth. Here in a nutshell is how it came down at the Convention.

According to the Virginia Plan, the working draft from the beginning (see Chapters 9–11), "a convenient number of the National Judiciary" would combine with the executive to form a "Council of Revision," which could veto acts of Congress. Madison, Wilson, and others thought that people might object to one man (the president) exercising veto power, but if he acted with a council of judges, who best understood laws, the public would accept his veto. "The aid of the judges will give more wisdom & firmness to the executive," Oliver Ellsworth argued. "They will possess a systematic and accurate knowledge of the laws, which the Executive can not be expected always to possess."

Absolutely not, other delegates proclaimed. "A knowledge of mankind, and of legislative affairs cannot be presumed to belong in a higher degree to the judges than to the legislature," argued Luther Martin. "As judges they are not to be presumed to possess any peculiar knowledge of the mere policy of public measures," said Nathaniel Gorham.

As delegates discussed the veto power of the proposed Council of Revision, they argued whether judges were the right people to evaluate laws up front, *before* those laws were finalized. But in the process, they revealed how they thought about judges judging laws *afterward*, when they tried cases on the bench. In effect, they were discussing judicial review.

A few delegates thought judges should never be able to nullify a law, either before or after it was passed. John Francis Mercer "disapproved of the doctrine that the judges as expositors of the Constitution should have authority to declare a law void. He thought laws ought to be well and cautiously made, and then to be uncontroulable." John Dickinson agreed with Mercer, but he also admitted he was "at a loss what expedient to substitute."

More delegates thought that judges would inevitably have to judge the laws that came before them, to make sure they were consistent with the Constitution. Their "exposition of the laws," said Elbridge Gerry, necessarily involved "a power of deciding on their Constitutionality." In fact, this became the main argument *against* the Council of Revision. "As to the Constitutionality of laws," Luther Martin observed, "that point will come before the judges in their proper official character. In this character they have a negative on the laws. Join them with the executive in the revision and they will have a double negative." John Rutledge said, "Judges of all men [are] the most unfit to be concerned in the Revisionary Council. The judges ought never to give their opinion on a law *till it comes before them*." Even James Madison admitted that the Constitution would, in certain limited cases, "oblige" judges to declare a law "null & void."

The Council of Revision was rejected, for fear of giving judges a "double negative." Best to leave them out of the law-making process and then let them rule on constitutionality at a later stage, once an act was being enforced.

And best to leave this implicit rather than spelling it out. To hold that judges must consider the Constitution while "expounding" laws was certainly acceptable, even necessary. To say, outright, that a few unelected men could declare acts of Congress unconstitutional and therefore null and void would be a hard sell to the people, as it was to delegates like Mercer and Dickinson. Logically, these two statements were very close, although not quite identical. Politically, they were miles apart. Delegates were understandably hesitant to take the extra step.

THEIR OWN WORDS

"No legislative act, contrary to the Constitution, can be valid. To deny this would be to affirm that the deputy is greater than his principal; that the servant is above his master; that the representatives of the people are superior to the people themselves." It therefore is the "duty" of "the courts of justice … to declare all acts contrary to the Constitution void. Without this, all the reservations of particular rights or privileges would amount to nothing."

—Alexander Hamilton, in *The Federalist #78*. Hamilton was one of the few framers to argue in public for judicial nullification.

Original Intent and Original Meaning

Everybody agreed that judges should consult the Constitution, which they must take an oath to support. But how should they read and understand that document? The framers did not offer a blueprint for this, and since then, the question has given rise to vigorous debate.

Some believe judges must adhere to a standard called "original intent." They should review not only the Constitution but all reports of what was said at the Constitutional Convention and any record these men left in their lifetimes, whether published works, letters, or other papers. They should consult Founding Fathers who did not appear at the Convention as well. If clarity were determined by word count, original intent would solve any number of legal disputes. But there are problems.

Vigorous thinkers all, our founding leaders were generally fond of documenting their opinions. Changing their own minds as months and years passed, they sometimes contradicted themselves. Through the course of the Convention, they certainly contradicted each other, disagreeing on just about everything. By rummaging through the enormous stack of materials the framers and Founders left behind, anybody can uncover comments to support his or her opinions. But in reality the sheer volume of their utterances might confuse, rather than elucidate, judicial interpretation.

The statesmen themselves did not think their intentions *should* be consulted. At the Constitutional Convention, absolute secrecy on proceedings was the rule. Notes and records were private, and delegates were forbidden to speak of what went on. Why? Think politics for a moment. Then as now, horse-trading was common, and delegates engaged in the practice, perhaps out of sheer necessity. Practically speaking, with dozens of delegates weighing in, how else could a nation be founded? Understandably, delegates didn't want a blow-by-blow account of all this to get out. James Madison summed up their thinking. "As a guide in expounding and applying the provisions of the Constitution," he said, "the debates and incidental decisions of the Convention can have no authoritative character."

"Original meanings" is cousin to original intent. People who adhere to this standard see the Constitution as a sacred contract between framers and those who agreed to the deal back in 1788, when the Constitution was ratified. Striving to uphold that contract, judges try to figure out how each and every one of its terms was understood by the people of those times. That way, they can hold the document fixed and absolute. The Constitution, said Thomas Jefferson, should not be treated as a "mere thing of wax in the hands of the judiciary which they may twist and shape into any form they please."

Some people say, though, that the original meaning approach holds the Constitution *too* fixed and absolute. A zillion things have changed since 1788, over two centuries ago. What can Revolutionary Era Americans tell us about the constitutionality of regulating the Internet? Or establishing no-fly zones? Or placing limits on biological engineering? Judges must respond to such rapid social transformations. What we need, these people say, is more of a "living Constitution," one that evolves with the times. Judges must interpret the document not only in the way people understood it back then, but also in a way that can help us adapt its core values to a changing world.

What is a judge to do? In actual practice, most respect all three standards. They consider the original intent of the framers, try to understand it as people of the time did, and figure out how to apply constitutional standards to an ever-changing world. Day by day, they look also to a body of law set in other court cases, known as precedents, which themselves are based on constitutional standards. Often, they have to weigh items of Constitutional law and precedent that appear to contradict each other, no easy task. People will disagree with this decision or that, but we can all agree that the United States Constitution, as amended by the people and interpreted by judges, is the oldest written constitution governing a nation today. The framers (I resort now to original intent) wanted the document they created to endure, and it has.

Enforcing the Constitution

Initially, in the aftermath of the Federal Convention, the Constitution itself was an extremely controversial matter. As we shall see in Chapter 14, the nation almost split apart when people of each state argued about whether to approve, or ratify, the new plan of government. In the end, it was endorsed, but by the narrowest of margins in the four most significant states. Possibly, the majority of Americans living at the time opposed it at the outset.

So how did they come to accept it? And who, in the people's minds, should uphold it?

Popular Constitutionalism

For 15 years after the Constitution was ratified, few people thought that the courts had the final say in upholding it. That matter, most felt, lay in their own hands. As primary parties to this new contract, they would interpret and enforce its rules.

But in doing so, they disrupted the normal flow of governmental operations. Juries ignored the instructions of judges. Crowds shooed away tax collectors. States nullified federal laws (more of this in Chapters 19 and 20). For now, let us simply note that whatever the Constitution said or didn't say about judges being its final arbiters, most Americans simply assumed that "the people themselves" were. Legal scholars call this philosophy "popular constitutionalism."

Marbury v. Madison

In 1803, the Supreme Court of the United States, headed by Chief Justice John Marshall, made a major pronouncement: henceforth, the court could void a law deemed to be unconstitutional. We will discuss this landmark decision, *Marbury v. Madison*, in

Chapter 22. The case proved critical to establishing the independence of the judiciary. The notion of judges judging laws, discussed but not finally determined in the 1780s, would eventually become the law of the land.

Activist Judges

If the Supreme Court declares a law unconstitutional, people who disagree with that verdict cry "foul!" and argue that judges, who are not elected, should not undo the work of the people's representatives. They complain about so-called "activist judges" who overturn laws and impose their own wills. But such complaints are often one-sided. If you are a staunch supporter of the right to bear arms (see Chapter 18), and your town decides to *permit* the carrying of guns in public, you don't want some activist judge to interfere. On the other hand, you *will* want the courts to interfere if your town *outlaws* the carrying of guns in public, which you think violates your constitutional rights.

What defines an activist judge? There are three possible meanings. A judge could be overturning a lower court ruling, a law or executive order, or an established precedent. The first is not really "activism" because appeals court justices are supposed to review lower cases. The second can sometimes be judicial activism, but it might also be necessary. If a judge nullifies a local ordinance that forbids German Americans from writing letters to the newspaper, it can hardly be called judicial activism. He or she is ruling according to a commonly accepted view of the First Amendment.

Only the third meaning—overturning precedent—is true judicial activism. In this case, the judge would be ruling against the collective wisdom of the judicial profession. Sometimes it might be called for, since times do change. By the mid-twentieth century it was clear that the 1896 "separate but equal" ruling in *Plessey v. Ferguson* made no sense. Separate schools for black and white children were rarely equal, and that precedent was overturned. But such cases are rare and should be approached with caution.

The framers certainly expected judges to be *judicious*—to be sensible, careful, cautious, and thoughtful, and to set aside personal inclinations and desires, whether political or religious or anything else. They did not want judges to act independently, without consulting the Constitution and each and every precedent relevant to the case before the court. They should explore the sum knowledge and understanding of all those who had made judgments before them. In this manner, Supreme Court justices would be vigilant guardians and prevent the nation from careening wildly from one side of the road to the other.

But the founders also knew they could never insulate us from our own disagreements. Although they gave us a nation based on law, how we actually *use* the Constitution will always be subject to debate. Benjamin Franklin, after leaving the Federal Convention the final time, was reportedly asked, "Well, Doctor, what have we got—a Republic or a Monarchy?"

"A Republic," he replied, "if you can keep it." It's a job for all, including judges who make the rulings.

The Least You Need to Know

- In colonial times, judges answered to the Crown, and in Revolutionary times, to state legislatures.
- In the 1780s, to check legislative overreach, some people suggested that judges be able to overturn laws that violated their state's constitution. Today, we call this "judicial review," but it wasn't called that at the time.
- At the Federal Convention, the notion of judicial review was tossed about but never firmly concluded.
- To understand the Constitution, some people turn to the "original intent" of its framers or the "original meaning" (how people at the time understood things), while others say the Constitution buttresses a body of law that is always evolving.
- Before federal judicial review was first practiced by the Supreme Court in 1803 *(Marbury v. Madison)*, many people thought that the people themselves were the final arbiters of the Constitution.

The Founders and Slavery

In This Chapter

- Representation in Congress: The three-fifths Compromise
- Slave importation and returning fugitive slaves
- Slavery in the South and the North
- Framers who owned slaves and framers who opposed slavery
- Slavery in the lives of Washington, Jefferson, Madison, and Monroe

How could a nation founded on freedom depend on slave labor?

In forming a new code of rules, would the Federal Convention condemn slavery or protect it?

In this chapter, you will see how delegates addressed, or didn't address, issues pertaining to the enslavement of other human beings. You will need to be especially alert. In the actual Constitution, the word "slavery" is never mentioned. It was an embarrassment, so code words were used instead. But in debates on the floor, the word was used time and time again. Slavery's rightness or wrongness, though, would invite only occasional comment in these discussions. As delegates designed an actual government, hard numbers were at issue, not "inalienable rights" or "liberty," the ideals celebrated in the Declaration of Independence.

Even most slaveholders knew slavery was wrong. To understand their troubling dilemma, we look at how four important men—presidents, in fact—struggled with their consciences and with the societal and economic constraints that bound them to an institution they abhorred.

Count 'Em: The Three-fifths Compromise

From the start, the issue of slavery placed delegates to the Federal Convention in a bind. Southern delegates wanted to count their slaves when determining how many representatives they had in Congress, but northern delegates insisted that would not be fair. Were slaves to be considered as people? If so, they should vote; if not, they should not be counted. Or were slaves to be considered as property? If so, why shouldn't "the cattle and horses of the North" also be counted?

Four years earlier, Congress had faced a similar situation when trying to determine how much money each state should contribute to the federal treasury. At that time, though, southerners maintained slaves should *not* be counted, while northerners thought they should (see Chapter 8). Now, both sides reversed their positions to suit their interests.

Back then, Congress had settled on a compromise: slaves would count as three-fifths of a free person. There was no particular logic to this figure, although some people tried to maintain that a slave was three-fifths as productive as a free person. Now, too, logic would fall by the wayside. "The labour of a slave in S. Carolina" was "as productive as that of a freeman in Massachusetts," observed Pierce Butler of South Carolina. Had slaves suddenly become more productive in four years time? Hardly. Although the sides had reversed, one thing that remained the same was that magical fraction. The Federal Convention determined that for purposes of representation in Congress, a slave would once again count as three-fifths of a person.

Of course, the 400,000 people held in bondage did not enjoy any of the power they brought to their states. Worse yet, from their perspective, the additional representation in Congress gave their masters increased influence in the new nation's affairs. In years to come, that influence would be used, in part, to perpetuate slavery.

BY THE NUMBERS

To count slaves or not? Here is what was at stake for Virginia, a slave state, and Massachusetts, a free state:

- 747,610—the population of Virginia in the first federal census, taken in 1790. This included 292,627 slaves.
- 378,787—the population of Massachusetts in 1790. It had no slaves, since slavery had been abolished by court order.
- Under proportional representation, counting slaves, Massachusetts would get only half as many congressmen as Virginia. Without counting slaves, it would get three fourths as many.

Slave Importation and Fugitive Slaves

Delegates from the Lower South pushed for further concessions. First, they wanted to prohibit Congress from passing any ban on slave importations. Charles Cotesworth Pinckney of South Carolina explained that without this provision, his state would refuse to become part of the union. Abraham Baldwin of Georgia argued that slave importation was a purely "local matter," and if "national powers" interfered, his state, too, would walk away. This tactic had worked for Delaware in the small state/large state controversy (see Chapter 10). Why wouldn't it work for South Carolina and Georgia here?

The threat took hold. Connecticut's Oliver Ellsworth said, "Let us not intermeddle," while his colleague, Roger Sherman, argued that no "public good" would be served by taking away "the right to import slaves," although he personally "disapproved of the slave trade." Elbridge Gerry of Massachusetts said the Convention "had nothing to do with the conduct of the states as to slaves," although it should "be careful not to give any sanction to it." New England, in short, ceded to the Deep South on this one.

John Dickinson, from Delaware, took a tougher stance: "It is inadmissible on every principle of honor & safety that the importation of slaves should be authorized to the states by this Constitution." Pennsylvania's James Wilson did not understand why all other imported items could be taxed, but not slaves. Besides, he did not think the renegade states from the Deep South would go through with their bluff.

What about Virginia, with twice as many slaves as any other state? George Mason spoke for the prevailing view among Virginia's elite slave owners, but he did not say what you might think. "Every master of slaves is born a petty tyrant," he admitted. Slavery would "bring the judgment of Heaven" on the country, and morality aside, "slavery discourages arts & manufactures."

But who was to blame? Originally, the "avarice of British merchants," and now "our Eastern brethren" (slave traders from New England) whose "lust for gain" led them to continue "this nefarious trade." Mason, with this argument, could take the moral high ground while avoiding blame. Left unsaid: Virginia already had more slaves than it needed, so many, in fact, that the sale of slaves to other states and to the Western territories was one of its leading industries. By banning slave importation, it would avoid foreign competition.

Responding to Mason, C. C. Pinckney said what most people at the time already knew: "As to Virginia she will gain by stopping the importations. Her slaves will rise in value, & she has more than she wants." Further, he claimed that the slave trade benefited the entire nation. "The more slaves, the more produce to employ the carrying trade. The more consumption also, and the more of this, the more of revenue for the common treasury."

FOUNDER ID

South Carolina's delegates to the Convention—**John Rutledge, Pierce Butler, Charles Pinckney,** and **Charles Cotesworth Pinckney**—came from the upper crust of their state's slave-owning, planter elite. How do we distinguish one from the other, particularly the Pinckneys? Madison called Charles Cotesworth "General," a commission he earned by defending Charleston from the British. The other Charles Pinckney was the son of General Pinckney's cousin (Colonel Charles Pinckney), making the two first cousins once removed. Had enough? We've only getting started. Charles the younger served multiple terms as the state's governor; he was preceded in office by Thomas Pinckney, the General's brother, and succeeded through history by seven of his own descendents. General Pinckney, sometimes called C. C. but often simply Charles (no matter that there was another Charles), ran as a Federalist for vice president in 1800 and for president in 1804 and 1808, while brother Thomas was the Federalists' vice-presidential choice in 1796. Cousin Charles, meanwhile, became disillusioned with the Federalists and campaigned against the General in 1800, possibly costing him the election (see Chapters 21 and 22). Got it? Good luck!

Delegates found themselves at another impasse. What was to be done? Rufus King said it most bluntly: "The subject should be considered in a political light only." That meant another compromise was in order, and here is how it all came down.

Congress could not ban slave importation until 1808, but after that it could. Why this date? That, too, took some haggling. The first date proposed was 1800, but South Carolina and Georgia, playing hardball, managed to buy eight additional years of slave trading.

Further, fugitive slaves would have to be returned to their owners, even if they had run to states in which slavery was illegal.

In return for these concessions from the North, southern delegates agreed to drop one of their demands. They were concerned that the eight northern states would gang up on the five southern states and pass commercial laws or taxes that interfered with slavery or favored northern merchants and manufacturers at the expense of southern farmers and consumers, so they wanted to require a two-thirds majority for any such measure. Do the math. With a two-thirds threshold, the southern states could have doomed any attack on their regional interests, including the preservation of slavery, through commercial regulation. But to gain 20 more years of slave importation and a fugitive slave clause, southerners let this one go.

The deal was complete, but it had been a deal with the devil, some would later maintain. Slavery would continue in the land of the free, unfettered by national law. Starting in 1808, if it wished, Congress could outlaw the slave trade, but there was nothing in the Constitution that authorized it to interfere with slavery in states where it already existed.

Slavery, North and South

To understand the relationship between the Founders and slavery, and why delegates to the Federal Convention failed to deal in a serious way with its immorality, we need to view these men in the context of their times. In 1787, slavery still existed in the North (the 1790 census listed over 40,000 slaves north of the *Mason-Dixon Line*), but several states had taken tentative steps toward *abolition.* Slavery had been outlawed by court order in Massachusetts in 1780; recent laws in Pennsylvania, Connecticut, and Rhode Island provided for the *emancipation* of slaves born after the enactment of the legislation once they had reached certain ages; similar laws had been introduced but defeated in New York and New Jersey.

In the South, by contrast, some 650,000 slaves were counted in 1790. Land and slaves passed from generation to generation, conferring privileges on an elite master class. The abolition of slavery would have necessitated a radical restructuring of society and the economy. Thomas Jefferson, while calling slavery a "disease," explained why the South could not easily be cured. "Where the disease is most deeply seated, there it will be slowest in eradication. In the northern States it was merely superficial and easily corrected. In the southern it is incorporated with the whole system and requires time, patience, and perseverance in the curative process." Patience, of course, meant one thing to a master and another to the men, women, and children he held in bondage.

Abolition in this context was politically impossible. Nobody could wipe out slavery in the South with the wave of a magic wand. If a particular slave master felt bad about the situation, though, he could *manumit,* or free, his own slaves. Robert Carter III of Virginia manumitted 452 slaves, not all at once, which would have stirred great resistance, but gradually. Other owners also freed slaves, some in their lifetimes, others in their wills.

DEFINITION

Abolition is the act of officially ending a law or practice, such as slavery. To **manumit** is to release one person, or a defined group of people, from slavery. An owner could manumit his slaves, but he could not abolish slavery. Any slaves who were freed, whether by abolition or manumission, were emancipated. The **Mason-Dixon Line,** drawn by two surveyors in the 1760s to establish the official boundary between Pennsylvania and Maryland, has been used historically to differentiate slave and nonslave states.

Manumission was not easy, however. There were tight legal restrictions, for two reasons. First, whites feared that free blacks would become a burden on society, so owners had to ensure that the men and women they freed would be self-supporting. Whites also thought free blacks might stir dangerous longings amongst slaves who had not been freed. Until 1782, no one could free a slave in Virginia unless the Assembly gave permission. When the Assembly did free someone, it was often for good deeds; one man gained freedom because he had turned in counterfeiters.

There were other problems as well. In an uncertain agricultural society depending on a market crop, slaves provided security. If you had inherited a plantation and a number of slaves to work it, but little cash (this was common), what could you do if untimely storms or temperatures wreaked havoc with crops? What happened if tobacco or rice or indigo prices dropped, or foreign creditors raised interest rates? In a financial pinch, you could sell slaves. But let's say you were a good master and wanted to keep slave families together. Instead of selling people off, you could choose instead to borrow money and use slaves as a lien on the debt. After that, even though these slaves continued to live on your plantation with their families, your creditor had a claim on the people you might wish to set free. Several well-meaning masters who hoped to manumit slaves found themselves constricted by such debts.

Slave Owners Among the Framers

Just over half of the 55 delegates to the Convention owned slaves. These can be broken into four groups, as follows:

- Men from the South who owned plantations that were worked by large numbers of men and women they held in bondage. Large-scale owners included: Daniel Carroll, Daniel of St. Thomas Jenifer, John Francis Mercer (MD); George Mason, George Washington, Edmund Randolph, John Blair, James Madison (VA); Richard Dobbs Spaight, William Blount, William Richardson Davie, Alexander Martin (NC); Charles Pinckney, Charles Cotesworth Pinckney, John Rutledge, Pierce Butler (SC); William Houstoun (GA). Richard Bassett and John Dickinson (DE), each of whom owned plantations in both Maryland and Delaware, can be included in this group.

- Men from the South who owned some slaves but were not dependent on an enslaved workforce. These included: Luther Martin (MD); George Wythe (VA); William Few (GA).

- Men from the North who owned, or had owned, a few slaves for "convenience," mostly as household servants. These men, some of whom became active opponents of slavery, included: William Livingston (NJ); Thomas Fitzsimons, Benjamin Franklin (PA); George Read (DE); Doctor William Samuel Johnson (CT).

- One man from the North whose business dealings involved him in slavery. This was Robert Morris, who invested in an orange plantation along the Mississippi worked by 100 slaves. Earlier, before the Revolutionary ferment, Morris had imported slaves on his ships.

Slavery's Opponents Among the Framers

Some delegates to the Federal Convention worked actively to oppose slavery. Most notable was Benjamin Franklin, who in 1787 helped revitalize the Pennsylvania Society for Promoting the Abolition of Slavery. (Benjamin Rush, an important Founder but not a Convention delegate, also worked with this group.) Franklin was typical of well-to-do northerners who kept a few slaves in their households. In the 1740s, long before the Revolution, he held two slaves, Peter and Jemima. In preparation for a trip to England in 1757, he purchased Othello to help his wife during his absence, but at the same time he drew up a will to set Peter and Jemima free at his death. This was a common balancing act from a man who found slavery an irresistible convenience, while believing it should be abolished. Late in life, when Franklin became an active abolitionist, he did so with a practical bent, as was his style. Slaves not only needed to be freed, he said, but also educated, trained, and employed. In this context, he promoted the cause of free blacks as well as slaves. As his very last public act, Franklin sent off a petition to the first Congress under the new Constitution, begging representatives to "promote mercy and justice toward this distressed Race."

Alexander Hamilton was an active member of the New York Manumission Society, founded in 1785 by a famous Founder who was not at the Federal Convention, John Jay. (See Chapter 19 for more on Jay.) William Livingston, Governor of New Jersey and delegate to the Convention, supported this organization. The Society lobbied for legislation for gradual abolition in New York, a move that failed narrowly in 1785 but finally passed in 1799. In the meantime, the Society was able to eliminate legal obstacles to private manumission, and it encouraged owners to do this. It also boycotted merchants who participated in the slave trade.

Luther Martin, who owned six slaves at the time of the Convention, helped found the Maryland Society for the Abolition of Slavery two years later. Samuel Chase (see Chapter 22) was also active in this group.

Rufus King of Massachusetts authored the provision in the Northwest Ordinance that outlawed slavery in the Western Territories north of the Ohio River.

On a personal level, George Washington, Benjamin Franklin, George Wythe, Luther Martin, John Dickinson, William Livingston, and Richard Bassett manumitted some or all of their slaves, some during their own lifetimes, others in their wills.

Despite a strong current of anti-slavery sentiments among the framers of the Constitution, only one man—Gouverneur Morris, a New York aristocrat representing Pennsylvania—launched an unequivocal assault on slavery at the Federal Convention, assailing all compromises (for more on Morris, see Chapter 11). Slavery was "a nefarious institution" and "the curse of heaven," he said in an impassioned speech on August 8, 1787. After detailing its degrading effects on society, and demolishing the illogical compromises concerning representation and importation, Morris presented with rhetorical flourish his own scheme for immediate emancipation: buy all slaves and free them. He "would sooner submit himself to a tax for paying for all the negroes in the U. States, than saddle posterity with such a Constitution," Morris announced to his stunned peers.

THEIR OWN WORDS

"Upon what principle is it that the slaves shall be computed in the representation? Are they men? Then make them citizens and let them vote. Are they property? Why then is no other property included? The admission of slaves into the representation when fairly explained comes to this: that the inhabitant of Georgia and S. C. who goes to the Coast of Africa, and in defiance of the most sacred laws of humanity tears away his fellow creatures from their dearest connections & damns them to the most cruel bondages, shall have more votes in a government instituted for protection of the rights of mankind, than the citizen of Pennsylvania or N. Jersey who views with a laudable horror, so nefarious a practice."

—Gouverneur Morris at the Federal Convention, August 8, 1787

Other delegates did not take Morris's idea seriously, and Morris, like the others, continued to work out the details of a Constitution that not only permitted slavery, but also offered slave states special dispensations. In fact, rather than walking out on the Constitution because of concessions to slavery, Morris wrote the final draft. Only by ignoring the evils of the "nefarious institution," delegates believed, could the union be preserved. An outright attack on slavery in the new plan would doom its possibilities for adoption, certainly in South Carolina and Georgia, and probably in North Carolina, Virginia, and Maryland. This would lead to two confederacies, not one "United States," delegates feared. In this manner, the new nation was held hostage by an institution few of the Founders actually condoned.

Presidents and Their Slaves

Four of the first five presidents were Virginians and inherited plantations. These prominent founders stood behind the nation's foremost principles—that men are created equal, deserve life and liberty, and have the right to pursue happiness. All inspected the institution of slavery through this Revolutionary lens and condemned the practice in no uncertain terms. Evidence is there; quotations abound.

Yet no matter what they said, each man kept slaves during the Revolution and for the years that followed. Blacks they held in bondage served their households, worked their vast fields, or put down new, shining floors in their mansions, as they had done for generations. Their privileged world would disappear if slavery did. "Justice is in one scale," Jefferson stated, "and self-preservation in the other." Only one of the four men freed all the slaves that he could in a will.

George Washington

Legally, George Washington became a slave owner at age 11, when he inherited a small farm and 10 slaves. With the death of his elder half-brother Lawrence a decade later, George inherited a share of a much larger plantation at Mount Vernon, along with the enslaved men and women who worked it. In 1759, when George married the rich widow Martha Custis, he gained control, but not ownership, over her 84 "dower slaves." (The wife of a deceased husband inherited one third of the husband's estate, including slaves. If a woman remarried, her new husband managed her dower slaves, although her husband's heirs would inherit them, along with the dower slaves' children.) Joining their resources, George and Martha more than doubled the land and labor force at Mount Vernon over the next 15 years, in the years leading up to the American Revolution.

George Washington was no stranger to the institution of slavery, but left no evidence in his early years of being plagued by feelings of guilt. During this time he set slaves to some horrendous tasks, such as clearing out a swamp for The Great Dismal Swamp Company in order to create a rice plantation. As was customary, he bought and sold people at will, had them whipped when he thought necessary, and spent no more than was required on their keep. He issued clothing once a year and food rations once a week, which slaves supplemented with produce from small slave-quarter gardens. He allowed slaves Sundays off, as well as Christmas and Easter Monday. He trained some in carpentry or blacksmithing or other trades, but set others to arduous work in the fields. Though more considerate than many masters, Washington treated the people he enslaved according to local customs and practices.

> **BY THE NUMBERS**
>
> George Washington's enslaved workforce at Mount Vernon:
>
> - 36—number of the enslaved workforce at Mount Vernon before Martha Washington arrived early in 1759.
> - 84—Martha's dower slaves when she married George.
> - 135—Washington's slaves (not including Martha's dower slaves) in 1774, just before the Revolutionary War.
> - 46—enslaved people purchased by George Washington in the 15 years before the war. (The rest of the increase was reproductive.)
> - 216—enslaved people at Mount Vernon in 1786, shortly after the war ended. 103 belonged to Washington himself, while 113 were dower.
> - 7—slaves taken to New York in 1789 to run Washington's presidential household.
> - 124—all of Washington's slaves in 1799, whom he freed in his will (pending the death of Martha).
> - 153—Martha's dower slaves in 1799, whom Washington could not free.

After 1772, as republican rhetoric took hold, Washington increasingly questioned slavery's morality. He wanted nothing to do with the slave trade. He set himself against selling Mount Vernon slaves, even when he found himself with an unprofitable "surplus." He was against purchasing slaves, too. On September 9, 1786, he wrote: "I never mean (unless some particular circumstances should compel me to it) to possess another slave by purchase; it being among my first wishes to see some plan adopted, by which slavery in this country may be abolished by slow, sure, & imperceptible degrees."

But in a slave society there were always "particular circumstances." Only two months later, expressing "great repugnance," Washington said he would accept payment for a debt from a man who had no money. "I will take six, or more negroes of you, if you can spare such as will answer my purpose …" Three weeks later, he added a stipulation, refusing payment-in-slaves if it would "hurt the feelings of those unhappy people by a separation of man and wife, or of families." By this time he had formulated firm and positive principles. He made a deal, breaking with those principles; he broke a deal, returning to them.

Washington was severely tempted to purchase a slave at another critical moment: a culinary crisis. His esteemed chef, Hercules, had served the Mount Vernon household with great flair, and Washington insisted Hercules accompany him when he became president. At the President's House, first in New York and then in Philadelphia, Hercules ordered several assistants about a bustling kitchen and conjured up elaborate meals. When Hercules escaped, Washington was at a loss: "The running off of my cook, has been a most inconvenient thing to this family; and what renders it more disagreeable, is, that I had resolved never to become the master of another slave by *purchase*; but this resolution I fear I must break." By chance, Washington was again able to hold to his beliefs. The new chef was white.

Washington's treatment of slaves was in some ways typical, but he also showed revolutionary backbone. He died in December of 1799 and left a will that said his own slaves would go free after Martha's death. He had no say over her dower slaves. In the will he provided for sale of parcels of his land to support the elderly people he turned free, train the children, and care and educate others. With this final act, he tried to fulfill ideals that had remained elusive during his life.

Thomas Jefferson

In 1757, when Thomas Jefferson was 14 years old, his father Peter died, bequeathing him a 5,000-acre plantation and some 40 slaves. In 1774, he inherited 135 additional slaves from his father-in-law, John Wales. By the time Jefferson died in 1826 at the age of 83, he had owned over 600 individuals, averaging about 200 at any given time. Many were born and died on his Monticello plantation.

Yet Thomas Jefferson, taking the ideals of the Revolutionary Generation seriously, detested slavery. In 1769, while serving his first term in the House of Burgesses, the 26-year-old lawyer wrote a bill that would let masters manumit slaves without getting permission from the Virginia Assembly, as was the practice. The bill was shouted down. That same year, in his private practice, Jefferson represented a mulatto who sued for freedom. "Charge no fee," he wrote in his casebook, and in court, he argued that "Everyone comes into the world with a right to his own person." The judge threw the case out. The following year, Jefferson refused to defend a white man accused of whipping a black woman so hard that she died.

In a draft for the new Virginia Constitution in 1776, Jefferson proposed that "no person hereafter coming into this country shall be held in slavery under any pretext whatever." Not surprisingly, his idea never made it to the final draft. Again in 1783, in another proposal for the Virginia Constitution, he stipulated that all people born into slavery after 1800 would be set free. This sort of gradual emancipation was finding favor in the North at this time, but in Virginia it got nowhere.

In 1784, while serving on a committee of Congress, Jefferson pushed for abolishing slavery in the western territories, both North and South. The resolution failed by one vote but was later adopted for the new states north of the Ohio River (the present-day Midwest). "The voice of a single individual would have prevented this abominable crime from spreading itself over the new country," Jefferson lamented.

While Thomas Jefferson loathed slavery and wished it would come to an end, he caricatured the African people whom Americans had enslaved. As the Revolutionary War was drawing to a close, in a book he called *Notes on the State of Virginia*, he cast his allegedly scientific eye toward the many black people at Monticello, whose racial characteristics were "fixed in nature." In reasoning abilities, blacks were "much inferior" to whites, he wrote. They had no imagination, making them "dull" and "tasteless." Because they secreted less by the kidneys, he explained, they had "a very strong and disagreeable odour." Because they lacked the "flowing hair," light skin color, and "elegant symmetry of form" of white people, they were wanting in their "share of beauty." Knowing this themselves, they preferred whites to their own kind, much as the male "Oran-ootan" in Africa chose "the black women over those of his own species."

Some of Jefferson's categorical assessments were not only ludicrous but also self-serving. "Their griefs are transient," he wrote. Their "numberless afflictions are less felt and sooner forgotten with them." On their faces, "that immoveable veil of black" covered "all the emotions." Forcing labor from these people, although not ideal, was less consequential than it might have been if they were white. Blacks also "require less sleep," he noted, for they chose "to sit up to midnight, or later," even though they would have to start work at dawn. (He would not acknowledge that evening was the only time enslaved workers truly belonged to themselves.) On the other hand, blacks had a marked "disposition to sleep" when "unemployed in labour." Overseers would do well, then, to keep workers on task. It would be difficult to imagine a people better suited to slavery than the ones Jefferson conjured up in *Notes on the State of Virginia*.

According to Jefferson, such people would never make fit companions for white Americans and, once freed, they should be removed to some other place. Even as Jefferson opposed slavery, he thought the only way to end it sensibly was for former slaves to be relocated to distant colonies. Fear played a role here, for Jefferson, like other masters, trembled at what might happen if blacks gained liberty and power. The resentment that liberated slaves must feel for their former masters, combined with their presumed racial inferiority, made their removal not only desirable but necessary, in his mind.

In 1778, when in the House of Burgesses, Jefferson codified the slave laws of Virginia: slaves could not bear arms, testify against whites, or travel without a pass from their master. These were old customs that Jefferson merely set to paper, but he also suggested some new laws of his own. Free blacks would not be allowed to enter the state; if already there, they would have to leave within a year. A white woman who bore a black child would also have to leave. Offenders would be placed "out of the protection of the laws," meaning they could be seized and enslaved. These new restrictions made it clear that in Jefferson's mind, free blacks should not live side-by-side with whites, no matter what the personal consequences. Fortunately, Jefferson's stringent addendums to the slave laws failed to pass.

Precisely because Jefferson, like most other whites of his times, regarded blacks as inferior, he believed they required his protection, care, and attention. He would treat his slaves well, he vowed, and in many ways he did. Conscientiously and meticulously, he tended to their physical needs with a precision shown by few other masters. But ultimately, his own needs came first. When selling off slaves, he tried his best to keep families together, but only "where it can be done reasonably," he admitted. Although he opposed miscegenation, it is very likely, according to DNA and circumstantial evidence, that he fathered offspring with a mulatto woman, Sally Hemings, he held as a slave and who was his deceased wife's half-sister. As with so many masters, Jefferson found it difficult to lead a life that accorded with his professed ideals.

Jefferson's special care for his slaves at times reflected self-interest. When ordering his overseers not to overwork "breeding women" and to allow young mothers to spend more time with their young children, he explained himself: "I consider a woman who brings a child every two years as more profitable than the best man of the farm. What she produces is an addition to capital, while his labors disappear in mere consumption." The increase in population served Jefferson in two ways. First, breeding slaves ensured a future workforce, and second, it provided extra capital when he needed or desired it. Over the course of his lifetime, Jefferson purchased fewer than 20 slaves yet sold off approximately 100.

THEIR OWN WORDS

"The loss of 5 little ones in 4 years induces me to fear that the overseers do not permit the women to devote as much time as is necessary to the care of their children: that they view their labor as the 1st object and the raising their child but as secondary. I consider the labor of a breeding woman as no object, and that a child raised every 2 years is of more profit than the crop of the best laboring man."

—Jefferson's instruction to his plantation manager, 1819

Ceding to political and military realities, Jefferson in time was less committed to the abolition of slavery. As governor of Virginia in 1780, he signed a bill that granted any white male who enlisted for the duration of the war "300 acres of land plus a healthy sound Negro between 20 and 30 years of age or 60 pounds in gold or silver." As Secretary of State in 1791, he pressured the Spanish government in Florida to return runaways. Two years later, he supported the first national Fugitive Slave Law, which committed the federal government to enforce slavery throughout the nation.

As President, Jefferson advocated the extension of slavery into the Louisiana Territory, which he had acquired from France. That great expanse offered possibilities for colonization, and permitting slavery there would make this more feasible. It would also diffuse slavery, Jefferson believed, and that would somehow lead to its demise. This was a complete reversal from his stance in 1784, when he favored outlawing slavery throughout the West. Jefferson became so devoted to the expansion of slavery that he refused to support the Missouri Compromise in 1820, which prohibited slavery in the northern portion of the new Western lands, while allowing it in the southern portions.

As Jefferson became ever more deeply in debt due to his architectural endeavors at Monticello and other extravagances, financial entanglements nearly prohibited his freeing slaves, even if he wanted to do so. During his lifetime, he commanded the labor of over 600 slaves, but manumitted only two before his death in 1826. Then, in his will, he freed five mulattoes, possibly his relations, but left more than 260 in bondage. Some 150 of these would be sold to pay his estate's debts.

James Madison and James Monroe

James Madison, our fourth president, owned the Montpelier plantation. The 1820 Census noted that 15 free whites and 106 slaves lived there. Despite his personal status, Madison, like Jefferson, opposed slavery. "The magnitude of this evil among us is so deeply felt, and so universally acknowledged, that no merit could be greater than that of devising a satisfactory remedy for it." His solution was also the same as Jefferson's: colonization. In retirement, Madison became president of the American Colonization Society, which underwrote the purchase of slaves in order to free them and settle them far away from whites, in Africa or in the West.

Madison thought about manumission, but he failed to take decisive action. His will did not free slaves. Records do show, however, that a few attained freedom during his lifetime. One was Billey, who went to Philadelphia with Madison while the Continental Congress was in session and remained with him for three years. In 1783, rather than bringing Billey home at the end of their stay, Madison sold him to a

Pennsylvania Quaker, knowing that Pennsylvania law would declare Billey free after seven years. Here's a good deed. But it's also calculated, for Madison realized that Billey was no longer a proper companion for plantation slaves back home. Philadelphia's freewheeling style had "tainted" his mind, he wrote.

James Monroe, our fifth president, also supported the American Colonization Society. Like Virginian presidents before him, he too, had inherited a plantation, although a modest one. He also inherited "a Negro boy Ralph." By speculating in various lands, he built up his fortunes, and in 1789, he acquired a 3,500-acre estate in Albemarle County, where Jefferson was his neighbor. Reportedly, he treated his own slaves well, but the supervision was left to others when he lived away from home, doing the nation's business. The overseers he hired drove slaves hard as they tried to produce income on lands that never did turn much of a profit, all for the support of an owner known for his lavish lifestyle.

Jefferson, Madison, and Monroe, with many others of their time, believed that because of past antagonisms, the outright freeing of all slaves would lead to racial violence. With many others of their class and time, they also believed that slavery was wrong but also that blacks and whites were inherently unequal in their abilities, if not their rights. They wished that slavery would simply go away, that blacks would disappear to some other place, and that the entire historic episode, a blemish on American virtue, would be forgotten. They shuddered when they realized it would not. Slavery was the Founders' unfinished business, a terrible problem they failed to solve.

THEIR OWN WORDS

"The whole commerce between master and slave is a perpetual exercise of the most boisterous passions, the most unremitting despotism on the one part, and degrading submission on the other. I tremble for my country when I reflect that God is just: that his justice cannot sleep for ever."

—Thomas Jefferson, *Notes on the State of Virginia,* 1781

It is difficult for us today to watch America's best statesmen struggle with an institution that damaged those caught up in it: slaves, most certainly, but also masters. We can learn from this. Our Founders, whom we justly revere in most respects, were limited by their times and not infallible. The documents they created were not infallible, either, most notably the Constitution, which incorporated slavery as part of the fabric of the nation. This demonstrates that our nation was, and is, a work in progress.

The Least You Need to Know

- The Constitution dodged the issue of slavery by compromising on key points and avoiding use of the word.

- Northern delegates wanted only free citizens to count for representation in Congress, while southern delegates wanted to count slaves as well.

- The Convention compromised by counting three fifths of all slaves, the same fraction used in 1783 to determine how much money each state should pay to Congress.

- Faced with a threatened walkout by South Carolina and Georgia, the Convention prohibited Congress from outlawing slave importation before 1808.

- Although more than half the delegates were slave owners, several delegates tried to end or limit slavery.

- Four of the first five presidents, slaveholders themselves, were deeply conflicted about how to deal with the institution.

The Launch

On September 12, five days before the Federal Convention adjourned, Doctor Samuel Johnson, on behalf of a five-man Committee of Style, presented a polished version of the new plan, written primarily by committee member Gouverneur Morris.

Tortuous sentences were now readable, and one in particular stands out. Initially, the opening words of the preamble had read: "We the people of the states of New Hampshire, Massachusetts ..." and so on, listing all thirteen states, from north to south. Morris turned this into the form we all know and love: "We, the people of the United States ..." The shift was more than a stylistic improvement. It confirmed the document's nationalist slant, and beyond that, it was politically necessary. What if one of the listed states failed to ratify the new Constitution? Would the first order of the new government be to rewrite its very first sentence? That would be a poor start indeed.

The fact is, the work of the Convention would come to naught if at least nine states did not approve, and approval was far from automatic. The framers had made one colossal mistake: they had failed to include a Bill of Rights. In this part, we will see that the nation paid a huge price for the framers' "what-were-they-even-thinking" blunder. The politics of ratification became extremely bitter, occasionally erupting in physical violence. The unifying force of an iconic figure, George Washington, and the speedy passage of a Bill of Rights prevented a meltdown, but bad feelings remained and would continue to plague the Early Republic.

This part concludes by discussing the historic meanings of two items in the Bill of Rights that are hotly debated today: the freedom of religion clause in the First Amendment and the right to bear arms in the Second Amendment.

Ratification

In This Chapter

- How Federalists and Anti-Federalists got their names
- Anti-Federalist arguments against the Constitution
- Federalist defense of the Constitution
- Press wars, including *The Federalist Papers*
- State-by-state rundown of the key ratification conventions

On September 17, the final day of the Federal Convention, Benjamin Franklin rose briefly with a prepared speech, but he was too weak to present it, so he handed it to James Wilson to read. "I confess that there are several parts of this Constitution which I do not at present approve," Franklin admitted, "but the older I grow, the more apt I am to doubt my own judgment." In the end, he gave the Constitution his approval "because I expect no better, and because I am not sure that it is not the best." All but three of Franklin's fellow delegates followed his lead and signed on, even though each of the signers had doubts about this provision or that. After four and a half months, the Convention had produced a government that looked viable. Delegates knew that the whole was greater than the sum of its parts and overcame their own misgivings.

The new plan could not become the Constitution of the United States, however, until "We the people" consented. Not all of the people needed to approve, nor even a majority in all of the states. Unlike the Articles of Confederation, which required all thirteen state legislatures to approve of any change, this plan would take effect if nine of the thirteen states gave it the nod.

But would the people buy into the scheme? An almost-king who might serve for life, if continually re-elected? All those extra powers granted to Congress, like taxing and regulating commerce? A central government that could trump state laws? A standing army, even in times of peace? All this, yet no declaration of rights? It would be a hard sell back home. In this chapter, you will read about the very mixed reception the plan received and the razor-thin votes in must-win states. Our Constitution, which is now so ensconced that we take it for granted, was almost nipped in the bud.

Taking Sides and Closing Ranks

The fate of the nation hung in the balance as supporters of the plan, calling themselves *Federalists*, faced the plan's opponents, the *Anti-Federalists*.

DEFINITIONS

At the Convention, people who wanted a strong central government were considered *nationalists* (see Chapter 9), while the few delegates who resisted it were called Federalists, because they wanted to continue the Articles of "Confederation." But because the meeting in Philadelphia was known as the "Federal Convention," people who liked its proposed Constitution started calling themselves **Federalists.** This was handy politically, for it meant their adversaries were tagged as **Anti-Federalists,** and that name, in the popular lingo, meant "obstructing good government." Opponents tried to resist their new label and call *themselves* federalists, as they were called during the Convention. But it didn't take hold, and the terms remained reversed. So-called Anti-Federalists lost the original and perhaps most significant spin war in our nation's history.

Returning home, most Convention delegates drummed up support in newspaper articles or in letters to key people they wanted to convince. Sometimes their sales pitch differed markedly from the positions they held during the Convention. Alexander Hamilton, in a complete turn-around, argued that the president was in no way a king, even though he had wanted the new office to be modeled on the British monarchy. James Wilson explained that popular election of the president was simply not feasible, even though he had pushed for it numerous times on the Convention floor. James Madison showed how states and the new federal government would share powers, and even that "state governments will have the advantage of the federal government," although at the Convention he had favored the increased centralization of authority.

Writing the Constitution and selling it were two different matters. Federalist delegates might be statesmen, but in this case they behaved as politicians. Madison, Wilson, Hamilton, and many others truly believed that the fate of the plan as a whole was the only real issue now. Like Franklin, they willingly embraced the entire package, even the parts they might not have liked. They saw the forest for the trees. Could they then be faulted for a flip-flop here and there?

One influential supporter of the Constitution stands out from the rest: George Washington. Federalists exploited his name brazenly. "Is it possible," asked one writer, "that the deliverer of our country would have recommended an unsafe form of government for that liberty, for which he had for eight long years contended with such unexampled firmness, consistency, and magnanimity?" Another proponent suggested "that the Federalists should be distinguished hereafter by the name of Washingtonians, and the Anti-Federalists by the name of Shayites." Those opposed to the Constitution were allegedly endorsing civil disorder and repudiating America's beloved idol.

Yet another advocate fabricated a tale that ignored the facts entirely. According to Madison's notes, Washington spoke substantively exactly once, and then but briefly. His job had been to preside over the Convention, not debate its points. Discarding the facts entirely, this writer reported that Washington had held the floor "two hours at a time, in speaking upon some parts of the proposed system," and "he advocated every part of the plan with all those rhetorical powers which he possesses in eminent degree."

Three delegates did *not* sign the Constitution, and two of these, George Mason and Elbridge Gerry, led the opposition. On September 12, as soon as the Committee of Style presented its almost-final draft, Mason and Gerry moved that the Committee also produce a Bill of Rights, similar to the ones many states had included with their constitutions. But the other delegates, weary and wanting to go home, could not be bothered at this late date. Not a single state delegation supported the notion.

Furious, Mason started scribbling a list of objections on the back of his printed copy of the Constitution's draft. He worked on these in the waning days of the Convention, and once it had adjourned, he showed his objections to Anti-Federalists in Philadelphia, who were beginning to organize a resistance. He also sent a copy to Richard Henry Lee, who was Virginia's representative and who then tried in vain to get Congress to add a Bill of Rights (see Chapter 16).

When Elbridge Gerry headed back to Massachusetts, he took a copy of Mason's objections and shared them with Anti-Federalists in New York on the way. In his home state, Gerry expected his old friend and political ally Samuel Adams, as well as others, to oppose a plan that placed so many new powers in the hands of a central government, without adequate guarantees of liberty.

FOUNDER ID

George Mason (1725–1792). Virginia House of Burgesses, 1758–1761. Virginia Committee of Safety, 1775. Virginia Convention, 1775–1776. Virginia Assembly, 1776–1780. Constitutional Convention, 1787. Virginia Ratifying Convention, 1788. Co-author, Virginia Nonimportation Agreement (1769), Fairfax Resolves (1774), Virginia Declaration of Rights and Constitution (1776).

Mason often worked closely with his neighbor, George Washington. In the House of Burgesses, they acted on behalf of the Ohio Company to pursue their common interests in Western development. Together, they penned Virginia's Nonimportation Agreement and the Fairfax Resolves. Together, they mobilized the local militia in 1775. But when Washington went off to war, Mason stayed home to help organize the new state. Weeks before independence, he penned a draft for Virginia's first state Constitution, prefaced by a Declaration of Rights that proclaimed, "All men are born equally free and independent." (Jefferson's similar words came a few weeks later.) Often, Mason was recruited to serve in the Continental Congress and other high posts, but he always declined, claiming poor health. At the Constitutional Convention, he and Washington parted ways politically. Mason, unlike Washington, opposed a single executive and favored a Bill of Rights. Outvoted on these and other counts, Mason refused to sign the Constitution. Mason lost the initial battle but won the war. After the Convention, "the genius of the people" insisted their rights be guaranteed.

FOUNDER ID

Elbridge Gerry (1744–1814). Massachusetts Colonial House of Representatives, 1772–1774. Executive Committee of Safety, Massachusetts Provincial Congress, 1774–1775. Continental Congress, 1776–1780, 1783–1785. Treasury Board, 1776–1779. Massachusetts House of Representatives, 1776–1777, 1780–1781, 1786–1787. Constitutional Convention, 1787. United States House of Representatives, 1789–1793. Envoy to France, 1797. Massachusetts Governor, 1810–1812. Vice President, 1813–1814.

A merchant allied with Samuel Adams, Gerry hated both imperial and popular rule. Active in the Committees of Correspondence and the Continental Congress, he was an early advocate of independence and helped supply the army. But in 1774, when a mob fiercely resisted his smallpox inoculation program, and in 1786, when Massachusetts farmers took up arms, Gerry came down firmly against "democracy." At the Constitutional Convention, he opposed popular elections but favored a Bill of Rights. Fearing the political and military power of the new central government, he refused to sign the Constitution. Politically unpredictable, he became a Federalist congressman, then bolted to the Democratic-Republicans. As Governor of Massachusetts, Gerry redrew election districts to favor his party. Although this had long been a common practice, a critic noted that one of Gerry's redrawn districts resembled a salamander and called it "gerrymandering," a term that has stuck to this day. Gerry died while serving as Madison's vice president.

The third nonsigner, Edmund Randolph, was a politically cautious fence-sitter, who waited to see what his home state of Virginia thought of the Constitution. There, former governor Patrick Henry joined with Mason in an impassioned resistance. In Virginia as well as New York and Massachusetts, initial polling (had there been any at that time) might well have revealed that supporters of the proposed Constitution were in the minority.

The fight was on. Leaders on both sides represented only the tip of the iceberg. Over the course of the following year, the entire nation participated for the second time in a grand debate that would shape the future. Through the first half of 1776, in taverns and meetinghouses and outdoor venues, the populace had debated independence. Now people congregated anew. Circumstances were different this time: the nation was on its own, and people were debating a proposal that had been conceived by a small group of their fellow citizens behind closed doors. But those doors had opened, and the last word lay with the people. They could elect representatives who would reflect their views, and then, at state conventions, these men would hash things out and give the proposed plan their okay—or not!

A Great National Debate: Issues

The framers concocted a multi-faceted government with separate seats of authority, each with some checks on the others. In the interest of national unity, they made necessary compromises, but in the end, it seemed that all the pieces fit together. So what was wrong with this plan in the minds of its opponents?

Anti-Federalist Concerns

People had grown accustomed to placing written restrictions on their governments. The British had done so back in 1689 (see Chapter 1). Most states, following independence, had done so when they devised their new state constitutions (see Chapter 6). So why, pray tell, was there no declaration of rights in the plan coming out of the Federal Convention? That was the most pressing question that adversaries posed.

Other questions followed. How could a few men, meeting in secret, with no accountability, replace the existing constitution with another? States had instructed their respective delegates to revise, not abolish, the Articles of Confederation.

Then there were substantive structural concerns. The states, it seemed, would be swept up by the new national government. The Constitution, together with any laws Congress saw fit to pass, would become "the supreme law of the land; and the judges in every state shall be bound thereby, any thing in the constitution or laws of any state to the contrary notwithstanding." This was too much for many loyal Virginians or New Yorkers or Pennsylvanians or … (Name your state.)

There was no "rotation in office" (term limit) for the presidency. One man could serve for life. In addition to his other powers, he would be Commander-in-Chief of a standing army, a dangerous institution in its own right. Was the president not then a thinly disguised monarch? Senators were elected by state legislators and not directly responsible to the people. Their terms lasted six years, and they could continue in office indefinitely. Was the Constitution planting the seed of a new aristocracy?

The Senate and the President, in tandem, determined Supreme Court Justices, appointed ambassadors, and made treaties. The people, through their representatives in the House, had nothing to do with any of these grave matters. A select few would rule, all others must follow. This was certainly not a democracy, and hardly a republic.

Finally, to support this new layer of government, Congress was empowered to pass its own taxes. The states and the central government would subject citizens to double taxation. This left no man's property safe. Federal tax collectors would comb the farthest reaches of the land, extracting from the people what should remain their own.

THEIR OWN WORDS

"A sole executive, who may be for life, with almost a negative upon ye legislature;—ye Senate, a principal part of the legislature, which may also be for life, occasionally a part of ye executive—these appear to me to be most unfortunate parts in the new constitution. I may be deceived, but they present to my mind so strong a stamp of monarchy or aristocracy, that, I think, many generations would not pass before one or the other would spring from the new constitution provided."

—Reverend James Madison, President of the College of William and Mary, and cousin to the man we know as *the* James Madison

Federalist Responses

To counter these objections, Federalists published pamphlets and flooded newspapers with arguments defending the webbed system of government in the proposed Constitution, with its shared powers and various checks and balances. The first major defense was James Wilson's October 6 address to "a very great concourse of people" in the State House Yard, right outside the room where the Constitution was conceived. Point by point, Wilson answered the Anti-Federalists' concerns.

Because the absence of the Bill of Rights was already emerging as the most serious challenge to ratification, Wilson addressed this first. The new constitution did not contain a listing of rights because it didn't need to, he said. All powers not granted to the government still lay with the people. In fact, if the document listed the people's rights, it would imply that others, not listed, now belonged to the government. It was best to steer clear of any such implication.

Wilson then took up other critiques. State governments, far from being annihilated, still maintained power over the selection of senators and the President. The Senate and the President would not augment each other's power by acting in unison, but check each other's powers. A standing army was not only appropriate but necessary, and in fact one already existed in the "cantonments along the banks of the Ohio." National taxation, far from being oppressive, would allow Congress to assume the states' war debts, which had proved so burdensome to the people.

Wilson's speech was reprinted in 34 newspapers in 27 towns, aided in part by George Washington, who arranged for publication in Virginia. Wilson was "as able, candid, & honest a member as any in the Convention," Washington commented, and his speech placed "the most of Colo. Mason's objections in their true point of light."

Mason's objections and Wilson's speech were only the beginning. Over the next 10 months, literally thousands of political pieces appeared in the nation's budding press, arguing on one side or the other. It's easy for us to imagine the excitement and concern. Think of how blogs and talk radio go wild over lesser issues today, then multiply this many times over, and you can catch a glimpse of the seriousness and extent of the debate back then. Not just this law or that, but the very ground rules for the fledgling nation were at stake.

The Federalist Papers

Federalists had their talking points down, but two New Yorkers, Alexander Hamilton and John Jay, wanted a full-bodied, detailed, and persuasive rendition to be put before the reading public. Their idea was to publish a series of essays, and in the end there were 85 of them. One by one these anonymous essays appeared in New York's Federalist newspapers. Once gathered together in two volumes, they became *The Federalist*, which we call today *The Federalist Papers*. The essays were signed "Publius" (a founder of the Roman Republic), but most were penned by Hamilton and James Madison, who was enlisted to help with the project. Jay fell ill and contributed only minimally.

If you took history in college, you might well have been assigned *The Federalist Papers.* Your professor wanted you to understand the complex thinking that went into the writing of the Constitution, but he or she probably neglected to tell you that *The Federalist Papers* were not nearly so big a deal back then as they are now. The essays were reprinted in only a handful of out-of-state papers, while many other pro-Constitution writings achieved much wider circulation. The bound volumes, meanwhile, sold fewer than 500 copies; by contrast, Thomas Paine's *Common Sense* had sold more than 100,000 back in 1776 (see Chapter 4).

Your professor might also have minimized the primary function of the essays: to sell a product, not to reflect the author's favorite ideas. Alexander Hamilton, who preferred a monarchy, argued in *The Federalist Papers* that the president was not in the least bit like a king. Madison, who had argued in the Constitutional Convention for a strong national government, now said the states would be at least as strong, or even stronger, than Congress and the President. Hamilton and Madison wanted people to approve the Constitution, so they painted it in terms they thought the people could accept.

The State Conventions

The fate of the Constitution lay with four key battleground states: Massachusetts, New York, Pennsylvania, and Virginia. Should Massachusetts bow out, New Hampshire would probably follow, and because Rhode Island was already opposed (it hadn't even sent delegates to the Convention), New England would be lost. If New York or Pennsylvania declined to join, the nation would be cut in two. If Virginia did not sign on, her neighbors would join her to form a separate confederacy of the slave states, with great access to the West.

THEIR OWN WORDS

"As the instrument came from [the Convention], it was nothing more than the draught of a plan, nothing but a dead letter, until life and vitality were breathed into it by the voice of the people, speaking through their state conventions."

—James Madison.

Pennsylvania

The Pennsylvania Convention met first. Surprisingly, the Constitution met resistance in the state that had hosted the convention that framed the Constitution. Western farmers, harboring resentments parallel to those of the Massachusetts Regulators (see Chapter 9), did not like more centralized taxation, the prohibition against debtor relief, and the lack of a Bill of Rights. Philadelphia, on the other hand, was the commercial hub of the nation, and the Constitution was certainly friendly to commerce. It would be a hot fight.

When Federalists tried to call for an early ratification convention in Philadelphia, the Constitution's home turf, two Anti-Federalist assemblymen refused to show up, thus denying the Assembly its quorum. Enter Robert Morris, aka THE Financier (see Chapter 8). Morris ordered one of his ship captains to hunt down the Anti-Federalist assemblymen and drag them back into chambers. The Assembly continued its business, the convention met in Philadelphia, and after considerable debates in which no minds were changed, it ratified the Constitution by a 2-1 margin.

That did not end the matter, however. In the interior town of Carlisle, Anti-Federalists broke up a Federalist victory celebration. The following day, Anti-Federalists burned effigies of James Wilson and Thomas McKean, the state Chief Justice. Four weeks later, 21 of the Anti-Federalist rioters were jailed, and when 7 of these refused bail, several hundred local militiamen marched on the jail to free them. Obviously, a Federalist victory "inside chambers" did not guarantee the assent of the body of the people "out-of-doors." The new Constitution was not entirely secure.

Massachusetts

Massachusetts was up next. Samuel Adams, President of the State Senate, did not look kindly on the centralization of power. "I confess, as I enter the building I stumble at the threshold," he said. "I meet with a national government instead of a federal union of sovereign states." In the towns, which voted on representatives to the state ratifying convention, skepticism was widespread. The town of Southborough was typical. Instructing its delegate to the convention, it said: "It is our opinion that the Federal Constitution, as it now stands ought not to be ratifyed, but under certain limitations and amendments it may be a salutary form of government."

When the convention met in the middle of winter, Anti-Federalists were in the majority, but their opposition in many cases was "soft." Governor John Hancock proposed a compromise: Massachusetts should ratify the Constitution, but it should also "recommend" nine amendments for future consideration. To the surprise of many, Samuel Adams supported Hancock's scheme. The amendments, Adams said, would "conciliate the minds" of opponents, particularly "the people without doors." Hancock's proposal managed to win over just enough Anti-Federalists to change the outcome. The final tally was so close that if only 10 of the 355 delegates had voted no instead of yes, the Massachusetts Convention would not have ratified the Constitution. And that, in turn, might well have affected the results in other states like Virginia and New York.

Virginia

By the time the Virginia Ratifying Convention met on June 2, 1788, delegates knew that seven other states had already signed on. Two days later, they learned that South Carolina had as well, making a total of eight. The fact that the Constitution was on the verge of becoming a reality changed the nature of the contest. No longer could Anti-Federalists simply oppose the plan outright, not after the majority of states had already come out in its support. The best they could do was offer amendments that would rectify the Constitution's shortcomings.

So the question came down to this: Should the Virginia Convention follow the lead of Massachusetts by approving the Constitution and suggesting amendments that could be added later? Or should it insist that the plan be amended *before* ratification? Federalists advocated the first approach; Anti-Federalists the second.

There was one unique twist to the three weeks of debates at the Virginia Convention: the topic of slavery. Patrick Henry, leader of the Anti-Federalists, warned that under the sweeping "general welfare" clause, Congress could "pronounce all slaves free." Because the majority of congressmen and senators came from the northern states, Henry said, "They have the power in clear unequivocal terms, and will clearly and certainly exercise it."

Virginia's Federalists played the slave card as well. Should their state not join the new union, they said, it would be vulnerable to Indian attacks, slave insurrections, and foreign invasions. Slaves, a large share of the population, could not be relied on for defense, while whites who could otherwise be soldiers had to stay home to lord over slaves. So, however productive and prosperous, Virginia was in no position to defend itself militarily without support from outside.

On June 25, by a 10-vote margin, Virginia voted to ratify the Constitution. The Convention did propose 40 amendments, far more sweeping in scope than those of Massachusetts, but it did not require that these be passed first. Delegates didn't know it yet, but four days earlier, New Hampshire had voted for ratification, making *it* the ninth state and activating the Constitution. That made Virginia the tenth.

BY THE NUMBERS

At the time, ratification of the Constitution was far from certain. Here are the vote tallies in various states. Note that the key states of Massachusetts, Virginia, and New York were very close:

- 30–0—vote of the Delaware Ratifying Convention, the first to approve the Constitution. Two other states to weigh in early, New Jersey and Georgia, were also unanimous.

- 187–168—vote to ratify the Constitution by the Massachusetts Convention. This was the sixth state to approve the Constitution. Federalists prevailed only by agreeing to propose nine additional amendments. After that, all remaining states offered amendments to the Constitution, even as they ratified it (see Chapter 16).

- 89–79—vote to ratify the Constitution by the Virginia Convention, which proposed 40 amendments before settling on approval.

- 30–27—vote for the Constitution by the New York Convention, which proposed 56 amendments and demanded a second Constitutional Convention to consider them.

- 2,711–239—vote by the people *against* ratification in Rhode Island, the only state to hold a popular referendum instead of a convention. Many Federalists boycotted the election, which they knew they would lose.

- 34–32—vote for ratification at the second Rhode Island Convention on May 29, 1790. This was 985 days after the Constitutional Convention adjourned on September 17, 1787.

The Federal Procession

The timing of the Virginia and New Hampshire ratification votes was perfect. Within days, the nation would be celebrating its eleventh birthday, so now it could celebrate its new Constitution as well. On the Fourth of July in Philadelphia, Federalists organized a victory celebration in the great tradition of Revolutionary street theatre. Each of 44 different groups—cordwainers, bricklayers, coopers, brewers, engravers, whip manufacturers, and so on—tried to outdo the others by constructing creative, gargantuan floats. Butchers marched two oxen side-by-side down the street, one labeled ANARCHY and the other CONFUSION. The banner hanging between their horns read, "The Death of ANARCHY and CONFUSION Shall Feed the Poor and Hungry," and at the conclusion of the parade, the men who led the oxen made good on their word by butchering the animals and feeding the crowd. The parade featured 5,000 participants and stretched for a mile and one half.

The featured display in this rambling performance was the "GRAND FEDERAL EDIFICE." Carried on a carriage and drawn by 10 horses, it rose to a height of 36 feet above street level. To accommodate the magnificent structure, workers had climbed and limbed trees along the course the previous evening. The large dome of the Edifice was adorned with a frieze showing 13 stars (one per state, of course), and supported by 13 Corinthian columns. Of these only 10 were finished. The others represented New York, North Carolina, and Rhode Island, states that had not yet ratified the Constitution. Federalist event organizers were delivering a potent and not-so-hidden message.

Unfinished Business

The Grand Federal Procession played well in Philadelphia, but it would not have done so everywhere. In Providence, Rhode Island, on the morning of July 4, a thousand Anti-Federalists confronted Federalists, insisting that revelers celebrate independence only, not the Constitution. After forcing this concession, Anti-Federalists staged their own party, and in toasts that preceded each new round of drinking, they refused to concede defeat. "May the sons of freedom in America never submit to a despotic government," one said. "May each state retain their sovereignty in the full extent of republican covenants," said another.

In New York, meanwhile, delegates to the state ratifying convention were locked in a heated battle, and the populace was as well. In Albany, on the day of the Grand Federal Procession, Federalists and Anti-Federalists engaged in street battle. Without New York, the new nation would be considerably weakened, and the outcome there remained very much in doubt.

In the end, the New York Convention ratified the Constitution by a razor-thin, three-vote margin. But it also called for a second Constitutional Convention to consider its own proposed amendments and those suggested by other states. North Carolina went further yet, refusing to ratify until a second convention actually *met*. It even elected delegates to such a convention. Rhode Island, meanwhile, would have none of all this. There, the issue of ratification was decided by the people themselves, and only one of every twelve voters supported the new plan.

If this was to be a united nation, there was much work to be done.

The Least You Need to Know

- "Federalists" hijacked that name, which originally referred to *opponents* of a centralized national government.

- Anti-Federalist complaints included the lack of a Bill of Rights, too little power for the states, a president and senators who could remain in office for life, national taxation, and a standing army.

- Federalists argued that specific rights did not need to be listed, and that multiple seats of authority, which checked each other, would limit any concentration of power.

- *The Federalist Papers,* although impressive, were among numerous political tracts in a national debate matched only during the build up to independence.

- The vote for ratification was extremely close in the battleground states of Massachusetts, Virginia, and New York.

- Several states proposed amendments, including guarantees that the new government would not interfere with basic rights.

The Father of Our Country

In This Chapter

- The first federal elections for Congress
- Field test for the presidential elector system
- The importance of Washington as a unifying icon
- Debates in Congress: taxes and presidential power
- Washington's selections for the first "cabinet"

With New York's ratification in midsummer of 1788, eleven of the thirteen states had signed on to the new Constitution, and people assumed this would force North Carolina and Rhode Island to do so sooner or later. It was time to put the Constitution into effect. But how do you stop one form of government and start another? There was plenty of room for doubt and apprehension.

What if George Washington, the obvious choice for first president, declined to serve? Would Federalists and Anti-Federalists ever agree on another candidate? And how would the new president address the rift in the nation, which had only deepened during the ratification debates?

Would Anti-Federalists, the opponents of the Constitution, ever *accept* this new government, which lacked a bill of rights? What if the electorate chose Anti-Federalist representatives and senators? Would Congress then try to bring down the new government from within?

The First Federal Elections

George Washington, for one, worried that "a considerable effort will be made to procure the election of Anti-Federalists to the first Congress in order to undo all that has been done." Some Congressional contests were close. Even James Madison, who had worked so hard to create the Constitution and shape it into a form that the states would accept, faced stiff competition from James Monroe, an Anti-Federalist. (Years later Monroe would succeed Madison as President.) But Madison did edge out Monroe and returned to his old haunts in Congress. Other veterans of the Convention, like Sherman and Gerry, joined Madison in the House of Representatives.

When state legislators chose the first federal senators, fully half turned out to be veterans of the Constitutional Convention. These people had provided themselves with jobs, taking seats in a new body that they themselves had created from scratch. Altogether, despite the concerns of Washington and others, Federalists won over-whelming majorities in both houses of Congress.

It was onto business, and time was of the essence. The nation, as usual, was broke, but before revenues could flow in, the governmental machinery had to be up and running. If all went well, that would start on March 4, 1789, the day the new Congress was slated to convene. On that date, the Senate was supposed to open and validate the official returns from the Electoral College, and then it could quickly pass some import duties. The new president could sign these into law before the spring importing season began, and money would start filling the national coffers. But none of this was automatic. The Electoral College remained untested. Indeed, Congress itself was untested. Would this two-chamber business work out? What if there were some hidden flaws the framers had not envisioned?

And for President?

The presidential election presented a unique set of challenges.

Nobody knew if the bizarre new system of electors would work. The Constitution stipulated that presidential electors would be chosen "in such a manner" as each state's legislature "may direct." Supposedly, the point of the elector system was to remove politics from the selection of the presidency, but in fact, this provision ensured that elections *would* be political. Legislators quickly learned they could game the system. In five of the eleven states then in the union, legislators chose electors of their own political persuasion. In two states the voters decided, but when no candidate received an absolute majority, the state legislators took over. In two other states voters also decided, but in districts men in the legislatures drew up and manipulated.

Only in Pennsylvania and Maryland did the people vote for electors without any meddling from state legislators. But here, too, the elections turned political. Federalist and Anti-Federalist conventions drew up slates of candidates pledged to their side, then staged barbecues and parades, just like today. Militia companies worked on get-out-the-vote campaigns. None of this was supposed to happen. Electors were supposed to be wise men who would make decisions on their own.

Why all the fuss, if Washington was everybody's first choice? Nobody dared oppose Washington, for fear of being perceived as unpatriotic, but Washington had not said he would accept the job, for fear of appearing over-eager. And if he declined, what then?

According to the elector system, there was no difference between first and second place votes. Let's say electors agreed on a slate, Washington for President and candidate XX for Vice President. If all electors marked their tickets with those two men, they would wind up in a tie. Worse yet, if even one elector held a grudge and left Washington off, candidate XX would then become president!

THEIR OWN WORDS

"Everybody is aware of that defect in the Constitution which renders it possible that the man intended for Vice President may in fact turn up President."

—Alexander Hamilton to James Wilson, January 25, 1789

Some former Constitutional Convention delegates, Alexander Hamilton included, realized they had committed a serious blunder in devising a system that could produce such a bizarre result. To prevent the system from yielding such a result, Hamilton urged his fellow Federalists to support John Adams for Vice President, but then he persuaded a few electors to leave Adams off their ballots so he wouldn't defeat Washington. The scheme worked. Washington was included on all 69 ballots, while Adams received 34 votes, making him vice president. Twelve years later, in a similar situation, the vote *would* end up in a tie, as Hamilton feared, and repercussions from that would cost him his life (see Chapter 21).

Please, General, Just Say Yes!

Americans had feared that the War for Independence might somehow promote a military takeover. At war's end, when Washington left his office of Commander-in-Chief, citizens were reassured and applauded that move. In the nation's eyes, he was a selfless hero who did not crave power. Now, if he accepted the presidency, could his efforts on behalf of a strong central government leave the impression that he had created a powerful new office so he could occupy it?

On the other hand, if he shunned the office, would he be letting the nation down? Hamilton, Washington's former aide and still his confidant, told his mentor that in supporting the Constitutional Convention and ratification, Washington had "*pledged* to take a part in the execution of the government." Again and again in the waning months of 1788, people like Hamilton urged Washington to accept an office that had been created under the assumption that he would be its first occupant. Washington responded that he would prefer to remain in private life, if possible. Only if no other candidate would be acceptable, and if his refusal would result in "some very disagreeable consequences" to "the good of my country," would he consent to come out of retirement and accept the presidency.

FOUNDER ID

George Washington, General and President, is known to us all. But what about Washington, the land developer? Frustrated by Virginia's tobacco-and-slave economy, Washington believed that America's future, and his own, lay in developing western lands, which put him in conflict with Native Americans. Early on, as the Ohio Company's surveyor and commander of the Virginia militia, he had challenged French and Indian control of the West (see Chapter 1). After the French and Indian War, although British officials had promised him lands for his service, they denied him his patents, leading him to join the patriots. After the Revolution, with his claims secured, he ventured West to remove squatters from his lands and locate a water route to the interior. His grand vision, embodied in his Potomac Canal Company, was to link the Ohio country with the Atlantic via Virginia, unifying and enriching the nation. Washington's political, military, and entrepreneurial goals were all of a piece. He thought that only an expanded nation could hold its own with European powers. (See Chapter 1 for more information on Washington.)

On the first day of 1789, Washington wrote that he would decline the presidency if it could be done "consistently with the dictates of duty." The very next day, he sent to James Madison, under the utmost secrecy, a 73-page draft of an inaugural address that he and his secretary, David Humphreys, had been working on for weeks. This didn't mean he had been hypocritical. As a military man, the General was always prepared for all contingencies. If duty did call, he had to be prepared to accept.

One week later, on a "raw & chilly" day, George Washington rode to the Fairfax County Courthouse to cast his vote for his district's presidential elector. The elector system spared Washington the embarrassment of voting directly for or against himself.

Four weeks after that, on February 4, electors cast ballots in their respective states. Washington soon knew he would be president, but he couldn't just pack up and go to New York, the seat of the government, because the outcome wasn't yet official. First, Congress would have to convene, hopefully on March 4. The President of the Senate would tabulate the official returns, and only then could a messenger ride to Mount Vernon with an official congratulatory message.

A Slow Start for Congress

It wasn't until April 14 that Charles Thomson, the longtime secretary of Congress, arrived at Mount Vernon with the formal job offer. Why the delay of more than five weeks? Partly, that's the way things worked in the eighteenth century, with horses and carriages traveling over lousy roads in the slushy time of year. But for whatever reason, the United States Congress, from the outset, just couldn't get it together.

On March 4, the date Congress was supposed to convene, neither the House nor the Senate had a quorum. Delegates who arrived on time were forced to wait around, doing nothing. One week later, when no additional senators had arrived, the eight who were present drafted a letter to the twelve who were not. "We earnestly request, that you will be so obliging as to attend as soon as possible," they wrote.

A week later, there were still only eight senators present. Once more they sent out a notice, this time guilt-tripping the laggards: "We again earnestly request your immediate attendance, and are confident you will not suffer our, and the public anxious expectations to be disappointed."

BY THE NUMBERS

Framers of the Constitution were eager to put their plan into effect, but others were less so. The Senate usually acts slowly, but never so slowly as at the very start:

- 8 senators showed up on March 4, allegedly the opening day of Congress. For a quorum, there needed to be 12. Of the dedicated group, 6 had been delegates to the Constitutional Convention.
- The same senators, and no others, were still there two weeks later, on March 18.
- 10 senators had arrived by March 21. Of these stalwarts, 8 had attended the Constitutional Convention.
- The twelfth senator, Richard Henry Lee, finally showed up on April 4.

Not until April 4 did both houses of Congress achieve a quorum and count the official votes of the electors. They were exactly one month late. While waiting for Charles Thomson to fetch Washington from Virginia, congressmen tried to settle on an official presidential title. In the Senate a majority preferred "His Highness," which was exactly the sort of high-toned snootiness that Anti-Federalists had feared from that body. The House, though, wisely concluded that such a monarchical term would offend the American people. Congress also discussed the inauguration ceremony and tried to figure out its own rules. To accomplish these tasks, it formed committees, dozens of them, following the tradition it had established at its inception in 1774.

Congress also considered the most urgent item of business on its agenda—how to raise money. On April 28, the House of Representatives presented a draft for scores of import taxes it wished to levy, broken down in excruciating detail. Teas imported on American ships were to be taxed less than those on foreign ships. Bohea tea, souchong tea, "superior" green tea, and just ordinary green tea would be taxed at different rates. The tax for superior green tea imported on a foreign ship was 30¢ per pound; for bohea on a United States ship, only 6¢ per pound. Taxes covered everything from "canes, walking sticks, and whips" to "distilled spirits of Jamaica proof."

BY THE NUMBERS

Here are just a few of the items on the House list of proposed taxes:

"It is the opinion of this committee that the following duties ought to be laid on goods, wares, and merchandises imported into the United States, IN CENTS:

- On Madeira wine, per gal. … 25
- On all other wines, per gal. … 15
- On every gallon of beer, ale, or porter, imported in casks … 8
- On all beer, ale, or porter, imported in bottles, per doz. … 25
- On boots, per pair … 50
- On all shoes, slippers, or goloshoes, made of leather, per pair … 7
- On all shoes or slippers made of silk or stuff, per pair … 10
- On hemp, per cwt. after the first of December, 1789, … 60
- On snuff, per lb. … 10"

If the tax list was specific, so were the demands of constituents. Petitions flooded in. "Merchants and traders" from Portland wanted to lower or eliminate the tax on molasses, which would "be attended with pernicious consequences to manufactures."

Philadelphia distillers also complained about the molasses tax, but they wanted a higher tax on imported rum that competed with their own product. Philadelphia shipwrights wanted to tax foreign ships so theirs would be more valuable, while "tradesmen and manufacturers" from Baltimore, Boston, and New York also requested "protecting duties," what we now call protective tariffs. But Virginia tobacco growers worried that giving preferential treatment to American shippers would increase the cost of exporting their product, while all protective tariffs would bump up consumer costs.

And so the horse-trading began. Molasses at six cents per pound? Outrageous! Do I hear five, four, three, two? No tax at all? But why then should loaf sugar be taxed? Congress debated for months the various duties, with each representative upholding the interests of his constituents, much as they do now. Not until July 6 were the nation's first import duties signed into law, too late, unfortunately, to cover the year's first round of imports.

Washington Takes the Helm

Back to the President-elect. Washington arrived in New York to great fanfare on April 23. Over the following week, Congress, the only operative branch of the new national government, put the final touches on the inauguration ceremony.

On Thursday, April 30, 1789, Robert R. Livingston, the Chancellor of New York, administered the presidential oath of office. According to tradition, Washington added the words "so help me God" to the oath he pronounced. Historians have found no firsthand evidence for this, but Washington did imbue this momentous event with a touch of religion. Following his taking the oath, to a joint session of Congress he offered his "fervent supplications to that Almighty Being who rules over the universe, … the Great Author of every public and private good." At the session's conclusion, Washington and members of Congress participated in "divine service" at St. Paul's Chapel. (For more on Washington, the Founders, and religion, see Chapter 17.)

In his speech, Washington also told congressmen that he trusted their actions would be motivated by "no local prejudices or attachments, no separate views, nor party animosities," but instead by "the pure and immutable principles of private morality." He tried to set a proper tone.

And he did lead by example. Recognizing the ill will that still existed between Federalists and Anti-Federalists over the issue of amendments, Washington proposed a middle way. He approved of the Federalists' desire to "carefully avoid every alteration, which might endanger the benefits of an united and effective Government," but urged them to honor the desires of the Anti-Federalist minority, who wished to secure "the characteristic rights of freemen." He hoped that "a regard for the public harmony" would "sufficiently influence" the deliberations of this new Congress. Translation: Don't be closed-minded, my fellow Federalists. We need to heal this nation, and a Bill of Rights might just be the way to do it. (For more on the Bill of Rights, see Chapter 16.)

Already, Washington was performing the job he was called upon to do. The president, by design of the framers, was supposed to be an "exalted character," above politics. This was certainly Washington's notion of the job, and part of the reason he took it. He wanted to exemplify what people called "republican virtue," or disinterested leadership. (For more on this, see Chapter 6.) He even declined to accept a salary, just to prove he was not after any sort of personal gain—although he did accept reimbursement for all his expenses, which were considerable.

Washington was a unifying icon. No question about that, but in Chapters 19 through 22, we'll see how difficult it was for the Founders, and even for this exemplary leader, to transcend politics.

The President Chooses His Team

To get the executive machinery up and running, Congress had to act first. There would be no state department, war department, treasury department, or courts before Congress established them. Then, and only then, could President Washington make executive appointments and start governing.

But Congress was a deliberative body, and debates took time. In establishing executive departments, congressmen found themselves at yet another impasse. Without question, the President had the power to make appointments, with the advice and consent of Congress. But did he also have the power to *remove* the men he appointed? The Senate discussed this over and over, as if they were at another Constitutional convention. When the matter finally came to a vote, it was a stalemate, ten-to-ten. Vice President John Adams broke the tie, giving the president the power of removal.

Meanwhile, Washington was beseeched with applications for several hundred jobs in the government. A stickler for decorum, he kept the reasons for his choices closely guarded, and he carefully avoided any appearance of favoritism. When his beloved nephew, Bushrod Washington, asked to become a federal attorney, the President told him point-blank that there were more qualified lawyers seeking the job. (Later, after his uncle left office, Bushrod would gain a seat on the Supreme Court.) The new president also distributed the jobs to people of different regions and even political persuasions, so long as the office-seekers were not confirmed foes of the Constitution.

It is not difficult to understand the reasons for Washington's major appointments. Thomas Jefferson was the current minister to France, and a man who knew Europe as well as any Founder except Franklin and Adams. Washington chose him as Secretary of State, head of the Department of Foreign Affairs.

Henry Knox would become Secretary of War. He had served with Washington since the outset of the Revolutionary War and was currently in charge of the federal army, numbering fewer than a thousand men now that the nation was not at war.

FOUNDER ID

Henry Knox (1750–1806). Colonel (1775), Brigadier General (1776), Major General (1782), and Commander-in-Chief (1783–1784) in the Continental Army. Confederation Secretary of War under the Articles of Confederation (1785–1789) and the new United States government (1789–1794). Founder and secretary-general of the Society of the Cincinnati (officers of the Revolutionary War), 1783–1799.

Knox was large (almost 300 pounds), lively, and loyal, both to his wife (who was nearly as large) and to Washington. A bookseller in Boston before the war, he read books about artillery and military engineering intended for British officers. When war broke out, he quickly became Washington's go-to man for artillery. The arms and ammunition that he and his men carted over rough terrain from Fort Ticonderoga allowed Washington to chase the British out of Boston. He was quickly promoted to general, and he commanded the artillery throughout the war. When Washington resigned, Knox took over, first as senior officer, then as Congress's Secretary of War, and finally as Washington's Secretary of War. In the mid-1790s Knox retired to manage and expand his vast land holdings in Maine. There, he evicted poor veterans (including Private Joseph Plumb Martin) who had been farming the land, but like other land speculators of the period, he was often financially pinched. Knox died from swallowing a chicken bone.

Of far more importance than the Secretary of War, and perhaps more important than the Secretary of State, was the Secretary of the Treasury because the nation was, of course, still deeply in the red. One man, Robert Morris, was extremely more qualified for this post than anyone else. THE Financier had bailed the nation out once before (see Chapter 8), but Morris had had his fill of nation-saving and didn't want the job.

Neither did Gouverneur Morris, Robert Morris's assistant, who was now partnered with his former boss and was representing their business interests abroad. Only one other man was qualified for the challenging post: Alexander Hamilton, who had served under Robert Morris in the early 1780s and had made an extensive study of private and public finance. Fortuitously, Hamilton was also a longtime associate of Washington, first as an aide-de-camp during the war, and now as a political ally and confidant.

The last major position in the Executive Branch, Attorney General, went to Edmund Randolph, who had served as Attorney General in Virginia, the nation's largest state. The job was brand new. Under the Articles of Confederation, there had been no federal laws, but now laws would proliferate and oversight was required. Randolph, who had ten years of experience as Virginia's Attorney General, was as well qualified as anyone. Randolph had opposed a single executive (see Chapter 11), and refused to sign the Constitution, but Washington wasn't the type to hold a grudge. Besides, Randolph's later support for ratification at the Virginia Convention had proved crucial.

And why didn't a post go to James Madison, who was closely allied with Washington and helped him write the inaugural address? Madison was in Congress, and the President wanted to keep him there—for good reason, as we shall see in the next chapter.

With his crew of department heads, who by 1793 would be called his "cabinet," Washington was ready to assume command of an active and independent Executive Branch. But could the President, his cabinet, and Congress place the nation on a firm financial footing, establish its standing abroad, and reduce the internal divisions of the 1780s, which had deepened during the ratification debates? These were tall orders.

The Least You Need to Know

- Federalists prevailed in the first elections for Congress.
- The presidential elector system, intended to negate political influence, immediately became politicized.
- Washington, the unanimous choice for President, wanted to unite a divided nation.
- The first job of Congress was to raise money, but it took months for special interests to agree on tax rates for imports.

- With Vice President John Adams breaking a deadlock, the Senate decided that the President could dismiss his own department heads.

- Washington's choices for the first "cabinet" were Thomas Jefferson (Secretary of State), Henry Knox (Secretary of War), Alexander Hamilton (Secretary of the Treasury), and Edmund Randolph (Attorney General).

Finally, a Bill of Rights!

In This Chapter

- Madison's changing views on a Bill of Rights
- Rights in colonial charters and state constitutions
- Amendments proposed by state ratification conventions
- Debates in Congress over constitutional amendments
- Congressional approval and state ratification

The nation would not heal without a Bill of Rights. George Washington knew it. Thomas Jefferson, the Secretary of State who was still in France, knew it. Even James Madison knew it, although he had originally opposed the concept. In fact it was Madison who introduced a draft for Constitutional amendments in the first session of Congress, only to meet stiff resistance from other Federalists, who held firm in their opposition. Out-of-doors, meanwhile, Anti-Federalists would not endorse their nation's Constitution until they felt their rights were secured. The fight was still on.

This chapter covers the creation of the Bill of Rights, the most talked-about and treasured part of our Constitution, and its genesis in an earlier history. Colonial charters from the 1600s had guaranteed rights. After independence, state constitutions had guaranteed rights. The ratification conventions had proposed more than 200 amendments, many of them guaranteeing rights. With such an abundance of precedents, how did the nation come to adopt the final ten?

Madison Comes Around

On September 27, 1787, ten days after the Federal Convention had adjourned, Richard Henry Lee suggested that Congress add a Bill of Rights to the Constitution before sending it out to the states for ratification. James Madison immediately objected. Because nothing in the Constitution deprived people of basic rights, he said, a separate listing would only jeopardize any rights *not* listed.

The following summer, at the Virginia Ratification Convention, Madison repeated this argument verbatim. He did say, though, that he was not opposed to amendments per se, if they were not "dangerous." He also agreed to sit on the Virginia committee that proposed Constitutional amendments, alongside nonsigners George Mason and Edmund Randolph (see Chapter 14).

By early January 1789, Madison had had a change of heart. He was engaged in a heated election campaign for a seat in the House of Representatives (see Chapter 15), and he had been roundly criticized for opposing a Bill of Rights. Because most of his constituents, including Baptists pushing for freedom of religion (see Chapter 17), wanted a Bill of Rights, he suddenly proclaimed he thought it was a fine idea after all. He had opposed all amendments before ratification, he explained, from fear that alterations in the proposed Constitution would lead to endless arguments and a "dissolution" of the new nation. But now, with ratification secured, he no longer thought amendments presented any great danger and they might even do some good.

Madison's turnaround worked. He won the election and headed off to Congress, where he would make good on his pledge to work for a Bill of Rights.

THEIR OWN WORDS

"Amendments, if pursued with a proper moderation and in a proper mode, will be not only safe, but may serve the double purpose of satisfying the minds of well meaning opponents, and of providing additional guards in favour of liberty."

—James Madison, January 2, 1789, explaining his change of heart on a Bill of Rights after the Constitution had been ratified.

Precedents

Imagine yourself a "soft" Federalist like Washington and Madison. You want amendments that will satisfy Anti-Federalists but not antagonize "hard" Federalists. This is "a point of no uncommon delicacy," as Washington put it. You want to include amendments that are "really proper and generally satisfactory," but none with "with such a spirit of innovation as will overturn the whole system." To these general ground rules, Washington added one firm restriction. There must be no amendment "which goes to the prevention of direct taxation." Congress needed to retain the power to tax. If the new national government had to rely on state "requisitions," as under "the old confederation," the entire purpose of the Constitution would be undermined.

So how do you proceed? It might help to know the rich history of guaranteeing rights in America, from colonial times to 1789.

Colonial Charters

In 1818, when discussing who might be considered "the author, inventor, discoverer of independence," John Adams came up with this reply: "The only true answer must be the first emigrants, and the proof of it is the charter of James 1." That charter, granted to the founders of Virginia in 1606, promised that people who emigrated to America would "have and enjoy all liberties, franchises, and immunities … as if they had been abiding and born, within this our realm of England." In subsequent years, the charters of New England (1620), Massachusetts Bay (1629), Maryland (1632), Connecticut (1662), Rhode Island (1663), Carolina (1663), and Georgia (1732) likewise promised that colonists would enjoy all the rights of Englishmen.

In 1641, the people of Massachusetts listed in great detail just which rights they were entitled to enjoy. The document they created, called the "Body of Liberties," reads like an extended Bill of Rights, except for the spelling. Here is one of the 98 liberties intended to guarantee the "tranquillitie and Stabilitie" of society: " No man shall be forced by Torture to confesse any Crime against himselfe nor any other unlesse it be in some Capitall case where he is first fullie convicted by cleare and suffitient evidence to be guilty." Other liberties familiar to us today include a thorough list of the rights of the accused, including bail, legal representation, presentation of evidence, a speedy trial by jury, appeal to a higher court, security against double jeopardy, and a prohibition against "bodilie punishments" that are "inhumane Barbarous or cruel." (This meant no more than 40 lashes, "unles his crime be very shamefull.")

The guarantees did not end there, and some are rather surprising. Foreigners escaping persecution were to be welcomed. Monopolies were prohibited. No man could be pressed into fighting an offensive war without his consent. A man could not beat his wife, except in his own defense. Parents could not "wilfullie and unreasonably deny any childe timely or convenient mariage." Servants could flee from cruel masters, and if a master "smite out" an eye or a tooth, the servant could go free. Witches, on the other hand, were to be put to death, as were blasphemers, adulterers, and homosexuals. The rights guaranteed by the Massachusetts Body of Liberties are all the more striking because they were promised by a Puritanical society we think of as exceptionally stern.

Declarations of Rights in State Constitutions

With independence in 1776, 11 of the 13 states drafted new constitutions (see Chapter 6). Seven opened with detailed lists of rights, somewhat reminiscent of the Massachusetts Body of Liberties from a century-and-one-third earlier. (So, too, did Vermont, a wannabe state that was trying to secede from New York.) All of these lists affirmed that government must be rooted in the people and that people could only be taxed by their own representatives. They also guaranteed, in one form or another, freedom of the press, freedom of worship, the right to bear arms, and various rights for people accused of crimes. Most, but not all, asserted that men are "born equally free and independent." A few included features we do not generally associate with those times: proportional taxation, whereby each citizen would be taxed according to his ability to pay, and a prohibition against all monopolies. In 1783, New Hampshire, the last state to prepare such a list, gave it a new title, a "Bill of Rights" instead of "Declaration of Rights." The people's rights had been around a long time; only the name was late in coming.

BY THE NUMBERS

Our Bill of Rights had plenty of precedents, some dating back to colonial times:

- 148 years before Madison presented a Bill of Rights to Congress, the people of Massachusetts were guaranteed 98 "Liberties," including many of the items in our Bill of Rights.
- All 11 of the states that adopted new constitutions following independence guaranteed certain rights for the people. Seven of these state constitutions, plus that of Vermont, opened with separate lists of the people's rights.

210 Amendments? Good Luck!

At the ratification conventions in 1787 and 1788, delegates from seven states prepared lists of changes and additions they wished to make to the Constitution. The Federal Convention, when it sent its handiwork out for approval, had told the states "take this or nothing" (in George Mason's words), but many folks did not want to play the game that way. Instead, they tried to put their own stamps on the new rules.

The first five states that ratified the Constitution proposed no amendments. (In one, Pennsylvania, Anti-Federalists submitted a dissenting, minority report and recommended 15 of them, but these were simply ignored by the majority.)

But the sixth state, Massachusetts, did propose amendments, and after that, as each state voted for ratification, and as people realized that the Constitution *would* pass, state conventions were seized by an amendment frenzy. The last four states to ratify offered a whopping 181 amendments and resolutions they called "principles," which read much like the state declarations of rights.

BY THE NUMBERS

Additions to the Constitution proffered at state ratifying conventions, in chronological order:

- Pennsylvania minority report: 15 amendments
- Massachusetts Convention: 9 amendments
- Maryland committee report: 13 from the majority, another 15 from the minority
- South Carolina Convention: 4 amendments
- New Hampshire Convention: 12 amendments
- Virginia Convention: 40 amendments
- New York Convention: 32 amendments, plus 24 "principles"
- North Carolina Convention: 46 amendments
- Total amendments and principles available to Madison when he drafted the Bill of Rights: 210
- Rhode Island Convention: 21 amendments, plus 18 "principles"
- Total amendments and principles offered by official bodies that wanted to improve the Constitution: 249

Many proposals appeared on several lists, a few on virtually all. The last four states broke their lists into two categories, one for "principles" that preserved the people's rights, the other for suggested changes in the workings of the new government. This latter group covered a wide range. New York's amendments, for instance, included such pro-democracy measures as a larger House of Representatives, prohibition of government-sanctioned monopolies, term limits for Senators and the President, restrictions on a standing army, a method for recalling Senators, more specific procedures for impeachment, open meetings of Congress, the frequent publication of Congressional proceedings, and returning authority over debtor relief to the states. Amendments from other states also had pro-democracy features, such as guaranteeing the right of citizens to instruct their representatives.

Federalists feared that these sorts of amendments might unravel the elaborate web the framers had woven at the Convention. One amendment, appearing on all lists, toyed with the very cornerstone of the Constitution: federal taxation. It stated that before taxing the people directly, the federal government would have to ask the state legislatures for funds, and only if the legislatures didn't come through, could Congress tax the people directly.

Federalists cringed. Amendments like these, which altered the Constitution's machinery, would undermine the entire enterprise.

Others amendments, however, just protected rights. Could they really do any harm? If these were added to the Constitution, Anti-Federalists would probably drop their other demands, and the essence of the Constitution would remain intact. Madison would make sure that "the structure & stamina of the government are as little touched as possible" by his amendments.

By May 1789, when Congressman James Madison sat down to compose additions to the Constitution, he could readily consult *the genius of the people*, embodied in 210 principles and amendments emerging from the state conventions. (A year later, the Rhode Island Ratifying Convention would add 39 more.) With this list in hand, and understanding both the deep tradition of rights in America and the political importance of securing those rights by amending the new Constitution, Madison set to work. He selected 19 amendments from the states' suggestions. These included ones that eventually became our Bill of Rights, as well as a handful that were structural.

> **DEFINITION**
>
> **The genius of the people** means public opinion. The Founders used the phrase often at the Constitutional Convention, usually when a speaker said that people would never consent to some measure that he opposed. Here are the oft-quoted words of George Mason, spoken at the Convention on June 4: "Notwithstanding the oppressions & injustice experienced among us from democracy; the genius of the people is in favor of it, and the genius of the people must be consulted."

Congress Selects the Finalists

Before going public with his list, Madison ran it by Washington, who gave his somewhat lukewarm endorsement. "I see nothing objectionable in the proposed amendments," the President responded. "Some of them, in my opinion, are importantly necessary; others, though of themselves (in my conception) not very essential, are necessary to quiet the fears of some respectable characters and well meaning men. … They have my wishes for a favourable reception in both houses."

And so, on June 8, 1789, Madison approached the House of Representatives, amendments in hand. His reception there was downright chilly. His Federalist friends called him a turncoat. They had won the battle over ratification, so why should they bow down to the other side now? Besides, the amendments weren't necessary, this wasn't the right time, and they were too busy with other more important business. In short, no deal.

Six weeks later, on July 21, Madison tried again. He "begged the House to indulge him in the further consideration of amendments to the Constitution." This time he managed to get a committee formed, but debate would not begin in earnest until mid-August. Finally, and reluctantly, the congressmen "indulged" Madison by considering his amendments. They quibbled about the wording and tightened the prose. They also made some significant changes. Madison wanted to interweave his amendments into the body of the Constitution. That was a bad idea, according to some; they would have to come at the end. Madison had written a verbose, 81-word preamble, copied almost word-for-word from Virginia's 1776 Declaration of Rights, which restated the ideas contained in the preamble of the Declaration of Independence. It was voted down. By deleting some provisions and combining others, Congress reduced Madison's amendments from 19 to 12. These finally passed both houses by the two-thirds margin required for Constitutional amendments, and on September 25, 1789, they went out to the states for ratification.

In a sense, the Bill of Rights crept in the back door. Once it was placed before Congress, representatives and senators knew they'd lose favor if they voted against it, and so, grudgingly, they passed it. What we regard today as the Founders' greatest triumph was for many in the Federalist majority an inconvenience at best.

THEIR OWN WORDS

"Whenever any government shall be found inadequate or contrary to these purposes, a majority of the community hath an indubitable, unalienable and indefeasible right to *reform, alter or abolish it.*"

—Virginia's 1776 Declaration of Rights, penned by George Mason.

"That the people have an indubitable, unalienable, and indefeasible right to *reform or change* their government, when it be found adverse or inadequate to the purposes of its institution."

—from James Madison's original Bill of Rights. Congress rejected this provision. Note the one major change between Madison's version and Mason's. Madison said it was fine to "reform or change" the government he had just helped establish, but not to "abolish" it.

Ratification by the States

Congress alone was not empowered to amend the Constitution. The framers had decided that such a momentous act would need to be approved by at least three quarters of the states. So on October 2, 1789, President Washington sent to the governor of each state the 12 amendments that Congress had just passed. If 10 states ratified the measures, they would be added to the Constitution.

How would these amendments be received? Most Americans probably agreed with all of them, but that did not mean the amendments enjoyed smooth sailing. Federalists hadn't wanted any amendments, while state ratification conventions had recommended many more than appeared on Congress's short list. Neither group could be entirely pleased.

The amendments were attacked from both sides. Staunch Federalists objected in particular to the first two, which enlarged the House of Representatives and prohibited congressmen from raising their own salaries. They did not want the people to fiddle with the machinery of the Constitution, although they would let the people protect their liberties. Radical Anti-Federalists, on the other hand, were not ready to sell out for this partial guarantee of rights. They had wanted more concessions, many more, and they thought (correctly) that once the first batch was passed, people would lose the drive to make more changes. In Virginia, a stronghold of Anti-Federalists, it took more than two years for the proposed amendments to clear the legislature.

But in the end, they did. On December 15, 1791, Virginia became the tenth state to ratify what we know today as the Bill of Rights, the first ten amendments to the Constitution. Those other two on Congress's list—adding more representatives and restricting congressmen's salaries—failed to make the grade.

THEIR OWN WORDS

"He [Mason] wished the plan had been prefaced with a Bill of Rights. It would give great quiet to the people; and with the aid of the state declarations, a bill might be prepared in a few hours."

—George Mason at the Federal Convention, September 12, 1787. Mason was voted down. Instead of a few hours, it took four years, three months, and three days for the Bill of Rights to become part of our Constitution.

The Ten Winners

Freedom of speech, religion, and the press. The right to bear arms. Protection against unreasonable searches and seizures. Bail, a jury trial, and other rights of the accused. No cruel and unusual punishments. Ever hear of these? You bet.

To understand how much Americans love their Bill of Rights, try this. Ask a bunch of people what they like best about the Constitution. More than likely, most items they think of first will not be from the body of the document, but from the Bill of Rights. It's difficult to imagine the American way of life without them and hard to believe that many of the Founders originally opposed them.

There is a plus side to the framers' neglect. It was the Constitution's opponents, the Anti-Federalists, who pushed for specific guarantees of the people's rights. This makes them, as well as the Federalists, true Founders. It wasn't one group or the other that created our guiding rules, but the creative dynamic between them.

Key to the success of the Bill of Rights were the last two. The Ninth Amendment said that a partial list of rights did not preclude others. This answered the Federalists' argument that listing only *some* rights might imply that others were not covered. The Tenth Amendment reserved all powers not mentioned in the Constitution to the states and the people. That is what Anti-Federalists had wanted all along, but Federalists could not safely oppose it for fear of appearing too tyrannical. In a sense, though the Federalists won the debate over the Constitution, the Anti-Federalists won the dialogue that accompanied that debate: The people, not the government, would always have the last say.

The Least You Need to Know

- Washington and Madison hoped that amendments to the Constitution would placate Anti-Federalists.
- From the beginning, colonial charters guaranteed certain basic rights to citizens, and after independence, the new state constitutions carried on this tradition.
- At the ratification conventions, people proposed numerous amendments to the Constitution, including but not limited to protections of rights.
- When Madison introduced a distillation of these amendments in Congress, Federalists objected, but in the end they refined Madison's list and sent it out to the states.

- It took two more years for the required ten states to ratify the first ten amendments, known as the Bill of Rights.
- Ironically, it was the Constitution's opponents who pushed for the features we most celebrate today.

Freedom of Worship

In This Chapter

- The Great Awakening and religious rebels
- Religion in the state constitutions
- Jefferson, Madison, and freedom of religion in Virginia
- The First Amendment
- Founders' views on the separation of church and state

Through history, when rulers insisted that there was only one true religion—their own—they attacked people they considered heretics. Endless numbers were victimized. Religious persecution ran rampant on the European continent, and it directly influenced the history of the United States. Some 20,000 Puritans fled England and its discriminatory laws. Catholics sailed to Maryland. Jews and Huguenots, who were French Protestants, came to New York. Quakers and banished German sects settled in Pennsylvania. A continuing stream sought sanctuary.

But once in America, those who had been persecuted sometimes became the persecutors. In Massachusetts, Puritans established strict codes and punished or banished those who questioned them. In Virginia, Anglicans attempted to impose "uniformitie throughout this colony both in substance and circumstance to the cannons and constitution of the Church of England."

Would the new nation, like European nations, establish one religion? Or instead, would government protect the "rights of conscience," allowing each individual the freedom to worship as he or she thought fit? It chose the latter route during the Founding Era, but as we shall see in this chapter, the path was not straightforward or easy. Americans who thought governments should play a role in enforcing piety clashed with those who thought governments should get out of the religion business altogether. Freedom of religion, as expressed in the First Amendment, was the most controversial component of the Bill of Rights at the time, and it is still debated today.

Intolerance and Tolerance in Colonial Times

Early on, in the 1600s, each separate colony was a stronghold for one particular faith. Faith fortified a colony, whose citizens were bound together by common religious practices and under common rule, and faith fortified individual believers, who faced terrible adversities. But such colonies were anything but bastions of religious freedom.

A colony gave financial support to a central, and often exclusive, church. It sometimes refused entry to those practicing another faith, and it fined, whipped, imprisoned, or exiled religious troublemakers. In Massachusetts, several Quaker women, caught preaching, were stripped to the waist and flogged until the blood flowed, and authorities hung four Quakers who returned after being banished. Puritans boasted of killing off "venomous weeds." In Virginia, a charge of blasphemy could result in a hot iron being plunged through someone's tongue. Anyone missing Sunday worship three times could very well end up on a galley ship, pulling at oars for months on end in penance.

Not all colonies were harsh, and some welcomed a multitude of denominations. "Providence Plantations," later to become part of Rhode Island, was founded in 1636 by Roger Williams, who had been forced into exile from Massachusetts Bay because of his "divisive, new, and dangerous opinions." Williams wanted to establish a "wall of separation" between church and state, and in dramatic language, he held that "forced worship stinks in God's nostrils." These views prevailed in the new colony, whose members pledged "to hold forth liberty of conscience" for all who came. And in Pennsylvania, although you had to believe in God, laws didn't specify *which* God.

 THEIR OWN WORDS

"All persons living in the Province, who confess and acknowledge the One Almighty and Eternal God to be the Creator, Upholder and Ruler of the World, and that hold themselves obliged in conscience to live peaceably and justly in *Civil Society,* shall in no wayes be molested or prejudiced for their religious per-swasion or practice in matters of *Faith* and *Worship,* nor shall they be compelled, at any time, to frequent or maintain any religious worship, place or ministry whatever."

—Pennsylvania's founding laws, 1682

The Great Awakening

For centuries, although many argued about *which* faith was the true one, few doubted there *was* one supreme faith. That changed in the decades immediately preceding the American Revolution with a religious revival movement called the Great Awakening. Itinerant, unlicensed lay preachers extolled the power of God's grace, encouraged personal conversions, and told common people that they could communicate directly with God. The faithful met in open fields or in town squares or wherever they chose; no church was required and no minister in robes held court. The converted were "Christ's Poor" and wore the title proudly, confident they had been "born again" to lead a new life in Jesus Christ.

One evangelical preacher, the English preacher George Whitefield, made seven tours to America between 1739 and 1770, attracting enormous audiences and even attracting the attention of Benjamin Franklin. Franklin gave Whitefield's sermons front-page coverage eight times in his paper, *The Pennsylvania Gazette*, and described his preaching 45 times more inside these pages. He would correspond with Whitefield for more than thirty years. Though he was hardly an evangelical believer, Franklin obviously liked the rambunctious, self-reliant spirit of Whitefield's message. Franklin questioned things this movement did—rigid church hierarchies and laws, denominational affiliations, state support of religion, licensing requirements, or the unquestioned pronouncements of elite, haughty church leaders. He always wanted people to rely on their own sound judgment, what Whitefield might term their "inner light."

Churches that embraced evangelicalism during the Great Awakening were known as "New Lights," while those that didn't were "Old Lights." At the local level, the tension between the two grew, and sometimes churches or parishes became embroiled in civil strife, especially in colonies where the *Church of England* was *established* as the official government religion. Bibles in hand, evangelicals challenged the *Anglican* authorities and attempted to disestablish their church. The government should not declare that there is only one official faith, proponents of *disestablishment* said, nor support a single, exclusive religion.

DEFINITION

An **established** religion was any single religious denomination adopted and funded by a state. Church districts, or parishes, served as local political districts, like townships. Many people wanted to strip the established church of its official standing and special privileges, a process called **disestablishment.** In several states, the **Church of England** was the established religion, and people who belonged to it were called **Anglicans.** Those belonging to sects that had bolted from the Church of England were called Dissenters.

For decades on end, authorities tried to keep evangelical preachers out of their parishes or colonies. Virginia, for instance, made a law that said that every minister needed to be licensed. Every place of worship needed a license as well, so any preacher who had somehow managed to weasel a personal license from Anglican authorities could only hold service in an official church, not an open field. Defying the ban, evangelicals preached anyway and sometimes paid a terrible price. While one Baptist preacher named John Waller was singing with his congregation, an Anglican parson attacked him and shoved a horsewhip into his mouth. Waller was yanked off the stage, had his head beaten on the ground, and was given twenty lashes by the sheriff. Reporting that the Lord had "poured his love into his soul without measure" during the ordeal, Waller staggered back, exultant. Another Baptist, James Ireland, spent five months in jail, where he preached through the bars to those gathering outside. Officials and bigots rode horses through the crowd to drive people away, but they kept returning. Officials were stymied. There seemed no way to stop these worshippers.

BY THE NUMBERS

In Virginia, according to one compilation, there were at least 153 recorded instances of serious persecution against Baptists between 1760 and 1778. Forty-five different preachers were jailed. One, John Waller, spent 113 days in four different jails. That didn't stop Waller from baptizing more than 2,000 persons, ordaining 27 ministers, and aiding the establishment of 18 Baptist congregations.

Religion in Revolutionary America

Evangelicals stood up for what they believed in and refused to back down, and in that they resembled the rebels who would soon confront British authority. In fact, some historians say that the Great Awakening helped create the American Revolution. Less deferential than ever before, born-again coopers and blacksmiths or farm wives and seamstresses determined their own religious fate and in time would want to determine their political fate. But if religious fervor inspired revolution, the continual religious quarrelling proved counter-productive, pitting Americans against Americans. Would opposing sects unite as one people in the face of British oppression?

Religious Rebels

In Virginia, evangelical Baptists and Presbyterians, growing in numbers and in political skill, pushed simultaneously for religious and political liberty. After all, King George III headed both the British Empire *and* the Church of England, Virginia's established church. In attempting to disestablish that church, religious insurgents opposed the Crown, just as their secular counterparts did, and they even used similar tactics.

Starting in 1770, Baptists and Presbyterians flooded the House of Burgesses with petitions. They claimed the right to religious protection under Parliament's Act of Toleration, which had been passed in 1689, along with the English Bill of Rights (see Chapter 16). Petitioners wanted the Burgesses to repeal the ban on night meetings and the requirement for preaching licenses.

In 1775, after the House of Burgesses had been dissolved, the Virginia Baptist Association sent a petition to the new Revolutionary body, the Virginia Convention. Signed by the oft-persecuted John Waller as clerk, it praised members as "guardians of the rights of your constituents" against "tyrannical oppression." Next, the petition requested "free liberty to preach to the troops … without molestation or abuse." The Baptists' pledge of solidarity, couched in Revolutionary-style language, was both sincere *and* good strategy.

Country First

In the opening days of the First Continental Congress in 1774, a delegate proposed that an Anglican minister open the next day's session with a prayer. New York's John Jay and South Carolina's John Rutledge objected. According to John Adams's report, it was "because we were so divided in religious sentiments, some Episcopalians, some Quakers, some Anabaptists, some Presbyterians, and some Congregationalists, that we could not join in the same worship." Adams stated that his cousin then took the floor. "Mr. Samuel Adams arose and said that he was no bigot, and could hear a prayer from any gentleman of piety and virtue, who was at the same time a friend to his country." When the time came, delegates set religious differences aside and prayed together. Country came first.

Nobody knew this better than George Washington. As Commander-in-Chief of the Continental Army, Washington frequently invoked God to rally his own men, but this was everybody's God, not the God of one sect or another. Refusing to tolerate the religious bigotry that divided the troops, he declared an end to the practice of burning effigies of the pope on "Pope's Day," a carnival-like festivity that gave free rein to anti-Catholic feelings. As a man, no doubt, Washington disliked such behavior. As a general, who knew Catholics fought in Maryland's militia and who wanted to keep his troops unified, he opposed it. As a tactician, trying to woo aid from Catholic

France and attract Canadian Catholics to the cause, he railed against it in no uncertain terms: "At such a juncture, and in such circumstances, to be insulting their religion, is so monstrous, as not to be suffered or excused." Effigies were out. Again, country came first.

State Constitutions

Once independent from Great Britain, states no longer honored the Church of England as the official religion, and before long the Church was officially disestablished. Meanwhile, 11 of the 13 states adopted new constitutions that called for the "free exercise of religion" or "liberty of conscience" (see Chapters 6 and 16). Siding with Roger Williams' concept of a "wall of separation" between church and state, several states also prohibited ministers or preachers from holding public office.

But freedom of worship was not absolute. Most states offered freedom of worship only to Christians. Several required public officials to swear to a belief in God or a Christian or Protestant God. In South Carolina, an office holder had to vow that he believed in "a future state of rewards and punishments," "that the Christian religion is the true religion," and "that the Holy Scriptures of the Old and New Testaments are of divine inspiration, and are of the rule of faith and practice."

Disestablishment was not absolute either. Some states permitted state governments to raise taxes for the support of public worship. Although they did not specify which church would receive the funds, if there were only one church in town, as was often the case, this amounted to government-sanctioned religion. Massachusetts called for the funding of public worship and allowed laws that required people to receive religious instruction. (This was by far the most controversial item in the Massachusetts Constitution.)

It was a time of transition. Of the 11 new constitutions, only Virginia's came out for freedom of religion without qualifications of any kind.

Virginia Leads: Jefferson, Madison, and the Baptists

Drafted by George Mason and James Madison in 1776, Virginia's Constitution said that *"All"* men" were *"equally* entitled to the free exercise of religion." It did implore people to practice "Christian forbearance, love, and charity toward each other," but a Jew or Muslim or Deist or even an atheist could do that. Baptists and Presbyterians, who had pushed so hard for religious liberty, were thrilled to find that the state could no longer *order* them to believe in Christ.

In 1779, Thomas Jefferson, then in the state legislature, composed a "Bill for Religious Freedom" that was more insistent than the state constitution. "Almighty God hath created the mind free," he proclaimed, "and free it shall remain by making it altogether insusceptible of restraint." All attempts by government to interfere with that freedom were accompanied by "hypocrisy and meanness." Government funding of religion was no more than "bribing." Because Virginians were in the midst of the Revolutionary War at that moment, and uneasy with such a confrontational approach, Jefferson's bill never received serious consideration.

Five years later, after the war, Patrick Henry countered Jefferson's call for the separation of religion and government. He introduced a bill that would allow public funding of any Christian religion, hoping to win the support of dissenting sects such as Baptists and Presbyterians. To his surprise, Baptists didn't buy it. Above all else they valued a personal bond with their God and feared that the state's contribution, even if well intentioned, diminished that sacred relationship. "Taxing the people for the support of the gospel," they said, was "destructive to religious liberty." They insisted that God meant for the political and religious spheres to be distinct and cited Christ's own command to render unto Caesar what was his and unto God what was God's. Presbyterians, at first tempted by public funding, eventually sided with the Baptists.

So did many others. Petitions opposing Henry's bill received some 10,000 signatures, while those supporting the measure had only 1,200. James Madison, in a pamphlet he called *Memorial and Remonstrance against Religious Assessments*, asserted that the support of religion with public tax money was "an offense against God, not against Man." For religion's sake, the state should stand aside because through history, the "legal establishment of Christianity" had always resulted in "superstition, bigotry, and persecution."

 THEIR OWN WORDS

"Who does not see that the same authority which can establish Christianity, in exclusion of all other religions, may establish with the same ease any particular sect of Christians, in exclusion of all other sects?"

—James Madison, *Memorial and Remonstrance against Religious Assessments,* 1785

Henry's bill was defeated, and seizing the moment, Madison dusted off Jefferson's 1779 Bill for Religious Freedom and reintroduced it in the legislature. (Jefferson was in France at the time.) This time, in 1786, it passed. Jefferson would have only three of his many achievements emblazoned on his tombstone: "Author of the Declaration of Independence, of the Statute of Virginia for religious freedom and Father of the University of Virginia." Obviously, he was particularly proud of his part in obtaining true religious freedom in Virginia.

Madison, though, was not yet finished. The wind was at his back. Soon, for the nation as a whole, he would extend freedom of worship, prohibit the establishment of an official church, and discard the restrictive qualifications contained in the constitutions of other states.

The Constitution and First Amendment

The nation was now ready for such steps. At the Constitutional Convention in 1787, Charles Pinckney of South Carolina moved that "no religious test shall ever be required as a qualification to any office or public trust under the authority of the United States." (His own state's constitution, by contrast, demanded that an office holder profess his faith in very precise terms.) Roger Sherman thought the motion was "unnecessary" because "prevailing" opinion had turned against religious oaths, but Gouverneur Morris and others wanted it, just in case. And so, by unanimous consent of the Convention, Article 6, Section 3 of the United States Constitution prohibits the federal government from demanding religious oaths.

Then, in the state ratification conventions (see Chapter 14), Anti-Federalists demanded further safeguards against government interference with religion. Proposed amendments from seven states protected freedom of worship, with New Hampshire's the most succinct: "Congress shall make no laws touching religion, or to infringe the rights of conscience."

James Madison originally resisted such amendments, but he had political as well as philosophical reasons for securing freedom of worship. He owed his election in Congress to Baptist constituents, having been their ally in the fight for religious freedom in Virginia, and now he owed them again. In 1788, these long-persecuted people had been less than enthusiastic about supporting the nation's proposed Constitution. John Leland, one of their prominent preachers, feared that Congress might some day "favour one system more than another" and "oblige all others to pay to the support" of Congress's favorite sect. "Religious liberty is not sufficiently guaranteed," he stated. Madison then assured Leland that it would be. Reassured, and taking Madison at his word, Virginia's Baptists supported the Constitution's ratification.

FOUNDER ID

John Leland (1754–1841). Baptist preacher. Licensed to preach in Massachusetts, 1775. Preached in rural Virginia, 1777–1791, and in western Massachusetts, 1792–1841. Author, *The Rights of Conscience Inalienable*, 1791.

At age 18, Leland claimed he was called by God to renounce the "frolicks or evening diversions" and pursue "the work that you have got to do." Baptized at 20, he spent the rest of his life preaching in rural Massachusetts and Virginia. Widely read and articulate, he lobbied the Virginia General Assembly for religious liberty and persuaded the Baptist General Committee to condemn slavery as "a violent deprivation of the rights of nature." Allied first with Madison and later Jefferson, he was a staunch advocate for the complete separation of church and state. "If government can answer for individuals at the day of Judgment, let men be controlled by it in religious matters," Leland wrote sarcastically. "Otherwise, let men be free."

Madison showed up in Congress in 1789 and made good on the promise he had given to Virginia Baptists. Here is the amendment he proposed:

> The civil rights of none shall be abridged on account of religious belief or worship, nor shall any national religion be established, nor shall the full and equal rights of conscience be in any manner, or on any pretext infringed.

Although Congress fiercely debated the *general* issue of amendments (see Chapter 16), this *particular* amendment stirred no great controversy. Congress briefly opted for an even more comprehensive and tolerant ruling—"Congress shall make no laws *touching* religion"—but in the end it settled on Madison's narrower, more restrictive concept. The final version, the one that we all know, is simple but eloquent: "Congress shall make no law respecting the establishment of religion, or prohibiting the free exercise thereof."

"*Congress* shall make no law"—but what about the states? Theoretically, state governments, acting on their own, would not be bound by the First Amendment until 1868, when the Fourteenth Amendment extended all Bill of Rights guarantees to the states.

Are We a Christian Nation? Six Founders Respond

Today, some feel that the Founders, all Christians, intended to create a fundamentally Christian nation, even if there was no "established" church. They say we have gone too far in erecting a "wall of separation between church and state." They note that this phrase appears nowhere in the Constitution or in its amendments, only surfacing in a letter written by Thomas Jefferson in 1802, 15 years later. (Recall, though, that Rhode Island's Roger Williams called for that wall in 1644, a century and a half earlier.) Not all Founders accepted Jefferson's interpretation of the First Amendment, they assert, and it is not the law of the land.

Founders and framers were in fact born and raised as Christians. They were familiar with the Bible and frequently requested God's blessing or protection. Practical men, wanting the nation's welfare, they were convinced that religion promoted good behavior. They hoped for a god-fearing citizenry sustained by prayer, virtue, good works, and allegiance to the Almighty. In his inimitable way, Benjamin Franklin spoke for all when he said, "If men are so wicked as we now see them *with religion* what would they be *without it*?"

But these men belonged to several different Christian denominations and held varying views on the relationship between church and state. Some Founders were decidedly devout, others less so. And some, swayed by Enlightenment thinking and the philosophy of *Deism*, believed in an Almighty Creator but rejected such notions as miracles or Christ's divinity.

DEFINITION

Deism was an Age of Enlightenment philosophy that attracted followers in the Revolutionary Era. A deist believed that God, whom they called a "Supreme Architect," created a universe and its natural laws, and then stood aside once those natural laws were in place and efficiently regulating the universe. Strict deists said God did not intervene in human affairs through divine revelations or miracles, or by sending Jesus to Earth. Though many deists regarded Jesus and his teachings with great respect, they thought him human, not divine. Deists did not usually speak therefore of "our Savior" or "the Redeemer" or "the Resurrected Christ" as orthodox Christians did, but they did use words like "Supreme Ruler of the World" or "the Almighty" or the "Creator."

But the *personal* religious beliefs of these men are not the issue. In fact, the Founders themselves felt it should never be the issue. That's why the Constitution expressly prohibits the administration of any religious oath and the First Amendment guarantees freedom of worship.

On the other hand, how the Founders viewed the relationship between church and state *is* a legitimate topic. Did they want church and state to remain entirely distinct, or was that just Jefferson's interpretation? Let's ask six of the most famous Founders.

Thomas Jefferson and James Madison

Jefferson thought that a wall should divide religion and government and separate the two spheres absolutely. Government shouldn't intrude unnecessarily in human affairs, and certainly not in the most personal affair of all—religion. Besides, religion didn't require regulation. "It does me no injury for my neighbor to say there are twenty gods, or no god," Jefferson wrote. "It neither picks my pocket nor breaks my leg." Government simply didn't *need* to jump over the wall into religion's territory and therefore it shouldn't.

Whenever government did jump the wall, it wreaked havoc, Jefferson felt. He could point to religious persecution on other continents or in times past, and even in Virginia and in his lifetime, he had seen evangelicals cruelly hounded. In Jefferson's eyes, Christ was "among the greatest of the reformers of morals," though not divine. But "moral principles," as taught by Christ, had little to do with "the dogmas of religion." It was the kings and emperors and governors and the quarreling religious leaders who came after Christ who were the problem. When they imposed one strict interpretation of his word on all, they aroused "inextinguishable hatred" and "made of Christendom a slaughter-house…" These were strong statements, almost heretical in their day, but they testify to Jefferson's real dread of the state's meddling in religion. No wonder he wanted government on one side of the wall and believers safely on the other side.

Unlike Jefferson, James Madison was close to church people and was more accepting of conventional religious beliefs. He hoped religion would flourish in this new nation, and he believed it would because of its "innate excellence." Dependence on governmental support would "weaken" it, however. For *religion's* sake, the state should offer no support, and if offered, churches should not accept it. That was what evangelicals themselves had said when they opposed Patrick Henry's effort to give churches tax monies.

Both of these Founders wanted to protect the state from religion and religion from the state, but fine lines at times divided them. In 1788, Jefferson sponsored a law prohibiting preachers from holding public office. He thought government should be entirely free from the influence of religious interests, and he stood on that principle. But Madison opposed the law. He stood up for the preachers, who should not be denied their rights as citizens.

John Adams and Samuel Adams

In New England, church and state had *not* been separated by a wall. They had coexisted within the same room—literally. Establishing a congregation of believers in each township, "Congregationalists" gathered within meeting houses to both worship *and* govern. John Adams had grown up within this tradition, and he embraced Puritan values. During the Revolutionary War he had feared that defeat would stem from "vicious and luxurious and effeminate appetites, passion and habits," while victory would come only "if we fear God and repent our sins." Later, In June 1776, he declared, "It is religion and morality alone, which can establish the principles upon which freedom can securely stand." For all his life he was a self-proclaimed "church-going animal."

According to John Adams and nearly everybody else, his cousin Samuel Adams possessed "real as well as professed piety." He ran his household like a Sunday school, saying grace, leading devotional services twice a day, and reading from the Bible. God was not simply a "supreme ruler," as deists would say, but the one who "has given us his son to purchase for us the reward of eternal life."

In 1779, both John and Samuel Adams were appointed to a three-man committee to draft a constitution for Massachusetts (see Chapter 6). They thought churches that produced good, upright citizens for the state did deserve payback. In a constitutional provision, they said that the state's citizens could pay taxes "for the publick worship of GOD, and for the support and maintenance of publick protestant teachers of piety, religion and morality." For these Founders, church and state were not separate but wedded.

Benjamin Franklin and George Washington

Franklin was a generation older than other Founders and two generations older than some. He had a strong sense of time's passage and of the nation's history. When asked about that marriage between state and church in Massachusetts, he wasn't in favor, but he wasn't particularly worried either. Gazing calmly back through time, he commented, "Yet, if we consider what that people were 100 years ago, we must allow they have gone great lengths in liberality of sentiment on religious subjects." (A hundred years ago? Yes, definitely, the people of Massachusetts *were* doing better than they did during the Salem Witch Trials.) He then gazed into the future and wisely pronounced, "We may hope for greater degrees of perfection, when their constitution, some years hence, shall be revised."

As to state support of the church, Franklin concluded wryly that only when a religion was a "bad one" and "cannot support itself," and when "God does not take care to support it," would it be "obliged to call for the help of the civil power."

If he did desire a wall between church and state, Franklin could also jump over it when absolutely necessary. At the Constitutional Convention, after a month of debating, Franklin saw how delegates were "groping as it were in the dark to find political truth, and scarce able to distinguish it." He asked, "How has it happened, Sir, that we have not hitherto once thought of humbly applying to the Father of Lights to illumine our understanding?" Then he suggested delegates do that. Just a tad of religion, applied at just the right moment, might reduce strife and promote harmony. (The Convention never voted on Franklin's proposal.)

George Washington, like Franklin, opposed religious bigotry, which divided people, and relied on religion when it united them. He attended a variety of churches—Catholic, Episcopal, Lutheran, Dutch Reformed, or Congregational. He declared himself "no bigot myself to any mode of worship" and expressed respect for Jews and Muslims. He took a pragmatic middle course that best served the nation's needs in a sensitive era, during its formation. When Patrick Henry asked for public support of religion in 1784, Washington said he was not "one of those who are so much alarmed at the thoughts of making people pay toward the support of that which they profess." At the same time he feared that the bill's passage would "rankle and perhaps convulse the state."

While president, in a letter in 1792, Washington said, "Of all the animosities which have existed among mankind, those which are caused by a difference of sentiments in religion appear to be the most inveterate and distressing." Concerns like this were public knowledge, but Washington's personal religious beliefs weren't. On that score he revealed far less than the extroverted, plainspoken Franklin or others. He refused to make religious pronouncements that could only divide the country's diverse people of faith. Instead, he always tried to reconcile them.

THEIR OWN WORDS

"The path of true piety is so plain as to require but little public direction. To this consideration we ought to ascribe the absence of any regulation respecting religion from the Magna Charta of our country. To the guidance of the ministers of the gospel this important object is, perhaps, more properly committed."

—George Washington, shortly after assuming the presidency

The Least You Need to Know

- Colonists came to the New World in search of religious freedom, but some, once they were here, persecuted those of other faiths.
- An evangelical movement called the Great Awakening extolled direct communication with God, independence of belief, and born-again conversion, and it divided the religious world in two.
- After independence, state constitutions provided for religious freedom, but with a few qualifications.
- The Revolution's emphasis on liberty and the fight waged by persecuted minorities, especially evangelicals in Virginia, eventually led to the First Amendment, guaranteeing the freedom of worship and prohibiting the establishment of religion.
- Founders differed as to how rigidly church and state should be separated.

The Right to Bear Arms

In This Chapter

- The background—standing armies and militias
- The right to bear arms in the state constitutions
- The Federal Constitution and ratification conventions
- Drafting the Second Amendment
- Competing interpretations

"A well regulated Militia, being necessary to the security of a free State, the right of the people to keep and bear Arms, shall not be infringed." So reads the Second Amendment to the Constitution.

At the time these words were written, terms like "well regulated militia" and "to keep and bear arms" were reasonably clear, but today, their implications are hotly contested. We wonder: What's this about a "well regulated militia?" Why do these three words get top billing, coming first? Were this amendment's "people" only those who served in the militia, or were they people who wanted to keep private arms in their own houses? Further, did the amendment provide insurance against tyranny by allowing people to arm and overthrow their government if need be? Or, quite to the contrary, was a well-regulated militia supposed to provide insurance against those trying to overthrow the government?

The only way to answer these questions is to understand the history that led to the passage of the Second Amendment. In this chapter, yo will first learn about the issues this amendment was supposed to address. Then you will see how these were treated at the Constitutional Convention, the state ratifying conventions, and the first session of Congress, which drafted the measure.

Finally, you will see how various people interpret the Second Amendment and how they support their views. Then, with all these tools, you can develop your own interpretation.

Concerns and Precedents

Citizens of the new Constitutional government knew they needed a strong military to compete on the world stage, but they were wary of centralization of that military, and with good reason. Before and during the War for Independence, the King's Army had oppressed the nation's inhabitants. The new rules had to prevent that from ever happening again.

The Bugaboo of Standing Armies

In the minds of Revolutionary Era Americans, a standing army was the devil incarnate. Check out complaints listed in the Declaration of Independence. The King had "kept among us, in times of peace, standing armies, without the consent of our legislatures," it said. Soldiers from these armies had been quartered "among us," against the will of the citizens. They had "plundered our seas, ravaged our coasts, burnt our towns, and destroyed the lives of our people." Worst of all, military practices allowed "foreign mercenaries to compleat the works of death, desolation, and tyranny."

But in the absence of a standing army, how could the nation protect itself from foreign enemies or domestic insurrections?

The People's Alternative: Militias

The King's Army was an ocean away in colonial times and couldn't be relied on for protection against Indians who lived nearby or French settlers and trappers just to the north. British colonists had to protect themselves, and to do this they gathered as citizen-soldiers in groups called *militias*. Militiamen collected arms, ammunition, and powder, and they drilled on a regular basis. "Militia days" served as anchors for the social and political life of each community. Men not only readied themselves for war, but also drank together and talked politics. Sometimes, too, they enforced law and order because there was no separate police force. Years later, as tensions with the Mother Country mounted, militias protected citizens from a new threat: professional soldiers in the British Army.

Unlike standing armies, militias elected their own officers, at least at the local level. During the Revolutionary War, the democratic structure proved both a blessing and curse. It allowed people to "own" their own military organization, but officers were beholden to the men who elected them and were not always obeyed. Washington complained that militiamen were too free (see Chapter 8).

Militias were the military embodiment of the people, although in some places, lower-class men were excluded. George Mason tried to keep them out in Virginia. In his draft for the state's Declaration of Rights, he said militias should be composed only of "gentlemen farmers." The Virginia Convention changed this to the more inclusive "body of the people." Only because they were the embodiment of the people were militias trusted with military authority. They were to be *well regulated*, official arms of the government, not spontaneous mobs.

DEFINITION

A **well regulated** militia was organized into formal units with a specific chain of command. It acquired and stored military wares and enforced military discipline. All militia companies trained according to fixed, standardized routines so companies could synchronize a joint military operation. State and federal lawmakers in the new nation tried to make sure that militias lived up to that ideal.

FOUNDER ID

Timothy Pickering (1745–1829). Lieutenant (1766) and Colonel (1774), Essex (MA) County Militia. Adjutant General (1777) and Quartermaster General (1780–1785), Continental Army. Board of War, 1777–1780. Indian Commissioner, 1790–1794. Postmaster General, 1791–1795. Secretary of War, 1795. Secretary of State, 1795–1800. United States Senator, Massachusetts, 1803–1811. House of Representatives, 1813–1817.

Timothy Pickering's long political career started in his county's militia. Not satisfied with British military drills, he developed his own, which he published in 1775 as "An Easy Plan for a Militia." The Massachusetts Provincial Army adopted his plan at the outset of hostilities, and the Continental Army used it until switching to Baron von Steuben's drills at Valley Forge. Pickering's manual stipulated that patriot soldiers should be "clearly informed of the reason of every action and movement," not treated like "mere machines" as the British soldiers were. Pickering performed administrative tasks during the Revolutionary War, and in the 1790s he filled three cabinet posts. As Secretary of State, he contradicted the foreign policy of President John Adams, who fired him. A staunch Federalist, Pickering became disillusioned with the nation after Jefferson's election in 1800 and tried to get New England to secede from the union (see Chapter 22).

Arms, Armies, and the Militia in State Constitutions

Several of the new state constitutions addressed the need for military protections. These were their dominant concerns:

- Standing armies are "dangerous to liberty" and "ought not to be kept up." Raise an army in an emergency, but stick with the militias for peacekeeping—that was their thinking.

- Soldiers should "not be quartered in any house" without "the consent of the owner."

- The military should be "under strict subordination" to "civil power."

- The people had both the right and the duty to "bear arms" for "common defence" of the "state," "free state," or "free government."

Pay attention here, because the exact wording in these and related documents loom large in the arguments over the Second Amendment. While all states spoke in some manner of the need for common defense, two used the term "*well regulated militia,*" which would turn up later in the Second Amendment. Five used the words "bear arms" or "bearing arms," while one, Massachusetts, referred to the "right to *keep* and bear arms," another Second Amendment term.

THEIR OWN WORDS

"That a well regulated militia, composed of the body of the people, trained to arms, is the proper, natural, and safe defense of a free state; that standing armies, in time of peace, should be avoided as dangerous to liberty; and that, in all cases, the military should be under strict subordination to, and be governed by, the civil power."

Virginia Declaration of Rights, 1776.

Other terms used in these declarations did not make it into the Second Amendment. Pennsylvania's constitution said "the people have a right to bear arms for the defence of *themselves* and the state," but the addition of "themselves" fell by the wayside when Madison drafted the Bill of Rights 13 years later. Thomas Jefferson wanted Virginia's Declaration of Rights to say, "No freeman shall be debarred the use of arms within his own lands or tenements." That wasn't adopted. Two towns in Massachusetts wanted to include individuals, not just militias. Northampton complained that the guarantee of the "right to keep and bear arms," as written in the state Declaration of Rights, was not expressed with "that ample and manly openness and latitude which the importance of the right merits." The townsmen suggested a more expansive wording: "The people have a right to keep and bear arms as well for their own as the common defence." The town of Williamsburgh echoed this idea. This language didn't make the final cut either.

Today, people who argue that the Second Amendment applies to *individuals* point to the Pennsylvania measure, Jefferson's proposal, and the suggested amendments by the two Massachusetts towns. These passages reveal how Revolutionary Era Americans felt about self defense, they say. On the other hand, those who argue that the Second Amendment was meant only for *common defense* remind us that the framers rejected such wording. If they didn't want it in the Second Amendment, we shouldn't try to stick it in either, they insist.

The state constitutions were written a decade and more before Madison drafted the Bill of Rights. For us, they provide a window into the thinking of the Revolutionary generation, and for Madison and Congress, they provided valuable precedents. We should note, though, that they were forged in the midst of a nasty war. Bearing arms at that juncture was seen more as a duty than a right, and the right was far from absolute. It did not extend to those giving aid to the British army, for instance. Less than a year after Pennsylvania guaranteed the right to bear arms, the state Assembly disarmed all men who refused to take a loyalty oath.

Army and Militia Talk at the Convention

The right to bear arms was not discussed at the Constitutional Convention, but military matters certainly were. Without a military, the nation might disappear; if military control fell into the wrong hands, liberty would vanish. Treading a thin line, delegates allowed Congress to raise and support a standing army and navy, but only with constraints. Congress could allocate money but only for two years, forcing military authorities to make a regular accounting to Congress. Only Congress could declare war, and the President would be Commander-in-Chief of the armed forces. The reins of military control, in short, would be firmly in civilian hands.

So far, so good, but for some, the safeguards were not enough. Elbridge Gerry and Luther Martin wanted to limit the peacetime army to two or three thousand men, but Jonathan Dayton said that would be impractical because "preparations for war are generally made in peace." George Mason's suggestion for a "select militia," a sort of hybrid between the militias and a standard army, got nowhere. Charles Pinckney answered those who preferred militias to a professional army by saying they had already tried this "experiment," which led "toward anarchy."

Seeking a middle ground, James Madison wanted to nationalize the militias: "As the greatest danger to liberty is from large standing armies, it is best to prevent them by an effectual provision for a good militia," he said. But Roger Sherman warned against the government seizing the militias, saying the people would never "be so far asleep" as to allow it, and Gerry predicted that nationalization would doom the Constitution and even lead to a civil war. The debate over who should control the militias was as sharp as any at the Convention.

And so, as usual, it was time to compromise. Congress would oversee the "organizing" and "arming" of the militia and provide a uniform method of "discipline" or training. It could also "call forth" portions of the militia "to execute the laws of the Union, suppress insurrections and repel invasions." But the states could appoint all militia officers and actually perform the training.

Was this good enough, or would the people want further safeguards against a military force?

Amendments Proposed by the States

The Convention's solution failed to satisfy George Mason. What if Congress failed to arm the militia, then used the failure of the militia system as an excuse to build a strong standing army?

 THEIR OWN WORDS

"Should the national government wish to render the militia useless, they may neglect them, and let them perish, in order to have a pretence of establishing a standing army. I wish that, in case the general government should neglect to arm and discipline the militia, there should be an express declaration that the state governments might arm and discipline them."

—George Mason, at the Virginia Ratification Convention

Pushing hard, Mason convinced Virginia's Ratification Convention (see Chapter 14) to propose an amendment to the federal Constitution almost identical to the one in Virginia's Declaration of Rights, which he had drafted a dozen years earlier. This time, though, he added a forceful opening, lifted from the Massachusetts Declaration of Rights: "The people have a right to keep and bear arms."

New York, North Carolina, and Rhode Island also dusted off their Declarations of Rights at their ratifying conventions and pointed to the words "to keep and bear arms." Like George Mason, they felt the word "keep" was significant. The people's right to "bear arms" would only be of use if they *possessed* them, and Anti-Federalists like Mason did not trust the federal government to arm the militia. With this wording, if Congress bailed on supplying the militia, the states could step up and arm their own militias.

Did "keep" also imply that people could keep *private* arms in their homes? Scholars and nonscholars debate this point heatedly. We'll discuss this below, but first, let's follow the evolution of the Second Amendment to its final form. We're almost there.

Drafting the Second Amendment

When James Madison presented his draft for constitutional amendments to Congress on June 8, 1789 (see Chapter 16), he no longer addressed questions about a standing army or its control by civilians. No need—the body of the Constitution covered that. To quell Anti-Federalist fears, he simply secured the right to keep and bear arms, and then affirmed the importance of a well regulated militia. Congress reversed this order but kept the words intact: "A well regulated Militia, being necessary to the security of a free State" came first, followed by a clear statement of the resolution itself: "the right of the people to keep and bear Arms, shall not be infringed."

So there we have it, the Second Amendment! It seemed like a done deal, at least for a time. After the amendment was ratified by the states (see Chapter 16), it caused little controversy for several generations. Now, however, it's a huge bone of contention, with people divided sharply on how to read it. So what's up? Why the confusion?

To Keep and Bear Arms: Alternative Interpretations

First, some feel the Second Amendment protects a *collective* right, granting us the right to form militias for our mutual protection. Others insist that it extends to individuals, protecting a *private* right as well as a collective one.

Second, some say the amendment allows people to arm so they can resist a tyrannical government if they need to. It implies a right to revolution, they claim. Others say the militias were supposed to suppress rebellions, not instigate them. People would never have passed a Constitutional amendment that blessed the destruction of their own elected, representative government. That notion is ridiculous, they say.

So who is correct?

An Individual or Collective Right?

In Chapter 12, we reviewed three ways of interpreting the Constitution: "original intent," "original meaning" and a "living Constitution." So let's use these methods now, starting with "original intent"—what did framers who wrote the Constitution intend?

Those who think the amendment *does* protect an individual's right to bear arms note that other amendments clearly guarantee individual rights, like free speech or trial by jury. This right is no different and it certainly applies to individuals. But those who feel the amendment does *not* protect an individual right to carry arms say that the members of Congress, who debated and passed the measure, talked only about the danger of standing armies and the need to strengthen militias. Those had been the issues at the Constitutional Convention as well. It's all there in the written record. The discussion was never about an individual's right to bear arms, so that couldn't have been the purpose for this amendment.

On to the second way of interpreting our Constitution, "original meaning"—how was the language within the amendment understood at the time? What did the people think they were signing on to?

Supporters of the individual interpretation point to various documents, like the minority report of the Pennsylvania Ratification Convention. That document tried to guarantee the people's right to bear arms "for the defense of themselves and their own state, or for the purpose of killing game." They also cite other passages like this, showing that people at the time valued their right to keep and use arms in capacities that extended beyond militia participation, such as protecting their own homes.

But those supporting the collective interpretation say we have to examine the language closely. Like "a call to arms," the terms "keep arms" and "bear arms" are military references. They make no sense when applied to an individual. "A person does not bear arms against a rabbit," they say, "or even against a criminal." As for the spotty references to early Americans wanting guns for hunting and personal protection, they respond bluntly: "So what?" If a minority of representatives at a state convention asked for a hunting guarantee, the majority never did. Hunting matters were covered in state laws, not Constitutional amendments.

THEIR OWN WORDS

A hunter who has already been convicted for violating game laws shall not "bear a gun out of his inclosed ground, unless whilst performing military duty." ("A bill for the Preservation of Deer," written by Thomas Jefferson and introduced in the Virginia Legislature by James Madison in 1785.) Supporters of the individual right to bear arms present this quote to show that Jefferson and Madison used the term "bear a gun." Their opponents bring forth the same quote to show that the Founders were perfectly fine with gun regulations. The Second Amendment, they argue further, talks only of bearing arms, not bearing a gun. Such are the fine points in the raging Second Amendment debate.

How can we apply any of this to conditions today? According to the "living Constitution" method, we should try to embrace the underlying values expressed in the Second Amendment, and then apply these to the current realities. This seems a nearly impossible task. Arms today include rapid-fire assault rifles, not just single-shot muskets with powder and a ramming rod, and the militia is no more. The National Guard, the militia's technical successor, does not represent "the body of the people" or play such a central role in protecting "the security of a free state."

That said, a "living Constitution" approach can bridge the partisan divide. Whether or not the Second Amendment addressed the issue of private ownership, Founding Era citizens would not argue with the right to own a gun. But all states had game laws and controlled the use of guns. In cities, fire wardens regulated gunpowder storage for fear of explosions. People in "actual rebellion" could be disarmed. Private rights were always balanced by public safety. In bringing the laws of those by-gone days forward, we can embrace the fundamental wisdom of the Founders on this score. We can have our guns and regulate them, too.

To Support Revolutions or Squash Them?

If we apply the "original intent" method, we can hardly imagine why Federalists in Congress would want to sanction the overthrow of a government they had just created. The role of the militia in that government was to "execute the laws of the union, suppress insurrections and repel invasions." The militia protected the government.

But the Anti-Federalists were the ones who pushed for the Second Amendment initially, even if they didn't write the final draft. And in their minds, it provided at least a minimal protection against extreme governmental abuse. If a haughty Senate joined with a power-hungry president to tyrannize the people, and if the citizenry had been disarmed, the people would have no recourse. Only if the people still possessed arms could they stand up to oppression, they reasoned, and that's why the Second Amendment was so important to them.

This leads to two very strange places. First, ironically, it means that today's most ardent Second Amendment enthusiasts, so fond of waving the Constitution, actually trace their political heritage to the men who *opposed* that esteemed document, not those who created it.

And second, it's difficult to see how this "right of revolution" would play out in contemporary times. In a true revolution, people unite against a common enemy, but not everybody would see the United States government as the enemy, so a civil war would be the more likely scenario. Then, armaments were primitive; now, they carry a terrible destructive capacity. Would the Founders have wanted mass destruction, Americans killing Americans by the tens or hundreds of thousands? Is that what they sanctioned in the Second Amendment?

More likely, the Founders would tell us to work within our representative government, if at all possible. That's what *they* did. Even though Anti-Federalists wished to retain the right of revolution, in fact they pushed for amendments through a peaceful process, and Federalists, who were in power, finally acknowledged the discontent and gave us the Second Amendment, among others. The system seemed to work. Federalists and Anti-Federalists, bickering as they did, accomplished at least that much. That's a lesson for our own times.

The Least You Need to Know

- Militias were the people's preferred alternative to standing armies.
- Several state Constitutions opposed standing armies, supported a "well regulated militia," guaranteed "the right to bear arms," and ensured civilian control over the military.
- The Constitutional Convention did not address the right to bear arms, but it did permit a standing army, place the military under civilian control, and divide authority over the militia between the state and federal governments.
- At the ratification conventions, Anti-Federalists proposed Constitutional amendments on the militia and the right to bear arms similar to the safeguards in the state Constitutions.
- James Madison managed to push a pared-down version of these—our Second Amendment—through the Federalist-dominated Congress.
- The sharp debates over interpreting the Second Amendment focus on two issues: First, did the right to bear arms extend to individuals, or did it refer to the people collectively, in their military capacity? Second, was it meant to sanction revolutions or suppress them?

Partisan Divide

James Madison, in *The Federalist* #10, argued that if the people ruled directly, selfish interests would prevail over the "public good." That's why the new Constitution placed governmental power in the hands of "a chosen body of citizens." These men, wiser than the rest, would "refine and enlarge the public views." Not swayed by "temporary or partial considerations," they would have the good of the nation at heart.

But the harsh realities of partisan politics soon made Madison's ideal of wise and disinterested leadership appear out of date. It was a new world. Political parties, once derided as the worst of all ills, came to dominate public life. In 1789, Thomas Jefferson said if he "could not go to heaven but with a party," he would not go there at all. A dozen years later, Jefferson rode to the presidency on the back of a political party. The Federalists, when in power, decried those who would bust up the union; then, when pushed from power, some wanted to secede.

This part will detail how all this happened and suggest some reasons why. We will follow the conflicts within Washington's administration, the epic battle between two emergent political parties, the dramatic showdown in the election of 1800, and the strange reversal of roles once power had changed hands.

Washington, His Cabinet, and the People

In This Chapter

- Hamilton's financial plan
- Madison's and Jefferson's break from Hamilton
- Another rebellion, in Pennsylvania this time
- Jay's Treaty and further divisions
- Washington's final plea for unity

Hoping to lead by example, George Washington tried to set partisan politics aside and govern for the good of all. Why, then, did the nation almost burst apart in its formative years under the Constitution?

The Constitution, by centralizing power, intensified the urge to take command. Acting on that urge was Alexander Hamilton, the nation's Treasury Secretary, who was certain he had the answer to the nation's financial woes. In response to Hamilton's bid for control, Thomas Jefferson, Washington's Secretary of State, resigned. In the past, when each state was sovereign, such differences of opinion would have been limited to local or state venues. Now, they consumed the nation.

In this chapter, you will see how Washington's aim to transcend partisan politics fell short. It wasn't just Hamilton against Jefferson. Newspapers criticized the president's administration. People in western Pennsylvania threatened a rebellion even larger than the one in Massachusetts that had triggered the Constitutional Convention. By the time Washington stepped down after eight years in office, he could only plead with his countrymen. If they did not end factional combat, they would destroy the union.

Hamilton Takes Command

President Washington assigned Alexander Hamilton the task of placing the nation on a firm financial footing, a job that dwarfed all others. Having studied public finance for a full decade, Hamilton claimed he knew exactly the course to take. But "Why Hamilton?" many wondered. Why would President Washington, so universally admired, place the fate of the nation into the hands of a bastard immigrant from the West Indies whose support for republican principles was minimal at best?

FOUNDER ID

Alexander Hamilton (1755 or 1757–1804; birth date is disputed by historians). New York Militia, 1775–1776. Continental Army, 1776–1781. Aide to General Washington, 1777–1781. Continental Congress, 1782–1783, 1788–1789. Founder, Bank of New York, 1784. Annapolis Convention, 1786. Constitutional Convention, 1787. New York State Legislature, 1787–1788. New York Ratification Convention, 1788. United States Secretary of the Treasury, 1789–1795. Major General, United States Army, 1798–1800. Co-author, *The Federalist,* 1787–1788.

Of all the Founding Fathers, Hamilton was the least keen on republican government. Growing up in the West Indies, he missed the early years of protest when an aroused populace condemned tyranny and demanded representation in government. Late in 1774, as a student at King's College (the future Columbia University), he joined the protest, but he soon became a professional soldier, more committed to military efficiency than to popular government. After the war, he continued to think people got in the way of government. "Republican government does not admit a vigorous execution," he wrote at the Constitutional Convention. "It is therefore bad; for the goodness of a government consists in a vigorous execution." Hamilton believed that in a society based on money rather than aristocratic privilege, men of merit would rise to the top, and if these wealthy men gained a stake in the government, they would secure the nation. In Washington's cabinet, he had the opportunity to implement these notions. He centralized the government's finances, but in the process, this strong-willed individual became deeply embroiled in partisan politics. By the late 1790s he was feuding with his own Federalist party (see Chapter 20), and in 1804 Aaron Burr, a long-time political antagonist, killed him in a duel (see Chapters 21 and 22).

Why Washington Trusted Hamilton

Early in 1777, the Commander-in-Chief had invited the budding military genius to join his "family," Washington's name for his inner circle. Soon he said that Hamilton was his "principle & most confidential aid." That is not surprising. Not only was

Hamilton bright, but he shared Washington's commitment to military virtues of bravery and honor. Nobody exceeded Hamilton in "probity and sterling virtue," his mentor said. Now, in 1789, Washington wanted someone with can-do energy in his administration, and Hamilton had argued convincingly for "energy" and "vigor" in government at the Constitutional Convention, in private letters, and in his *Federalist* essays.

Besides, Hamilton knew his stuff. After leaving the army back in 1781, he had worked under THE Financier, Robert Morris, who had kept Washington in the field throughout the war (see Chapter 8). Morris was Washington's top pick for the Treasury post but declined the offer. Fortunately for Washington, Hamilton embraced all of Morris's goals and would eventually deliver a warmed-over version of THE Financier's programs. Back in 1781, of course, Morris had used his own personal credit to restore public credit (see Chapter 8), a super-human feat that Hamilton was in no position to pull off. Instead, Hamilton would have to create a viable system of public finance that could function on its own. Washington believed he could do it.

Hamilton's Financial Plan

First off, Mr. Hamilton, tabulate the nation's debt, both state and federal. Second, prepare a plan "for the support of public credit." In the fall of 1789, that's what congressmen asked the incoming Treasury Secretary to do, and then they took a few months off, leaving Hamilton behind to work it all out. Early the following year, an inventive Hamilton presented the first of two reports that showed how the credit of the United States could be placed on a firm and lasting footing.

Here, in brief, was Hamilton's scheme:

- Congress would assume all state debts. This highly controversial measure, called assumption, placed the national government at the center of the nation's finances.

- All public debts would be funded at par. This meant Congress would pay off government notes and bonds at their face value, plus accumulated interest.

- Congress would pass an excise tax on distilled liquor to raise money for funding the debt. Thirty-five years earlier, in his Albany Plan, Benjamin Franklin had suggested that liquor could finance a national treasury (see Chapter 7), and now Hamilton wanted to do it.

- Congress would establish tariffs that would stimulate American manufacturing while providing additional public funds.

- The federal government would establish a national bank. This would tempt rich men to provide capital for growth and link private capital to government. Notes issued by this bank could circulate and function as currency.

- The government would establish a national mint that would provide coins for everyday transactions.

These proposals all furthered Hamilton's overall goal: to centralize the government's financial sector and tie it to the country's commanding financiers, the leaders of industry and commerce.

In broad strokes, that was his scheme, but the fine points need more attention. First, there was no way that Congress could pay off all its debts at once, Hamilton figured, so instead it would create a continuing fund to pay off the interest at regular intervals. When people realized the government was paying interest on all of its debts, they would have faith in it. Second, the nation could pay down some principal, but only for a few notes at a time. That ensured that the holders of government notes—men with money—would have a vested and lasting interest in keeping the nation solvent while they collected their interest and waited for *their* notes to come due. Finally, because people could trust the government to honor its obligations, these stable notes would circulate as currency. All this came not from eliminating the government's debt, but from stabilizing and regulating it.

But most of the debt was held by wealthy speculators who had purchased them at a fraction of their face value. If the government paid those notes off at full value, speculators would grow rich on taxpayer money (see Chapter 9). Among the populace, particularly in western and rural regions and among debtors and farmers, this measure alone made Hamilton's financial plan wildly unpopular. But the moneyed men who held the notes threatened never to loan Congress another dollar if they were not paid in full.

In Congress, James Madison sided with outraged commoners and suggested that the government only pay speculators half the face value of the notes (the original recipients would get the other half), an idea called "discrimination." Most congressmen sided with the investors, however, and Madison and the taxpayers lost.

BY THE NUMBERS

Most of the public debt was held by a small percentage of large speculators, as you can see from these numbers:

- In Massachusetts, 7 percent of the creditors held notes of over $10,000. These amounted to 62 percent of the total state debt. 91 percent of the notes for over $25,000 were *not* held by their original owners, but by investors who had purchased those notes.

- In Maryland, 5 percent of the creditors held notes of over $10,000. These amounted to just over 50 percent of the total state debt. 97 percent of the notes for over $25,000 were *not* held by their original owners, but by investors who had purchased those notes.

- In debts listed with the federal treasury department, 9 percent of the creditors held notes of over $25,000. These amounted to 59 percent of the debt listed in these registers.

A National Capital: The Compromise of 1790

Congress might have been willing to pay off speculators, but it wasn't exactly eager to assume the debts of the states. If states didn't pay their own debts, Hamilton's opponents argued, they wouldn't be deciding whom and what to tax, and how much. The central government would. Always mistrustful of power concentrated at the top, Anti-Federalists were particularly wary. The old fissures were still there, with Federalists and Anti-Federalists bickering over state versus national control.

The assumption plan created a new political division between states with large unpaid debts, like Massachusetts and South Carolina, and those who had already paid off most of their debt, like Virginia, Maryland, North Carolina, and Georgia. Naturally, states that had retired their own debts didn't want to be burdened with the debts of others.

Early in April 1790, after heated debate in the House of Representatives, assumption was defeated by just two votes. This triggered some political haggling. Thomas Jefferson said he staged a dinner party in late June to broker a deal between Madison and Hamilton: Madison would back off from his opposition to assumption if Hamilton would get northerners to allow the nation's capital to be located in the South, somewhere along the Potomac River. Many historians doubt that Jefferson had quite the influence on this issue that he claimed, but they all acknowledge that horse-trading did occur. Two groups were essentially bought off. Congressmen from Pennsylvania agreed that the permanent capital could be on the Potomac, so long as it was located for the first ten years in Philadelphia. Meanwhile, four congressmen from districts bordering the Potomac—Daniel Carroll and George Gale of Maryland and Richard Bland Lee and Alexander White of Virginia—suddenly supported assumption; in return, they got the nation's capital.

That's why Washington, D.C., is where it is. Ironically, the city is named after a man who believed that wise rulers, with no interests at stake, should decide matters according to reason and virtue, but the so-called "Compromise of 1790" was made because a handful of congressmen cut a deal. To this day, the city named after our first president is associated with just the sort of politicking that created it.

BY THE NUMBERS

Only after the national capital was located on the Potomac did the House of Representatives agree to assume state debts, as we see from these three votes:

- House of Representatives vote on national assumption of state debts, April 12, 1790: 29 in favor, 31 opposed.
- House of Representatives vote on locating the national capital on the Potomac, July 9, 1790: 32 in favor, 29 opposed.
- House of Representatives vote on national assumption of state debts, July 26, 1790: 34 in favor, 28 opposed. Four key votes in favor came from congressmen who had originally opposed assumption, but whose districts bordered the Potomac.

Hamilton vs. Madison and Jefferson

In December of 1790, Hamilton submitted the final components of his plan, which called for a national bank. Once again, this triggered fears of over-centralization and a takeover of the government by wealthy men, but public discontent did not translate into discontent within Congress. The bank passed the House by a two-to-one margin and breezed through the Senate.

Yet some of Washington's closest advisors balked. Madison, Jefferson, and Attorney General Edmund Randolph said that the Constitution did not give Congress the power to charter a national bank. Hamilton admitted that there was no *explicit* provision but said the Constitution did empower Congress to stabilize finances, and so its authority was *implied*. Washington sided with Hamilton. "Implied" was good enough for him.

There was a subtext to this debate and to debates over Hamilton's entire program. Hamilton was all for commercial development while Jefferson, Madison, and others thought that wealthy investors and potentially corrupt commercial interests shouldn't decide the fate of a republic. For them, the future of the nation lay in the hands of small, hardworking, and independent farmers—"yeomen," in the parlance of the times. On almost every count, these differing visions of America led to competing policy positions.

The rift magnified when Hamilton offered Washington advice on matters of foreign policy, presumably the province of Secretary of State Jefferson, who was already disturbed by Washington's apparent favoritism of his rival. Of particular concern was the American response to the recently declared war between Britain and France. In April 1793, Washington issued a proclamation of neutrality, accepting Hamilton's counsel and rejecting Jefferson's. Jefferson, along with Madison, thought the president didn't have the right to do such a thing. Proclamations of neutrality were not a president's business. According to the Constitution, they were the business of Congress, which could declare war, or just the Senate, which alone could ratify treaties. Under the name of "Helvidius," Madison wrote essays to the newspapers complaining that the president had gone too far. Hamilton, writing as "Pacificus," responded with essays supporting the president's powers.

Five years earlier, Hamilton and Madison had collaborated in *The Federalist* (see Chapter 14). Now they were totally at odds. As personal tensions mounted, Washington asked cabinet members Hamilton and Jefferson to mend their quarrel, but to no avail. At the close of 1793, Thomas Jefferson resigned his position as Secretary of State. Madison, though, continued in Congress.

THEIR OWN WORDS

"I deserted Colonel Hamilton, or rather Colonel H. deserted me. The divergence between us took place from his wishing to administer the Government into what he thought it ought to be; while, on my part, I endeavored to make it conform to the Constitution as understood by the Convention that produced and recommended it, and particularly by the state conventions that *adopted* it."

—James Madison, discussing his break with Hamilton

Rebellion Yet Again: Western Pennsylvania Erupts

Sharp differences "in-chambers" were reflected "out-of-doors." Hamilton's financial program angered most debtors and farmers. When Congress approved Hamilton's excise tax on distilled liquor, the livelihood of farmers in western Pennsylvania was seriously threatened. Wheat and corn didn't pay off unless these men produced whiskey from their crops and sold it.

In 1794, tax-resisting Pennsylvania rebels, once again calling themselves "Regulators" (see Chapter 9), tried to play back the American Revolution, step-by-step. They threatened the tax collectors with humiliation and bodily harm. They erected Liberty Poles and formed into local "patriotic societies," which communicated with each other through "committees of correspondence." Fiercely democratic, the crowds voted at every turn, just as earlier crowds had done during the Massachusetts Revolution of 1774 (see Chapter 3). On August 1, somewhere between 6,000 and 9,000 men marched to Braddock's Field, where they hoped to seize stockpiles of arms and ammunition at nearby Fort Pitt, now Pittsburg.

Hamilton and Washington Clamp Down

Alexander Hamilton, whose policies had triggered this resurgence of revolutionary fervor, labeled the movement the "Whiskey Rebellion," a denigrating label that has stuck to this day. He urged the President to squash the rebellion with military force before it spread to Kentucky, Maryland, Virginia, the Carolinas, and Georgia, where other backcountry farmers were also expressing their discontent. Washington hesitated. "To array citizen against citizen," he said, was a step "too delicate, too closely interwoven with many affecting circumstances, to be lightly adopted." But in the end he relented and marched at the head of an armed force totaling 12,950 militiamen, gathered from four states. The mere presence of this massive force, larger than the Continental Army during much of the Revolution, made the rebellious farmers give in. By clamping down, Washington delivered a powerful message: the American Revolution was over. There would be no repeat performances. This government, embodied under authority of the people themselves, would enforce its laws.

Blame Game: Washington and the Democratic-Republican Societies

Washington was a Federalist who put his faith in strong and efficient government. He believed that the path Hamilton followed would strengthen and save the nation. The rebels in Pennsylvania were stirred not by their own legitimate grievances, he thought, but by dozens of "Democratic-Republican" societies organized by his political enemies, "the same set of men endeavoring to destroy all confidence in the Administration." The agitators were simply diehard Anti-Federalists who hoped "to disquiet the public mind."

Divisive issues had plagued the nation in the 1780s (see Chapter 9), and during the ratification debates (see Chapter 14), and the nation's wounds had not yet healed. Disgruntled farmers, political activists from the Democratic-Republican clubs of the mid-1790s, and influential leaders like Jefferson and Madison still hoped to defeat the Federalist agenda and reshape the nation. Lines were drawn, and in spite of all his honorable intention to avoid partisanship, President Washington had entered the fray.

Politics Yet Again: Jay's Treaty

Shortly after the farmers' rebellion in western Pennsylvania, Washington sent Supreme Court Chief Justice John Jay on a special diplomatic mission to London. Jay returned with a treaty that established favorable commercial terms with Great Britain and required her to abandon military posts along the Great Lakes.

FOUNDER ID

John Jay (1745–1829). Continental Congress, 1774–1776. New York Provincial Congress, 1775–1777. Chief Justice, New York Supreme Court, 1777–1779. President, Continental Congress, 1778–1779. Minister to Spain, 1779. Peace Commissioner, Treaty of Paris, 1782–1783. Secretary of Foreign Affairs, 1784–1789. President, New York Society for the Manumission of Slaves, 1785–1790. Chief Justice, United States Supreme Court, 1789–1795. Envoy to Great Britain, 1794. Governor of New York, 1795–1801. Co-author, New York Constitution (1777) and *The Federalist* (1787–1788).

John Jay, from New York's upper crust, was a cautious patriot who originally opposed independence but then became one of the most influential statesmen of the Founding Era. Today, Jay is remembered primarily for the 1794 treaty that bears his name, but that was actually his third treaty. With Adams and Franklin, he had negotiated a treaty with Britain that ended the Revolutionary War. He proposed yet another with Spain, although Congress refused to ratify it because it gave away American rights to the Mississippi River. A descendant of Protestant Huguenots who had been persecuted by French Catholics, he harbored a grudge and favored Britain over France in his international dealings, as did most other Federalists. In 1789, Washington asked Foreign Secretary Jay to become the nation's first Chief Justice. He served for several years, but he left that job to help Federalists defeat the Anti-Federalists in New York. In 1800, John Adams, at the end of his presidential term, asked Jay to lead the Supreme Court once again, but Jay declined because he thought the court was too weak. That's how John Marshall, architect of a powerful Supreme Court, became Chief Justice (see Chapter 22).

England was at war with France, and France was the sentimental favorite for many Americans. That country had given invaluable aid to the United States during the Revolutionary War, had recently overthrown a king, and was trying to establish a republic. While most Americans wanted nothing to do with the military conflict, many did want to put economic pressure on Britain, much as the rebellious colonies had in pre-Revolutionary years. The commercial agreements in Jay's Treaty ended those hopes. In addition, the treaty solidified a system of tariffs that fortified Hamilton's controversial financial plan.

To convince the Senate to reject the treaty, opponents flooded the press with letters, held mass meetings, and submitted petitions with thousands of signatures. Federalists were taken off guard by such resistance, but they soon responded in kind with rallies and petitions of their own. The raucous polarization that had characterized the ratification debates returned with a vengeance. In the end, the Senate ratified the treaty with the minimum vote required and Washington signed it into law. Anti-Federalists in the House tried to kill the treaty by not funding its provisions, but they lost out narrowly.

Washington's Farewell, with a Plea

George Washington had wanted to retire after one term in office, but he stayed in office at the urging of people on both sides of the growing political chasm. Without a unifying icon, all agreed that the nation would surely split apart. In spite of his presence, however, the partisan divide continued to widen.

In 1796, near the end of his second term as president, the 64-year-old Father of our Country announced that he was finally done with public life. In his Farewell Address—delivered in writing, not orally—Washington warned the nation of the dangers it faced; first and foremost was "the spirit of party."

THEIR OWN WORDS

"It [the spirit of party] serves always to distract the public councils and enfeeble the public administration. It agitates the community with ill-founded jealousies and false alarms, kindles the animosity of one part against another, foments occasionally riot and insurrection. It opens the door to foreign influence and corruption, which finds a facilitated access to the government itself through the channels of party passions."

—Washington's Farewell Address, September, 1796.

James Madison had prepared an early draft of this address back in 1792, when Washington first told his friends he wanted to resign. Four years later, Washington asked Alexander Hamilton to help him revise the speech. How ironic that Madison and Hamilton contributed to a polemic against "party passions." Their own disagreements had intensified a skirmish that both men, and Washington, decried.

The Least You Need to Know

- Hamilton, Washington's most influential advisor, created a financial plan that empowered the federal government to assume state debts, levy taxes, create a national bank, and honor government bonds on terms that rewarded speculators.

- Madison and Jefferson opposed much of Hamilton's financial plan and Hamilton's notion that the president commanded foreign policy.

- When farmers in Western Pennsylvania rebelled rather than pay taxes that benefited speculators, Hamilton convinced Washington to lead a massive military force against them.

- Jay's Treaty, which stabilized commercial relations with Great Britain, angered Americans who favored France.

- To prevent internal strife, Washington agreed to serve a second term, but the divisions remained, and when he finally did retire, he warned that "party passions" could destroy the government.

- Although Washington aspired to nonpartisanship, his support of Hamilton and his major decisions revealed he was firmly in the Federalist camp.

Politics and Parties: The Adams Years

In This Chapter

- The heated presidential election of 1796
- The Federalist and Republican political parties
- Politics and the press
- Americans divide over a war in Europe
- The Federalist crackdown and Republican response

During the tumultuous debates over ratification of the Constitution and through the rancorous 1790s, all Americans agreed on one fundamental tenet: the president, whoever he may be, was to be *everybody's* president, not the ally of any particular faction, party, or interest group. George Washington certainly aspired to that ideal, even if he had difficulty realizing it.

Could the *second* president avoid taking sides when cantankerous debates consumed public life?

Not likely. In order to become president, a candidate had to gain the support of either Federalists or Republicans; there were no other options. These groups were of approximately equal strength. In the election of 1796, the first one in which Washington did not run, the Federalist candidate, John Adams, defeated the Republican candidate, Thomas Jefferson, by only three electoral votes.

Not surprisingly, the nation did not unify behind President Adams. He had as many enemies as friends. When the opposition railed relentlessly against his administration and its policies, Adams and his fellow Federalists, who controlled Congress, tried to outlaw dissent. This only made matters worse. Two states, Virginia and Kentucky, openly threatened to disobey federal law.

In this chapter, we will see how a young nation that was not yet stable almost fell—not at the hands of some outside enemy, but from turmoil within.

The First Election *Sans* Washington

The framers of the Constitution rightly feared that congressmen would divide into various groups, each representing the interests of local constituents. That's where the president came in. They had great hope for the office. The president was to be a truly national leader who could check partisanship and act as a referee, not a participant. So went the theory.

In practice, unfortunately, the office of the presidency actually triggered division and the creation of clamorous political parties. Here's why. Obviously, any *faction* that elected one of its own as president would enjoy an advantage over all competitors because he would command exceptional powers. But to capture this plum of an office, a group had to organize and engage in political warfare on a national scale. Set on securing the presidency, those adversaries formed themselves into *political parties*, which made their first appearance in the United States in the 1790s.

DEFINITION

A **political party** is an organization that promotes an agenda by electing candidates to public office. It does this by nominating one person for each office, then pushing for that candidate against all competitors. Political parties, as we know them today, existed only in embryonic form at the birth of the nation. Although the Constitution does not recognize political parties, and the framers abhorred them, factions congealed into two national parties during the 1790s, Federalists and Republicans.

A **faction** is a group favoring a specific interest or position. Political factions have always existed and always will, however much people complain about them.

Political parties congealed in the contested presidential elections of 1796 and 1800. In 1796, Federalists chose John Adams, Washington's vice president, as their standard bearer, although Alexander Hamilton promoted South Carolina's Thomas Pinckney instead. Hamilton assumed that he would have little influence over Adams, but Pinckney was another matter. If Pinckney were elected, said one of Hamilton's confidants, the new president would be "completely in our power." Hamilton's scheming infuriated Adams and had political repercussions, as we shall see.

The *Republican Party* settled on Thomas Jefferson, who had emerged as a leading opponent of Federalist policies even while serving in Washington's cabinet. Fortuitously, Jefferson had also been the primary author of the Declaration of Independence. This allowed Republicans to claim that *they* were the truly patriotic party, even though they opposed the policies of the existing government.

> **DEFINITION**
>
> The **Republican Party** of the Founding Era was not the same as the Republican Party founded in the 1850s and still in existence today. The first Republicans formed in opposition to the dominant Federalists, who had favored ratification and who controlled most government offices in the first years under the new Constitution. Many years later, historians called the first Republican Party the Democratic-Republican Party to distinguish it from the current one, but in the 1790s "Democratic-Republican" referred only to special clubs of radical political activists (see Chapter 19), not to a national party. Because Federalists used the term "democratic" as an insult, equating it with mob rule, the Republican Party did not embrace that label until the early nineteenth century.

Neither candidate campaigned on his own behalf. According to the custom of the times, that would have been poor form. But each candidate's supporters campaigned for him, and, more often than not, campaigned *against* his opponent. According to Federalists, Jefferson was a deist and a terrorist who was under the influence of violent revolutionaries in France. According to Republicans, Adams was a closet monarchist who would force a king and ruling aristocracy on the United States if given half a chance. Negative campaigning was alive and kicking in the nation's first true presidential election.

When the dust had settled, Adams won with 71 electoral votes, compared with 68 for Jefferson. The voting was along strict regional lines. The North, with the exception of Pennsylvania, supported Adams, while the South, except Maryland, went for Jefferson.

> **BY THE NUMBERS**
>
> Electoral votes for president, 1796:
>
> - John Adams   71
> - Thomas Jefferson   68
> - Thomas Pinckney   59
> - Aaron Burr   30
> - Samuel Adams   15
> - 8 others   total of 33

By the rules laid out in the Constitution, Jefferson was to serve as vice president under the man who had just defeated him. Initially both men embraced the partnership. Adams recalled that he and Jefferson had worked "together in high friendship" when they pushed Congress to declare independence, and he thought he could depend on Jefferson's "ancient friendship, his good sense and general good disposition." Jefferson, for his part, was willing to accept "a secondary position" under a man who was his senior and who might, he hoped, "be induced to administer the government on its true principles and to relinquish his bias to an English constitution." Meanwhile, the men shared one common goal: to keep Hamilton from wielding influence.

Some began to imagine that a bipartisan Adams-Jefferson team would smooth out the inter-party fighting. A writer for a Republican newspaper that had attacked Federalists during the election wrote optimistically, "ADAMS and JEFFERSON, lately rivals, appear in the amiable light of friend. Surely this harmony presages the most happy consequences to our country."

Party Brawls

President John Adams had the best of intentions. He had always thought that a functioning government needed to have a persuasive and independent executive who could mediate between the legislative branches, the upper house representing the well-to-do and the lower house representing the common people. The Constitution had created just such an office, and he, as president, would intercede and settle any disputes between those bodies. In his inaugural address, he promised to serve "virtuous men of all parties and denominations" and to oppose "the spirit of party" and "the spirit of intrigue."

But two weeks later, John Adams told his wife Abigail that the "jealousies and rivalries" he encountered in Congress were "beyond all my former suspicions or imaginations." There had always been bickering and heated debate between men who weren't afraid to speak their minds or battle for their constituents. In the wake of the 1796 elections, however, Congress was sharply divided into two voting blocs, with the combat fierce and most issues decided along strict party-line votes. It was a contentious new world, and not one the Founders had intended.

THEIR OWN WORDS

"You and I have formerly seen warm debates and high political passions. But gentlemen of different politics would then speak to each other, and separate the business of the Senate from that of society. It is not so now. Men who had been intimate all their lives, cross the streets to avoid meeting, and turn their heads another way, lest they should be obliged to touch their hats."

—Thomas Jefferson to Edward Rutledge, June 24, 1797

Press Wars

In 1800, printers sent out 20 times as many issues of newspapers as they had in 1770. Increasingly partisan, the press fueled party divisions. Initially, Federalist papers outnumbered those of the opposition, but by the end of the decade, Republican writers and editors were battering the Adams administration.

Notable among Federalist newspapers was John Fenno's *Gazette of the United States*, first published in 1789 and supposedly following "INDEPENDENT and IMPARTIAL PRINCIPLES." But in declaring its editorial policy, the *Gazette* promised "to strengthen and complete the union of the states, to extend and protect COMMERCE, [and] to restore and establish the PUBLICK CREDIT"—in other words, to support the Federalist party line. Fenno, in fact, wanted his paper to become *the* official newspaper of the nation, financed by government contracts. When his press ran into financial difficulties, it was an ardent Federalist, Alexander Hamilton, who raised funds to help it out.

Not to be outdone, Thomas Jefferson and James Madison enlisted the services of Philip Freneau, whose *National Gazette* toed *their* party line. This *Gazette*, with no government financing, lasted only two years, from 1791 to 1793, but it inspired a barrage of increasingly belligerent opposition papers.

One, known today as the *Philadelphia Aurora* but originally titled the *General Advertiser,* was published by Benjamin Franklin Bache, grandson of Benjamin Franklin. While other papers were "in praise of monarchical and aristocratic institutions," Bache wrote, his paper spoke to "all true friends of liberty." Unlike other critics of the government, Bache challenged Washington himself. He felt that Federalists were using Washington as a shield for their self-interested policies and that someone had to call them on it. In 1797, on the day the first president left office, Bache had the gall to bid him a not-so-fond farewell:

If ever there was period for rejoicing, this is the moment. Every heart … ought to beat high with exultation, that the name of WASHINGTON from this day ceases to give a currency to political iniquity, and to legalize corruption. This day ought to be a JUBILEE in the United States.

FOUNDER ID

Benjamin Franklin Bache (1769–1798). Printer/editor/publisher of Philadelphia's *General Advertiser,* 1790–1798 (also called *Aurora* after 1794). Correspondence committee, Democratic Society of Pennsylvania, 1794–1795.

The son of Benjamin Franklin's daughter, Sarah, and Richard Bache, young Benjamin left home at age seven in the company of his celebrated grandfather. He was off to Europe to obtain a superior education. Returning to Philadelphia at 16, he attended the University of Pennsylvania, which the older Franklin had founded. Two years later, 81-year-old Benjamin Franklin set up 18-year-old Benjamin in the printing business. After his grandfather's death, Bache used some of the inheritance Franklin had left him to publish his own newspaper. He started by printing debates in Congress and translating foreign documents, and in 1795 he leaked the controversial text of Jay's Treaty (see Chapter 19). Federalists called him "Lightning Rod Junior," and one combative editor said he should be dealt with like "A TURK, A JEW, A JACOBIN [French extremist], OR A DOG." In 1798, Bache was prosecuted under the Sedition Act (see page 242), but before being tried, he died in a yellow fever epidemic. His widow Margaret and assistant William Duane continued the *Aurora* without him. Had Bache lived past the age of 29, he undoubtedly would have played a major role in Republican politics.

Competing July 4 Celebrations

Federalists and Republicans, going head-to-head, took the fight out-of-doors to Fourth of July celebrations, where each party commandeered the patriotic imagery of the nation's birth. On July 4, 1795, while Philadelphia Federalists rallied behind the usual parade of Revolutionary War officers, Republicans paraded with a huge image of Federalist John Jay, with these words written beside him: "Come up to my price and I will sell you my country." (This referred to Jay's Treaty, explained in Chapter 19). That night the marchers burned Jay's picture and hurled rocks at Federalist cavalrymen who tried to disperse the crowd.

For the next few years, the parties held separate parades, dinners, and toasts. In 1798, Boston Federalists raised a toast to "John Adams—may he like Samson slay thousands of Frenchmen with the jawbone of Jefferson." Republicans countered, toasting "the immortal Jefferson," who had written "the original object of the public anniversary"— the Declaration of Independence.

A Scuffle in Congress

Republicans and Federalists literally tussled in the hallowed halls of Congress, where allegedly wise and virtuous leaders settled serious matters of state. There, on January 30, 1798, Matthew Lyon, a Republican representative from Vermont, spat in the face of Roger Griswold, a Federalist representative from Connecticut, who had just made a joke about Lyon's questionable service in the Revolutionary War. In defense of his spitting, Lyon said, "I did not come here [to Congress] to have my --- kicked by everybody." Two weeks later, Griswold started caning Lyon on the floor of Congress, whereupon Lyon grabbed a pair of fireplace tongs. The two men lunged at each other with their makeshift weapons, then wrestled till they were pulled apart. In the aftermath, Federalists tried to expel Lyon for "gross indecency," but Republicans stood by their man.

FOUNDER ID

Matthew Lyon (1749–1822). Green Mountain Boys, 1774–1776. Continental Army, 1776–1778. Vermont Assembly and various administrative posts, 1778–1789. Publisher, *Farmer's Library*, 1793–1797. Congressman from Vermont (1797–1801) and Kentucky (1803–1811).

Matthew Lyon was no gentleman, and that's what so infuriated Federalist members of Congress. Born in Ireland, Lyon came to America as an indentured servant and was at one point traded for a pair of stags. Genteel congressmen mocked his origins, his accent, and his uncouth manners. They called him "Ragged Matt, the Democrat," a "beast," and a "Lyon" who needed to be caged. Lyon, in turn, mocked the pomp and circumstance of their official proceedings. His ways were more down-to-earth. He had been one of the Green Mountain Boys, who muscled their way free of New York to form their own state of Vermont. Unlike most of his colleagues, he dirtied his hands in work. He built a sawmill and paper mill, a blast furnace and an iron foundry. He owned a tavern and printed a newspaper, the *Farmer's Library*, which criticized Federalist policies and promoted his own political career. In 1801, he moved to Kentucky, where he once again promoted himself, his business enterprises, and Republican politics. A self-made man and a new breed of politician, Lyon threatened the old order.

Choosing Sides over Europe

Washington, in his Farewell Address, had warned the nation "to steer clear of permanent alliances with any portion of the foreign world." The United States should be particularly wary of "interweaving our destiny with that of any part of Europe," he said, for meddling Europeans would likely "tamper" with America's "public councils." In spite of that admonition, the nation divided into opposing camps over a continuing war in Europe between Britain and France.

THEIR OWN WORDS

"I should say that full one third were averse to the revolution … An opposite third conceived a hatred of the English … The middle third, composed principally of the yeomanry, the soundest part of the nation, and always averse to war, were rather lukewarm both to England and France."

—John Adams to James Lloyd in 1815 describing American opinion toward the French Revolution in 1797. In 1908, historian Sydney George Fisher misinterpreted Adams's reminiscence, thinking it applied to the numbers of patriots and loyalists in the *American* Revolution, not popular sentiments about the *French* Revolution two decades later. Many textbooks ever since have passed this mistake along. In letters to Benjamin Rush in 1812 and Thomas Jefferson in 1813, Adams did say that Congress in 1774, two years before independence, was divided into thirds, but he never said that only one third of Americans supported independence in 1776 or that only one third of the people sided with the Americans in the Revolutionary War. If that had been true, the rebels would certainly have lost the war.

The "Quasi War" with France

Always pro-commerce, Federalists backed Britain, America's most frequent trading partner. Republicans preferred France, the country that helped out during the American Revolution and that led the charge against monarchy in Europe. But when Jay's Treaty cemented friendly commercial relations with Britain, France started capturing American trading vessels on the open seas. According to France's new Revolutionary government, ships that carried goods to and from France's declared enemy were open game. Besides, the French were angry because the United States refused to pay back the money it had borrowed during the Revolutionary War and to honor the defensive treaty it had signed with France in 1778.

Hoping to avoid war, Adams dispatched a diplomatic team to France. There, the American envoys were approached by French agents, known in official correspondence as "X, Y, and Z," who made harsh demands and asked for a bribe. When news of the insulting "XYZ Affair" leaked out, impassioned Federalist hawks in Congress immediately went on the offensive. They rescinded the French-American alliance, commissioned armed vessels that could confront the French Navy, and created an army called the "Additional Army" or "New Army." Congress also authorized a "Provisional Army" that could fight if war was declared. But war was *not* declared, so the naval skirmishes with France and the military buildup at home became known as the "Quasi War."

Hamilton vs. Adams

The Additional Army was headed by none other than George Washington, whom Hamilton persuaded to answer his country's call once again. Washington then asked President Adams to let Hamilton serve immediately under him. Reluctantly, Adams ceded to Washington's request. But Washington, now 66 years old, was worn out, and if the Additional Army ever marched to war, it would probably be under General Hamilton, the man who had schemed against Adams in the 1796 election and who was constantly trying to influence Adams's own cabinet.

Now more than ever, as they vied for control of the Federalist Party and indeed the nation, there was no love lost between Adams and Hamilton. The two traded barbs. Adams said Hamilton was "proud spirited," "conceited," and "as great a hypocrite as any in the U. S." Hamilton, who had once called Adams a "firm honest independent politician," now called him "vain," "jealous," and "as wicked as he is mad."

 THEIR OWN WORDS

"He is a man ambitious as Julius Caesar. A subtle intriguer, his abilities would make him dangerous if he was to espouse a wrong side. His thirst for fame is insatiable. I have ever kept my eye upon him. He has obtained a great influence over some of the most worthy and amiable of our acquaintance."

—John Adams, describing Andrew Hamilton, in a letter to Abigail Adams, December 31, 1796

Alien and Sedition Acts

In the summer of 1798, at the height of the war hysteria, Federalists seized on the "spirit of patriotism" to inhibit dissent and create "national unanimity." (These are Hamilton's words.) They enacted four repressive laws, collectively labeled the Alien and Sedition Acts. Three of these were aimed at foreign residents, who could henceforth be deported by the President if he considered them dangerous or if they happened to come from an enemy nation.

The fourth controversial law, the Sedition Act, muzzled criticism of government officials and policies. It said that citizens could not "oppose or defeat" any law of the United States, nor could they "write, print, utter or publish … any false, scandalous and malicious writing or writings against the government of the United States, or either house of the Congress of the United States, or the President of the United States."

Notably *absent* from the list of offices that were shielded from criticism was the vice presidency. Currently, of course, that position was held by a Republican, Thomas Jefferson. Federalists could vilify him to their hearts' content, without fear of arrest, but Republicans could not target President Adams. Nor could they speak out against laws they deemed unfair—such as the odious, in their opinion, Sedition Act.

Although the Sedition Act managed to silence a few Republican newspapers, the partisan intimidation soon backfired. The 25 people arrested under the law, and in particular the 10 who were convicted, became martyrs and heroes. Matthew Lyon, the earthy Irishman described in this chapter's earlier pages, was re-elected to Congress while sitting in jail for violating the Sedition Act. Further, the law antagonized printers and editors who had formerly been neutral. They turned against the Federalists who had tried to silence them and joined forces with an ever-more hostile opposition press.

Nullification and a Constitutional Crisis

For many Republicans, the Alien and Sedition Acts proved that Federalists were willing to betray the principles of the Revolution and defy the First Amendment. Was it time to turn against the central government, which they thought the Federalists had hijacked, and reaffirm state sovereignty?

Jefferson and Madison thought it was. Because the federal government had overstepped its bounds, the states must "interpose" themselves on behalf of the people and "void" federal law. Jefferson drafted a resolution that he sent to legislators in

Kentucky, a hotbed of republicanism. Lawmakers there toned it down a bit, but in the end they declared that the Sedition Act was "void, and of no force."

Madison sent a similar resolution to the Virginia legislature. After some debate, lawmakers there pronounced that because the "alarming" Alien and Sedition Acts violated the Constitution and the First Amendment, Virginia would take "the necessary and proper measures" to preserve "the authorities, rights, and liberties" that the Tenth Amendment reserved to the states and to the people.

The "Kentucky and Virginia Resolutions" shocked the nation by suggesting that states could overrule the federal government. What if the "necessary and proper measures" of opposing the Sedition Act included military resistance? Could this be the beginning of the end of the United States of America?

Yet *Another* Rebellion

While Republican statesmen were passing resolutions, common folk protested the taxes they were supposed to pay to finance the military buildup for the Quasi War. Congress authorized a $2 million direct tax, to be proportioned according to the number of windows in a person's house—a measure of a person's wealth. (Recall, in Chapter 8, that Robert Morris had suggested this almost two decades earlier.) The tax infuriated those opposed to the war. When federal tax collectors rode through the heavily German areas of Eastern Pennsylvania to count the windows in each home, angry crowds bullied them in a manner reminiscent of the Stamp Act resistance in 1765 (see Chapter 2), and the Pennsylvania Regulation of 1794 (see Chapter 19). As with the so-called Shays' Rebellion in Massachusetts, opponents named this resistance after one of its leaders, John Fries.

In March of 1799, President Adams sent in troops to suppress "Fries Rebellion." That was the end of the uprising. The rebels hoped that common folk in other areas would rise up, but they didn't. Similarly, legislators in Kentucky and Virginia hoped other states would join them in declaring the Alien and Sedition Acts unconstitutional, but none did. This did not indicate a lack of opposition to Federalist domination, but only a difference in tactics. There was one remaining way to end Federalist rule: the ballot box. Republicans began to hope that this peaceable route would prove more effective than violence or defiance of law.

Politically, the Federalists were in trouble. They had pushed so hard that they antagonized many among the citizenry, and party feuds pitted Hamilton and his allies, called High Federalists, against more moderate Federalists, like the president himself.

Republicans realized that their opponents might have sealed their own doom. In this fractious climate, if they took advantage of Federalist spats and popular discontent, they might have a real shot at a Republican victory in the national election of 1800.

The Least You Need to Know

- In the nation's first contested presidential election, John Adams eked out a narrow victory over Thomas Jefferson, who became vice president.
- Although political parties were abhorrent to the Founders, the bitter contest over the presidency helped shape two opposing parties, called Federalists and Republicans.
- Partisan division in the late 1790s was reflected in press wars and even competing Fourth of July celebrations.
- Despite Washington's warning to avoid European entanglements, Republicans favored the French, Federalists favored the British, and the nation came to the brink of war with France.
- Federalists cracked down on the opposition by passing the Alien and Sedition Acts, which allowed for the deportation of immigrants and outlawed dissent.
- Legislatures in Virginia and Kentucky resolved that the Sedition Act was unconstitutional and protestors in Pennsylvania refused to pay federal taxes, but most Republicans chose to challenge the Federalists at the polls.

System Failure: The Election of 1800

In This Chapter

- The candidates: Adams and Pinckney vs. Jefferson and Burr
- The cumbersome workings of the elector system
- State-by-state returns, with a very strange result
- Thirty-six ballots in Congress
- For the first time, Federalists in defeat

It was a battle to the end, the final showdown. Both sides treated the presidential election of 1800 as a winner-take-all affair. The Alien and Sedition Acts proved that the United States had yet to accept the concept of a "loyal opposition." The party that prevailed would *own* the government, and the party that lost would be suppressed. Talk about red states and blue states! Now, if one party loses, we assume it will live to fight another day. Not so in the nation's second contested presidential election. Imagine how tempers would flare today if we all thought that whoever won the next election would virtually outlaw the losing party.

In this chapter, you will learn the epic story of the most bizarre elections in the nation's history. We like to think that the framers of the Constitution created a well-oiled machine, but in 1800 that machine failed one of its first major field tests. That presidential election was a "magnificent catastrophe," as one recent historian has called it—so bad, in fact, that Americans quickly passed a Constitutional Amendment to make sure such a thing would never happen again.

A Deist or a Monarchist for President?

At first glance, it might seem that the presidential election of 1800 was merely a replay of 1796. Same candidates, familiar issues. In fact, several of the issues had been around since the ratification debates of 1788 (see Chapter 14). Would the central government overpower the states? Would it trample their basic liberties? Would a standing army protect people or suppress them?

The sectional divisions were also familiar. Northern and eastern states saw things one way, southern and western states another. This had been true at the Constitutional Convention (see Chapter 10), in the frenzy over Jay's Treaty (see Chapter 19), and the election of 1796 (see Chapter 20). Now, once again, the nation was split on regional as well as ideological grounds.

But this time, the stakes were higher yet. The worst fears of Republicans had been realized. The threat of a peacetime army was no longer conjectural; a real one had actually been formed, with Alexander Hamilton at its head. Suppression of speech and the press was no longer just a possibility—it had actually happened. In fact, Federalists had even tried to pass a law (called the Ross Bill, after James Ross, a Federalist senator from Pennsylvania) that would have given Federalist officials the power to referee the upcoming election. Had that bill passed, the election would have been a sham.

Federalists saw things differently. Republicans were already defying federal law and threatening to break up the union. What, pray tell, might these people do if they actually *won?* Heads might tumble, as during the French Reign of Terror. Worse yet, a Republican victory might lead to a revolution like the one in Haiti, where blacks rose up to slay their white masters. In 1800, a rebellion in Virginia led by a slave named Gabriel proved that such things could happen here.

All the fears, all the paranoia, focused on two individuals: the Federalist and Republican standard-bearers for president. Republicans had little difficulty in settling on theirs: Vice President Thomas Jefferson, whom they viewed as their national leader since the previous election. Federalists had more difficulty settling on a candidate. Hamilton and his hardliners, who pushed for war and suppression, thought John Adams was egotistical and too weak a leader. But there were no primaries to determine a candidate, and when Federalist leaders caucused early in 1800, they decided to stick with Adams, the sitting president.

Unlike George Washington, neither candidate had been a military hero. Unlike Patrick Henry, neither was a great orator. Jefferson was aloof, Adams temperamental. So instead of concentrating on its candidate's strength, each party spent most of its energy tearing down the opposition. Jefferson, once again, was painted as a French "Jacobin" (the extremists in the French Revolution) and a deist (not a true Christian; see Chapter 17). Adams was portrayed as a monarchist, as in 1796, and also as a hotheaded president who had virtually lost his mind. Whichever man won, close to half the country would be thoroughly disgusted with the nation's president. This is not what the Founders had intended.

For vice presidential candidates, Federalists settled on South Carolina's Charles Cotesworth Pinckney, brother of the 1796 vice presidential candidate Thomas Pinckney. Republicans, meanwhile, chose New York's Aaron Burr, who had been a candidate for vice president the last time around. Would these choices prove significant? Oh, yes!

FOUNDER ID

Charles Cotesworth Pinckney (1746–1825). South Carolina Commons House of Assembly, 1769–1775. South Caroline Provincial Congress, Committee of Intelligence, 1775–1776. Regimental captain, South Carolina Provincial Army, 1775. Colonel (1776–1782) and Brigadier General (1783), Continental Army. Prisoner of War, 1780--1782. South Carolina House of Representatives, 1783–1790. Constitutional Convention, 1787. South Carolina Ratifying Convention, 1788. South Carolina State Senate, 1790–1796, 1800–1804. Minister to France, 1796–1798. Major General, Additional Army, 1798–1800. Federalist candidate for Vice President (1800) and President (1804 and 1808).

Pinckney was the Federalists' favorite southerner. Educated at the best schools in England from ages 8 to 24, he returned to America in 1769 and joined the fighting against imperial authority. During the Revolution, he became a regional hero by pugnaciously resisting British intrusions in the South, and at war's end, he was promoted to Brigadier General. Re-entering politics, "General Pinckney" (as he was fondly called) opposed equal representation for western farmers, resisted paper money and debtor relief, and favored moneyed interests. After protecting the institution of slavery at the Federal Convention (see Chapter 13), he helped sell the Constitution to his home state. Pinckney turned down Washington's offers to become a Supreme Court justice or Secretary of War, but he agreed to go to France to negotiate for peace. When that failed, he served as third in command in the Additional Army, just under Washington and Hamilton. General Pinckney came a hair's breadth from the presidency in 1800, but when placed at the head of their ticket two more times, he was thoroughly trounced.

Aaron Burr (1756–1836). Continental Army, 1775–1779. New York Assembly, 1784–1785. New York Attorney General, 1789–1791. United States Senator, 1791–1797. New York State Senate, 1798. Vice President, 1801–1805.

History has not been kind to Aaron Burr. He pursued his political career more overtly, if not more strenuously, than other public figures of his day, and he also earned the enmity of Alexander Hamilton. The two clashed politically in New York, and when Burr defeated Hamilton's father-in-law for a Senate seat in 1791, they continued their fight on the national level. Burr opposed Hamilton's policies, while Hamilton fought on the personal level. Burr was "unprincipled," he said, and wanted only "to make his way to the head of the popular party." Burr did exactly that. In both 1796 and 1800, he was placed with Jefferson on the Republican national ticket to provide regional balance. (For the messy story of what happened with that, see below.) When Burr ran for governor of New York in 1804, Hamilton renewed the vendetta with public slurs. Burr then challenged Hamilton to a duel, Hamilton accepted, and Burr prevailed. Charged with murder, Burr fled to the West, where he spearheaded a secessionist movement. He was captured and tried for treason, but acquitted. In the telling of history, Hamilton's version of the feud has prevailed. Lost in the story are Burr's admirable military record, his contributions to the Republican Party in the North, and his pioneering of grassroots political campaigning.

The Longest Election

Election day in 1800 was December 3, but that's not when people voted for president. That's when *electors* met in the separate states to cast their votes for president. The real contest started much earlier. Because the Constitution left the manner of selection up to the state legislatures, the election really began in the early spring, when people voted for their state legislators. Those were the men who would determine the outcome of the election.

Further, the election of 1800 did not end on December 3, but on February 17, 1801. It was America's longest and zaniest presidential election.

Choosing Electors, State by State

To understand this election, we must first learn the complicated ground rules the framers had made. Pay close attention. If you don't know the following rules, you'll be as lost as many Americans were at the time:

- **Step 1:** State legislatures determine how to choose electors. They can either choose the electors themselves or set up special elections so the people can choose them.

- **Step 2:** Electors meet separately in their respective state capitals on December 3, and each casts two ballots.

- **Step 3:** If one candidate appears on the majority of the ballots, he's the president, and the next highest vote-getter is vice president.

- **Step 4A:** If no candidate appears on the majority of ballots, the House of Representatives decides from among the top five, with each state delegation having one vote.

- **Step 4B:** If two men appear on the majority of ballots but have the same number of votes, the House of Representatives decides between them, with each state delegation having one vote.

Why did the framers construct such an elaborate system? Their idea was to place the election of the president at some distance from the people, whom they didn't trust with such a momentous decision (see Chapter 11). Instead, wise, virtuous, and disinterested "electors" would each choose two men who would make a good president. The electors were not supposed to be swayed by personal favoritism, special interests, or political maneuvering.

But that's not the way it worked out. By 1800, because competing parties now dominated the political arena, an elector did not "choose" of his own free will. He had already pledged to vote for the party that made him an elector. He was merely a cog in the wheel, a pawn in the game. The game itself had been played out in the choice of electors.

And a game it was, with each party trying to "game the system." In the lead-up to the state-by-state elections, Federalist legislatures in New Hampshire and Massachusetts, as well as Republican legislatures in Virginia and Georgia, suddenly changed the rules to benefit their own party. Republicans in North Carolina and Federalists in Maryland also tried to switch the rules midstream, but the people raised such an uproar that these attempts failed. When all was said and done, people in only 5 of the 16 states were allowed to vote directly for their electors.

As with our elections today, and like the election of 1796 (see Chapter 20), only a handful of "battleground" states were "in play." One of these was New York, which voted for its state legislators in the weeks before May 1. Thanks to a door-to-door campaign in New York City organized by Aaron Burr, Republican candidates there beat out a slate of Federalists chosen by Hamilton. This gave Republicans control of the state legislature, thereby ensuring that New York's presidential electors would be pledged to Jefferson. Four years earlier, New York had voted for Adams and provided his margin of victory, so this was a huge turnaround. For his part in delivering New York, Burr earned a slot on the Republican national ticket.

Alexander Hamilton, stunned by the news, refused to abide by the results of the New York election. He asked the Federalist Governor John Jay (his old friend and co-author of *The Federalist*) to call an emergency session of the outgoing Federalist legislature so *it* could choose the electors, thereby upstaging the incoming Republicans. Jay did not buy it. He, too, was upset by the Republican victory, but he was not into election tampering.

BY THE NUMBERS

Did the people really vote for the president in 1800? Not exactly. Politicians in state legislatures determined how electors were to be chosen, and in most cases they decided to select the electors themselves. Here are some details:

- In 11 of the 16 states, electors were chosen by the state legislatures.
- In two states, electors were determined by statewide popular elections.
- In three states, legislatures established special districts, and electors were chosen by popular elections within these.
- Each of 138 electors cast 2 votes.
- The minimum number of votes to win was 70.

Results from other states came in from May through October, with no huge surprises. Federalists did manage to pick up a few seats in the South, which had voted solidly Republican in 1796. These helped offset the loss of New York. By the end of October, most states had selected their electors, and the four candidates were locked in a virtual dead heat.

Four candidates? Exactly. Because each Republican elector was pledged to vote for both Jefferson and Burr, and each Federalist elector for Adams and Pinckney, all four men had an equal number of electors in tow. The Constitution had not asked electors to distinguish between their choices for president and vice president.

Hamilton Writes a Letter

That's where matters stood when Alexander Hamilton decided to vent his rage on President John Adams. There had been bad blood between them for years (see Chapter 20), but now Hamilton was particularly upset because the president had sent a peace commission to France, hoping to settle matters without a war. Even worse, Adams had just bowed to Republican pressure and disbanded the Additional Army, which Hamilton headed. Unable to contain his anger, Hamilton penned a rambling rant against the president. Hamilton's political allies, who also disliked Adams, counseled him not to write the letter, but he did it anyway. Republicans then wasted little time in exploiting the letter for their own political gain.

THEIR OWN WORDS

"There are great and intrinsic defects in his [Adams's] character, which unfit him for the office of Chief Magistrate. … He is often liable to paroxysms of anger, which deprive him of self command. … He has made great progress in undermining the ground which was gained for the government by his predecessor [President Washington], and ……it might totter, if not fall, under his future auspices."

—Letter from Alexander Hamilton, Concerning the Public Conduct and Character of John Adams, Esq., President of the United States, October 24, 1800

The strangest part of Hamilton's letter was its conclusion. Electors should vote for both Adams and Pinckney, he said. Why, after dumping on the president for some 15,000 words, did Hamilton then endorse him? People were baffled at the time, and historians have remained puzzled ever since. Here are two possible explanations.

Theory #1: Hamilton cracked. George Washington had just died. Hamilton never wielded power except through his mentor, who kept him close during the Revolutionary War, appointed him Treasury Secretary, covered his back politically, and even managed to twist Adams's arm to secure his command of the Additional Army. With Washington gone, Hamilton had to stand on his own. If Adams, who hated Hamilton, gained a second term in office, Hamilton would be totally outside the corridors of power. This prospect unhinged him so much that he could not even see the disconnect between the body of his letter and his endorsement of Adams.

Theory #2. Hamilton understood perfectly well what he was doing. Everyone knew he wanted to make Pinckney president, but he could not come right out and say it. Most of the votes were in, and the Federalists had a reasonable shot at victory. If they did win, and if he could steal just one or two votes from Adams on December 3, his man Pinckney would win.

The Cousins' War for South Carolina

If Hamilton did in fact hope for a Pinckney presidential victory (theory #2), it was not just wishful thinking. By design, Federalists had placed Pinckney on their ticket to carry his home state of South Carolina, deep in the heart of Jefferson's southern stronghold. General Pinckney was so popular there that both Republicans and Federalists might vote for him. If Republican electors placed Jefferson and Pinckney on their tickets, and Federalist electors voted for Adams and Pinckney, Pinckney might outpoll both Jefferson and Adams.

But this scheme faced a problem. *Charles Cotesworth Pinckney's* popularity was offset by that of his cousin *Charles Pinckney,* who had become a Republican a few years earlier because of Jay's Treaty (see Chapters 13 and 19). The two Charles Pinckneys had been colleagues at the Constitutional Convention, when they stood shoulder-to-shoulder to support slavery, but now they would not even talk with each other. The Republican Charles Pinckney placed party above family and actively opposed the candidacy of his own Federalist cousin.

Surprisingly, Charles Cotesworth Pinckney opposed the scheme that might have made him president. He said that electors who supported him should cast their second vote for Adams, even though he was a Yankee, rather than Jefferson, a fellow Southerner and slaveholder. By 1800, party affiliation had become so strong it could trump family, region, and class loyalties.

In the end, South Carolina remained in the Republican column. Republicans controlled the state legislature, and none of the eight electors they selected cast a vote for the state's native son, General Pinckney. This meant that Republicans prevailed nationwide by an eight-vote margin. Jefferson had won!

An Unexpected Tie

Actually, "Jefferson had won" is not a correct statement. Jefferson *and Burr* had won, each with 73 electoral votes, while Adams trailed with 65 and Pinckney 64. The exact numbers are significant. In order to avoid a tie, Federalists had the foresight to hold back exactly one vote from Pinckney, but Republicans failed to do that with Burr.

What did the Constitution say would happen in case of a tie? Consult ground rule 4B, above. When there was no clear-cut winner, the framers said the House of Representatives should make the final call. But to placate small states, who had little say in the House, they gave each state delegation exactly one vote. The House would vote until more than half the state delegations settled on a winner.

Congress Settles the Matter? Not so Fast!

More than half, that was the key. Republicans constituted a majority in 8 of the 16 delegations. (Vermont, Kentucky, and Tennessee were now part of the union). Federalists held 6 states, and two were evenly divided. So for Jefferson to become president, he would need the support of at least one state delegation that was not Republican.

But Federalists held firm. They saw an opportunity to deny Jefferson the presidency by casting all their votes for Aaron Burr. If they could convince just a few Republican congressmen to go with Burr, he would become president—and he would owe them for placing him there.

As Jefferson-hating Federalists lined up in support of Burr, one prominent leader refused to toe the party line: Alexander Hamilton, who wrote a spate of letters to his fellow Federalists. Burr was absolutely corrupt, he said, and he could not be trusted. "Burr loves nothing but himself, thinks of nothing but his own aggrandizement, and will be content with nothing short of permanent power in his own hands." Of the two evils, even Jefferson was better than Burr.

No Federalists listened to what Hamilton said. Like the boy who cried wolf, Hamilton had lost his credibility with his various character assassinations. Few Federalists had any great love for Burr, but they would do absolutely anything to keep Jefferson from power.

What did Aaron Burr think of the designs to make him president? That's what everybody wondered at the time and what historians still argue about today. Some say he stayed on the fence, neither endorsing the Federalists' scheme nor saying point-blank he refused to serve as president. Others note that according to some Federalists, Burr foiled their scheme by refusing to play along. In any case, Burr's political star dimmed, and after the election of 1800, he pulled little weight with either party.

Let the Balloting Begin

At 1 P.M. on Wednesday, February 3, 1801, in a capitol building still under construction, the House of Representatives cast its first ballot to break the tie. Both Republicans and Federalists hoped to pick up some defectors, but there were no surprises. Sure enough, 8 state delegations voted for Jefferson, 6 for Burr, and 2 split evenly. Jefferson was one state shy.

Members politicked and caucused. Republicans worked on Federalists they thought they could sway, and vice versa. Deals were offered, but none accepted. Congressmen voted again, but the results stayed the same.

Again they split up, came back together, and heard the results: no change. Pressure mounted on members most likely to switch their votes. They took another vote, then still another. Evening came, more votes. Members remained in their makeshift chamber through the night, each side hoping the other would tire. By 8 the next morning, after casting 27 ballots, the House finally recessed.

Voting resumed on Friday, and again on Saturday. Not until Sunday, the Sabbath, did members take a full break. By then they had voted 33 times.

Who would blink? At first glance, it appeared the deadlock favored the Federalists. They still controlled the Senate, and if the House could not settle the matter by March 4, the day the new president was supposed to assume his office, the Senate could choose its own president pro tem and make him President of the United States. All the Federalists had to do was stall.

This prospect made Republicans so angry they threatened to use military force. Republican governors of the two largest states, Virginia and Pennsylvania, made moves to mobilize their militias. Federalists countered by boasting that these greenhorn crews would be no match for the well-drilled militias of New England.

THEIR OWN WORDS

"Militia would have been warned to be ready, arms for upward of twenty thousand were secured, brass field pieces etc. etc. and an order would have been issued for the arresting and bringing to justice every member of Congress and other persons found in Pennsylvania … concerned with the treason."

—Thomas McKean, Governor of Pennsylvania, explaining to Jefferson the actions he would have taken had Congress settled on Burr.

This is exactly the sort of talk that finally settled the election. A handful of moderate Federalists from key states decided that obstructionist tactics must end before they led to civil war. Preserving the union, after all, was the centerpiece of Federalist ideology, and these men, true to their stated beliefs, refused to continue the battle. At noon on Tuesday, Feb. 17, on the 36th ballot, the House of Representatives declared that Thomas Jefferson would be the next president.

It wasn't pretty. The framers had created a confusing and cumbersome method for choosing the president, and the system had essentially failed. The elector scheme had done nothing to remove politics from the presidency. If anything, by encouraging each side to game the system, it made the process *more* political. And voting for two candidates, with no distinction between president and vice president, just didn't work. It had to be changed, and soon it would be. The Twelfth Amendment to the Constitution, ratified in 1804, established separate ballots for president and vice president. The Electoral College, on the other hand, remains with us to this day. We claim to have a democracy, but we *still* don't vote directly for our president.

The peculiarities of the Constitution affected the election of 1800 in yet another manner. Remember that bit in Chapter 13 about slaves counting for three fifths of free people? That's how Jefferson won. If slaves had not been counted, the southern states would have been entitled to fewer electors, and Adams, not Jefferson, would have won.

BY THE NUMBERS

Federalists dubbed Jefferson "The Negro President," not because he represented the interests of black people, but because counting slaves had thrown the election his way. Here's the math:

- Jefferson 73, Adams 65—vote of the presidential electors in 1800.
- Adams 63, Jefferson 61—vote of the presidential electors if each slave had not counted for three fifths of a free person when allocating the electors amongst the states.

Will the Federalists Accept Defeat?

President-elect Jefferson thought the Federalists had displayed characteristically poor form with their obstructionist tactics. Why couldn't they just accept defeat, as he had done four years earlier? What riled him most, strangely, was the manner in which they conceded defeat. Rather than cast votes for Jefferson, moderate Federalists just withdrew from the process. Jefferson was incensed by their symbolic resistance to his victory. "We consider this therefore as a declaration of war on the part of that band," Jefferson wrote to Madison the day after the final ballot.

The rancor would continue, but there would be no civil war. Federalists didn't have enough support. Although Federalists wanted to cast Republicans as just a bunch of slave-owning hypocrites who preached about liberty but didn't practice it, the party appealed to large swaths of the population in all regions, even the North. The nation was still overwhelmingly rural, and the Republican notion that small, independent farmers should control the nation was easy to sell.

Even without violent confrontation, Federalists devised a strategy for keeping some power. Although they would no longer control the executive and legislative branches of government, they could still dominate the judicial branch. In their last days in office, the Federalist Congress greatly expanded the national judiciary, and President Adams appointed a bundle of "midnight judges" to fill the new positions.

Then Adams went home. At 4 A.M. on the day of inauguration, he boarded a stage and left town. He did not want to honor the new Republican president.

The Least You Need to Know

- In the election of 1800, Federalists put forth John Adams and Charles Cotesworth Pinckney, Republicans countered with Thomas Jefferson and Aaron Burr, and both sides, believing the fate of the nation was at stake, vilified the opponents.

- With the people voting directly for electors in only 5 of the 16 states, and with most states firmly in one column or the other, the election turned on political maneuvering in the legislatures of a few "battleground" states.

- Because electors were not supposed to distinguish between presidential and vice presidential candidates, Republicans Jefferson and Burr wound up in a dead heat.

- In the House of Representatives, where ties were to be broken, Federalists lined up with Burr to keep their arch-rival Jefferson from the presidency.

- After a six-day deadlock, on the 36th ballot, a handful of Federalists abstained, and that threw the election to Jefferson.

- Defeated, Federalists in Congress expanded the judiciary, and President Adams, in his final act, appointed Federalist judges to those new posts.

Outsiders Move In: Jefferson's Administration

In This Chapter

- The nation's first transfer of political power
- The fight to control the national judiciary
- The Louisiana Purchase
- Reasons for the Embargo, and why it failed
- Political overreach and its consequences

After Jefferson's election to the presidency, Federalists feared a revolution and some Republicans hoped for one. Republicans now held a sweeping 69 to 36 majority in the House of Representatives and a narrow but sufficient 18 to 14 margin in the Senate. Whether they were expectant or anxious, people saw March 4, the date of Jefferson's inauguration, as the beginning of a new era.

When Republicans were out of power, it was easy for them to claim the high moral ground. Could they continue to do so while actually running the country? In this chapter, we will see what happened when Jefferson and his party were put to the test. It was a new day in a host of ways, but reality would take its inevitable toll on wide-eyed idealism. The nation was not some Garden of Eden, but a contentious and expanding empire, dedicated in theory to liberty, but in practice still subject to political pushes and pulls.

Changing of the Guard

"We have called by different names brethren of the same principle," Thomas Jefferson said in his inaugural address to Congress. "We are all republicans: we are all federalists." Partisanship must cease, the president preached, and he would lead the way. Now that Republicans were in the majority, they would not suppress dissent, as the Federalists had done, nor would they act vindictively toward their political foes.

THEIR OWN WORDS

"Let us then, fellow citizens, unite with one heart and one mind. Let us restore to social intercourse that harmony and affection without which liberty, and even life itself, are but dreary things."

—Thomas Jefferson's inaugural address, March 4, 1801

Jefferson's conciliatory attitude encouraged the citizenry and even many Federalists. "His public assurances have inspired us to hope that *he is not the man we thought him*," wrote one Federalist editor. "We thought him a Virginian, and have found him an American. We thought him a partisan and have found him a president." But this was Jefferson's "honeymoon phase," as we now call it. What would former opponents say when Jefferson tried to implement the Republican program?

Also in his inaugural address, Jefferson laid out his values and goals:

- Government should be "wise and frugal."

- Government should "restrain men from injuring one another," but otherwise leave them "free to regulate their own pursuits of industry and improvement."

- Government should not "take from the mouth of labor the bread it has earned."

- Freedom of speech, religion, and the press should be preserved.

- The public debt should be paid off.

- Commerce should be the "handmaid" of agriculture.

- A "well disciplined militia" should be the first line of defense, and a professional army the last.

Sound familiar? Here was the standard critique of Federalist policies, item-by-item. Jefferson viewed these commandments not as the Republican Party platform, however, but as a clear statement of how government must function in a republic. "The republicans are the *nation*," he wrote, not just one side of a partisan dispute.

Federalists, of course, saw it differently, but Jefferson was president and Republicans held power in the Senate and House, and they were no longer calling the shots. Although Jefferson did not interfere conspicuously in Congressional affairs, he did work with Republican leaders behind the scenes to attain the party's goals. Internal taxes, including the hated excise tax on whiskey, were repealed, and 400 tax collectors lost their jobs. The army was reduced to a mere 3,000 men and the navy was similarly diminished. The Naturalization Act, one of the Alien and Sedition Acts, was repealed, so immigrants once again needed to wait only 5 years, not 14, before becoming citizens.

A revolution? Not exactly, but government was certainly moving in a different direction.

Jefferson vs. Hamilton, Final Round

Jefferson was distressed by the seemingly evil spell Hamilton had cast on the nation. "When the government was first established, it was possible to have kept it going on true principles," he said, but the "half-lettered ideas of Hamilton destroyed that hope in the bud." He would have liked to dismantle Hamilton's entire financial edifice, but couldn't. The banking system now played a valuable role in the economy. The central government had long ago assumed state debts, which of course created a huge federal debt that had to be managed. Jefferson did ask his Secretary of the Treasury, Albert Gallatin, to devise a plan to "set afloat" (pay off) the national debt, but that would take many years, Gallatin told him.

THEIR OWN WORDS

"We can pay off his [Hamilton's] debt in 15 years, but we can never get rid of his financial system. It mortifies me to be strengthening principles which I deem radically vicious, but the vice is entailed on us by the first error."

—Thomas Jefferson, 1802

If Jefferson was distraught, so was Hamilton, who now found himself outside the corridors of power. In his view, Jefferson and the ruling Republicans were undoing his life's work. In a deep funk, he wrote to his friend and fellow New Yorker Gouverneur Morris. "Perhaps no man in the U[nited] States has sacrificed or done more for the present Constitution than myself," he said, but now he received only "curses" from Republicans and "murmurs" from fellow Federalists, whom he had antagonized during the previous election (see Chapter 21)." Every day proves to me more and more that this American world was not made for me."

But "this American world" was in an enduring sense Hamilton's, too. He had erected a rudimentary economic structure that still stood, as we see from Jefferson's own complaints. At Hamilton's urging, rich men had taken a stake in a nation that had *not* gone belly-up as once feared. They still influenced its workings as Hamilton had wanted, if not always to the degree he would have liked.

Although it was difficult for Hamilton to acknowledge, he had helped create the very political climate he now deplored. Republicans had prevailed in part because of his policies and political strategies of the 1790s. Rich bankers and speculators, whom he had favored, were thought to have wrecked the Constitution. To understand how Hamilton lost the battle for the American mind, look at how people today trash-talk "Wall Street." When you hear those populist groans, think "Hamilton." He did not single-handedly create the anti-intellectual, anti-Eastern, anti-elite, anti-Wall Street tenor of political discourse in America, but he certainly helped foster it.

Who finally prevailed in this epic battle for America? Much of the language we hear in politics today is Jefferson's: less government, lower taxes, greater liberties, local control, equal treatment for all, belief in the American people. Hamilton never fully grasped the importance of "the people" in politics, and Jefferson did. In Hamilton's world, the "vigor" of government depended on its ability to impose its will on the populous. He could not see that a government supported by the people could be far stronger than one buttressed by a powerful executive or military might.

But if popular discourse shows Jefferson's influence, current realities give Hamilton at least a draw. Increasingly, American society has been dependent on commercial vitality and the flow of money rather than agricultural production. The national debt will never disappear, nor will a standing army and a strong central government. Further, the government remains to this day closely linked to those with money, who wield great influence, whether playing their part at the center of the stage or behind the scenes. That was as it should be in Hamilton's mind, for their wealth would produce stability. Hamilton's notion is difficult to refute, even if it's hard for some to stomach.

The Tussle over the Judiciary

In the nation's first twelve years, the Supreme Court did not attract much attention, nor did prominent men seek an appointment to it. A few justices who did serve resigned after a short stint to seek greener pastures elsewhere. During the early years of Jefferson's administration, however, because the judiciary was all the Federalists had left, they vowed to make the most of it. The "least dangerous" branch of government, as Hamilton called the judiciary in *Federalist 78*, became a new battlefield in an old political war.

The Judiciary Act that Federalists had passed in the waning days of the Adams administration (see Chapter 21) greatly expanded the judicial arm of the federal government. Simultaneously, in a deft display of partisanship, it actually reduced the number of Supreme Court justices from six to five, simply to deny Jefferson the opportunity of appointing a new judge when one retired. Then on March 3, 1801, the evening before Jefferson's inauguration, President Adams filled numerous new positions in lower courts with trusty Federalists. The new appointees were called "midnight judges," which was approximately accurate—Adams was last seen signing the commissions of 42 justices of the peace at 9 P.M.

Republicans in Congress cried foul, and as soon as they took power, they tried to undo all this. Because the Constitution gave Congress the authority to create courts, they said that Congress could disband them as well and moved to repeal the Judiciary Act of 1800. Then, of course, it was the Federalists' turn to cry foul. They insisted that if Congress wanted to remove judges legally, it would have to impeach them, not just take away courts.

Republicans in Congress managed to repeal the Judiciary Act, by a wide margin in the House but only narrowly in the Senate. They followed immediately with another assault on the Federalist-controlled judiciary, delaying the upcoming session of the Supreme Court for more than a year. Federalists of course complained that Congress had no right to interfere with the courts this way.

Marbury v. Madison: John Marshall's Brilliant Ploy

Jefferson's executive department also entered the fray. Through an administrative oversight, commissions for some of the midnight judges had been signed by President Adams, and then sealed, but the Secretary of State had not actually delivered the documents to the appointees. When Jefferson assumed the presidency, he ordered his Secretary of State, James Madison, not to deliver the commissions.

William Marbury and three other appointees immediately sued Madison, demanding he deliver their signed commissions so they could start work. *Marbury v. Madison,* heard in the Supreme Court, created a political dilemma for John Marshall, the Federalist Chief Justice. If he ruled in favor of the plaintiffs and ordered Secretary of State Madison to deliver the commissions, Jefferson would probably tell Madison to disobey the court order and *not* deliver them. In the ensuing battle, Jefferson and the Republicans, at the height of their popularity, would undoubtedly prevail. On the other hand, as a Federalist, Marshall did not want to bow to Republican pressure and deny Marbury and the others their rightful commissions.

With a stroke of political genius, Marshall figured a way out. Rather than ordering Madison to deliver the commissions, Marshall declared that the court had no jurisdiction in the matter. According to the United States Constitution, only certain types of cases could be tried directly in the Supreme Court, and this was not one of them. This apparent retreat was in fact a masterful offensive. Marbury and the other plaintiffs, in bringing their case forward, had based their case on a law that said the Supreme Court *did* have jurisdiction, but Marshall overruled Congress and threw that law out. (Previously, the court had overturned state laws, but never a federal law.) The justices could not "close their eyes on the Constitution," Marshall wrote in the unanimous opinion.

Marshall had conceded the battle in order to win the war. Republicans could go ahead and deny the commissions, but Federalists, who still controlled the courts, had the final say in determining whether a law was Constitutional or not. *Marbury v. Madison* established what we now call "judicial review" (see Chapter 12). Far from bowing, Marshall had established both the strength and independence of the judiciary.

FOUNDER ID

John Marshall (1755–1835). Lieutenant, Virginia Minute Men (1775–1776) and Continental Army (1776–1780). Virginia House of Delegates, 1782, 1784–1785, 1787–1791, 1795–1797. Virginia Council of State, 1782–1784. Virginia Ratification Convention, 1788. Commissioner to France, 1797–1798. Congressman from Virginia, 1799–1800. United States Secretary of State, 1800–1801. Chief Justice, United States Supreme Court, 1801–1835. Author, *The Life of George Washington* (five volumes, 1804–1807).

With George Washington, Marshall was one of the few leading Virginians who always favored a strong central government. He fought in the Revolutionary War, studied law for a single term at William and Mary College, and in 1780 received his license to practice. In 1788, while arguing for the new Constitution, he said that judges could check excesses of Congress by declaring a law unconstitutional, a view he would establish as precedent in *Marbury v. Madison.* Marshall turned down Washington's offer of an appointment to the Supreme Court because he could not afford to give up his law practice, but in the waning days of Adams's administration, he agreed to serve as Chief Justice. During his long tenure, Marshall helped establish the court as a co-equal branch of government. His rulings cemented federal law as the "supreme law of the land." They nullified state laws and overruled state courts. Marshall also upheld property rights and the obligation of contracts at all costs. Using the interstate commerce clause of the Constitution, he allowed for a broad expansion of federal power. The Constitution, he said, was to be interpreted liberally to achieve its stated goal: a strong but fair national government.

The Impeachment of Samuel Chase

Following Marshall's adept maneuvering in *Marbury v. Madison*, radical Republicans in Congress embarked on a more direct challenge to Federalist judges: impeachment proceedings. William B. Giles, a senator from Virginia closely allied with Jefferson, said that if Federalist judges went so far as "to declare an Act of Congress unconstitutional," Congress had "the undoubted right" to impeach and remove them. Any judge holding "dangerous opinions," he said, should not be allowed to remain on the bench.

At first Jefferson shied away from such a frontal assault, but when he heard that Samuel Chase, Associate Justice of the Supreme Court, had harangued a grand jury in Baltimore with a political tirade against equal rights and universal suffrage, he warmed to the idea. Chase was an easy first target. As a Supreme Court justice, he had concurred with the decision in *Marbury vs. Madison*. In trying cases under the Sedition Act, he had bullied defense lawyers and issued blatantly partisan rulings. From the bench, Chase had removed from the jury "any of those creatures or persons called democrats" and forced Federalists to serve on juries, even if they admitted prior bias.

After the Republican-dominated House issued eight articles of impeachment, Chase faced trial in the Senate. There, Republicans commanded an impressive 24–10 majority, more than the two thirds required for conviction. Unfortunately for the Republicans, however, the Constitution said Chase could be removed from office only if convicted of "treason, bribery, or other high crimes and misdemeanors." That would be tough to prove.

The trial opened on the second day of 1805, with Vice President Aaron Burr presiding. Because Burr was currently under indictment for killing Alexander Hamilton in a duel (see Chapter 21), Federalists joked that a murderer was trying a judge, instead of vice versa.

At stake was not just one man's career, but the future role of the judicial department. Republicans argued that if judges did not answer to elected officials, the will of the people would be subverted. Federalists countered that impeachment for merely political reasons would undermine the independence of the judiciary, make judges subject to the temporary whims of the populace, and destabilize the nation. The Federalist argument was enough to sway six moderate Republicans, so Chase was acquitted.

The Chase trial made future impeachments less likely. If Samuel Chase, with his blatant bias, couldn't be convicted, who could? On the other hand, the trial did give notice to all judges, present and future, to lay off politics. An independent judiciary was necessary, but it required judicial restraint.

Samuel Chase (1742–1811). Maryland Assembly, 1765–1766, 1768–1771, 1773–1788. Committee of Correspondence, 1773–1775. Continental Congress, 1774–1778. Maryland Ratification Convention, 1788. Judge, Maryland General Court, 1791–1796. United States Supreme Court, 1796–1811.

Chase was a volatile fellow. Before the Revolution, he was an extreme opponent of British imperial policies. One royal official called him a "busy, restless incendiary, a ringleader of mobs, a foul mouthed and inflaming son of discord and faction." In 1776, he helped engineer Maryland's vote for independence (see Chapter 4). Although he was a merchant and speculator, he opposed the Constitution in 1788 because he thought wealthy merchants would have too much influence in the new government. But sometime between then and 1795, Chase had a change of heart. Revolutions suddenly scared him, and he became an ardent Federalist. Washington appointed him to the Supreme Court, and during the Adams administration he clamped down on political dissenters, even though he had once pushed for the Bill of Rights. On the bench he was a bully but not a party hack. His opinion in *Calder v. Bull* (1798) helped pave the way for judicial review by proclaiming that a legislative act was not "law" if it contradicted the "first principles" of government. Following his impeachment trial, Chase continued on the Supreme Court until his death six years later.

The Expansion of Federal Powers

In Jefferson's inaugural address, he described the United States as "a rising nation, spread over a wide and fruitful land." Under his watch, and by his efforts, that nation would nearly double in size. But if it were to acquire land, defend it, develop it, administer it, and keep the numerous regions of the sprawling nation in sync, the nation required more than a minimalist federal government. Wouldn't that challenge Jefferson's pledge to keep government small?

In the last decade of the eighteenth century, the population of the western territories increased almost tenfold, while the overall population of the United States did not even double. Here are the numbers:

- 35,691—U.S. population, excluding Indians, of the western territories (between the Appalachians Mountains and the Mississippi River), from the 1790 census.

- 335,411—Population of the same region, from the 1800 census.

Purchasing Louisiana: By What Authority?

As the nation expanded westward, it encountered French, Spanish, and Native American people who lived in, or had an interest in, Louisiana and the Mississippi Valley. Even though more Indians than Europeans lived there, Spain claimed that it owned the land. In 1801 it ceded the Mississippi River and lands westward to France. But France was busy, not only trying to conquer Europe but trying to put down a revolution of former slaves in Haiti, where some 20,000 French soldiers died of yellow fever. Napoleon wanted out of America. "Damn sugar, damn coffee, damn colonies," he said. "I renounce Louisiana. It is not only New Orleans that I cede; it is the whole colony, without reserve."

Meanwhile, war hawks in the United States were talking about conquering Louisiana by force. Jefferson didn't want that, but he did want Louisiana, so he empowered his minister to France, Robert R. Livingston, to look into a peaceful transfer, and he asked special envoy James Monroe to join the negotiating team.

FOUNDER ID

Robert R. Livingston (1746–1813). New York City Recorder, 1773–1775. New York Provincial Congress (1775) and Convention (1776–1777). Continental Congress, 1775–1776, 1779–1780, 1784. Chancellor, State of New York, 1777–1801. United States Secretary of Foreign Affairs, 1781–1783. New York Ratification Convention, 1788. Minister to France, 1801–1804. Founder, New York Society for Promotion of Agriculture, Manufactures, and the Useful Arts (1793) and American Academy of Fine Arts (1801).

Livingston believed the future of America lay in land. He knew a thing or two about land, having inherited a swath larger than the state of Rhode Island in New York's Hudson Valley and Catskill region, much of it worked by tenant farmers. One of New York's powerful elite, he was appointed the state's first Chancellor (similar to a Chief Justice, but with some political power), a position he held for a quarter-century. "The Chancellor," as people called him, was also a national figure. At the close of the Revolutionary War, as Secretary of Foreign Affairs, he tried to secure the Mississippi River for Americans—a goal he would achieve 20 years later. In 1788 he played a critical role in New York's ratification of the Constitution, and a year later, the Chancellor administered President Washington's oath of office. Favoring land over commerce and France over Britain, while opposing assumption of debts and Jay's Treaty, he naturally fell in with the Republicans. Then, as Jefferson's Minister to France in 1803, he finally secured the Mississippi and a whole lot more. A busy entrepreneur, Livingston financed early steamboat navigation, for which he obtained a monopoly on both the Hudson and Mississippi Rivers.

> **FOUNDER ID**
>
> **James Monroe (1758–1831).** Virginia militia, 1775. Lieutenant (1776) and Colonel (1777–1778), Continental Army. Virginia House of Delegates, 1782, 1787–1789, 1810–1811. Virginia Council, 1782–1783. Continental Congress, 1783–1786. Virginia Ratification Convention, 1788. United States Senator, 1790–1794. Minister to France, 1794–1796. Governor of Virginia, 1799–1802, 1811. Envoy to France, 1803. Minister to Britain, 1803–1807. United States Secretary of State (1811–1817) and Secretary of War (1814–1815). President of the United States, 1817–1825.
>
> The Louisiana Purchase was a pivotal moment in James Monroe's political career. He had opposed the Constitution in 1788 and Federalist policies in the 1790s, but Washington made him minister to France to appease his Republican critics. Monroe proved too pro-French for the Federalists, however, and was soon recalled. After Republicans took over, he got his second shot at treating with France. Upon arriving in Paris, he joined the negotiations over Louisiana, which were well underway. Both during and after the proceedings, Monroe and Livingston jockeyed for who would get the major share of credit. Monroe emerged a hero and figured prominently in national affairs thereafter. When tensions mounted with Britain a few years later, he beat the drums of war. During the War of 1812 he served simultaneously as Secretary of State and Secretary of War. That placed him in line for the presidency, which he won with minimal opposition in 1816. In office, he assumed the aggressive foreign policy that bears his name: the Monroe Doctrine. European powers were warned to stay out of American affairs—and by "American" he meant the entire Western Hemisphere.

Napoleon offered to sell the Louisiana Territory for a "mere" 80 million francs, or $15 million. Fearful that the quixotic Emperor might change his mind, Livingston and Monroe took the deal, even though they had been instructed to obtain only the Mississippi River and Gulf Coast, not the vast lands to the west. It was the largest real estate transaction in American history and also one of the quickest.

The United States Senate had to ratify the treaty, however, and Federalists in that body grumbled. We could have had it virtually for free, they said, if only we had just taken it by force! In truth, Federalists didn't like the deal for two reasons: Jefferson and the Republicans got all the credit, and it would diminish the importance of the Northeast in national politics. They also presented a third very disingenuous reason: the Constitution did not specifically authorize the President to acquire foreign lands. For years, they had been arguing for a *loose* construction of the Constitution (see Chapter 19), and now, suddenly, they demanded a strict interpretation.

Jefferson, to his credit, agreed with Federalist critics. He had "done an act beyond the Constitution," he freely admitted. "The Constitution has made no provision for our holding foreign territory, still less for incorporating foreign nations into our Union."

But Jefferson thought he was doing the right thing, and he knew most of his countrymen were behind him. All could be made well by amending the Constitution to grant the necessary powers, he suggested. His friends counseled him otherwise. That would delay Senate ratification of the purchase, and Napoleon might renege on the deal. Jefferson capitulated, but in doing so he sacrificed a dearly held principle. In the end, this president set an example *for* a broad construction of the Constitution, which he had previously opposed.

"Empire of Liberty"

In 1783, at the close of the Revolutionary War, the Treaty of Paris doubled the size of the United States. Twenty years later, the Louisiana Purchase almost doubled it again. This was the fastest-growing empire in the world, and an "empire of liberty," in Jefferson's words. It would revolutionize society and government as it spread, the people themselves taking charge and the government fading into the background.

There was some truth to the idea, but this empire, like other empires, depended on military conquest. Although France had ceded Louisiana, the people who lived there hadn't and were obviously going to resist intrusion by people who now claimed Native American lands. And the government wasn't about to fade into the background either. The purchase increased the national debt, and there were still roads to build, lands to develop, and soldiers to employ in fighting native inhabitants. Small and independent farmers *needed* government, now more than ever.

Republican Fiasco: The Embargo

Washington, Adams, and Jefferson all warned against European entanglements, but during Jefferson's second term, with the Napoleonic Wars in full swing, the nation couldn't avoid them. France and Britain, although foes to each other, each declared open season on American vessels that traded with the enemy. Both sides seized ships, confiscated cargoes, and impressed American seamen into foreign service.

In 1807, Jefferson didn't want a military war, and he thought he could use economic warfare instead. The United States would cease trade with both belligerents until they agreed to lay off American ships. Americans had used economic warfare to great effect in Revolutionary times, forcing Parliament to withdraw oppressive taxes (see Chapter 2), so why not try it again?

Late in 1807, Congress passed the first of three *Embargo* Acts, each stricter than the last. American vessels were forbidden to travel to foreign countries. To make sure they didn't stray beyond domestic ports, their owners had to post bonds that eventually totaled six times the worth of their vessels and cargo. Owners who violated the Act would be fined $10,000 and forfeit their cargoes.

DEFINITION

An **embargo** is a governmental restraint of trade. It can be applied to a specific item or to trade with a specific nation, or it can be a sweeping prohibition against commercial ships entering or leaving ports. The Embargo Acts of 1807–1808 prohibited all foreign trade with the United States.

However well intentioned, Jefferson stood yet again on shaky Constitutional grounds, his only defense a broad interpretation of its rules. The Constitution allowed Congress to *regulate* commerce but said nothing about *prohibiting* commerce. The Embargo was also in clear violation of the Fourth and Fifth Amendments when it allowed government agents to seize cargoes *without warrants* on the mere *suspicion* that owners or captains were *contemplating* a transgression. That was even worse than the blanket Writs of Assistance, which had initiated the resistance to British imperial policies back in 1761 (see Chapter 2). At least those were warrants; now, none were needed.

Practically, although many traders complied, the Embargo was difficult to enforce and smuggling seductively easy. To reach Canada and British jurisdiction, goods only needed to travel from Maine to New Brunswick, or by giant rafts across the Great Lakes, or by a rag-tag combination of boats, wagons, and sleds on and near Lake Champlain.

Jefferson determined to clamp down. Using the extraordinary powers Congress granted him, he determined what could be shipped, and where. Flour could no longer be sent from smaller ports to those engaged in foreign trade, for fear the cargo would be sent abroad. With commerce interrupted, many went hungry. Twenty to thirty thousand seamen were out of work.

The president's orders proved too much for William Johnson, Associate Justice of the Supreme Court. Denied clearance for a routine shipment of cotton and rice from South Carolina to Maryland, a ship owner sued in federal court, and Justice Johnson ordered the government to allow the vessel to sail. Jefferson not only disobeyed the court order but chided Johnson, a fellow Republican, for interfering in executive matters.

THEIR OWN WORDS

"The Embargo law is certainly the most embarrassing one we have ever had to execute. I did not expect a crop of so sudden and rank growth of fraud, and open opposition by force, could have grown up in the United States. … This law ought to be enforced at any expense."

—Thomas Jefferson to Treasury Secretary Albert Gallatin, August, 1808.

As in the American Revolution, repressive measures had the unintentional effect of increasing resistance. Throughout New England, people gathered in their town meetings to protest the administration's harsh measures; one Boston meeting, reminiscent of Revolutionary days, attracted 4,000 angry citizens.

Confrontations sometimes turned violent. On Lake Champlain, local lumberjacks recaptured a raft of lumber that had been seized by the government, but Jefferson declared a state of insurrection and had the miscreants tried for treason. When fighting broke out in upper Maine and on Lake Ontario, the president deployed the Navy and the militia, and in September 1808 he even dispatched a contingent of army regulars.

Jefferson believed his Embargo was like the nonimportation campaigns of the 1760s and 1770s, when patriots forced recalcitrant Tories to comply—but it was not the same. Then, local committees selected by the body of the people had brought their neighbors into line. Now, enforcement was the work of a distant government. Through most of his public life, Jefferson had tried to bring government and the people together, but the Embargo separated them. Suddenly Republicans, the supposed inheritors of the Revolution's ideals, had become the oppressors, and Federalists reclaimed the high moral ground. Wealthy merchants, by smuggling, could once again feel like patriots.

Role Reversal: Federalists Talk Secession

The Embargo revitalized the Federalist Party, and in the election of 1808, they regained control of state governments in most of the North while also capturing 70 percent of the North's congressional seats, excluding Pennsylvania.

Emboldened, Federalists got the Massachusetts legislature to declare that the methods used to enforce the Embargo were "unconstitutional, and not legally binding." Connecticut quickly followed suit. Both states echoed the Virginia and Kentucky Resolutions of 1798–1799, which had been penned in secret by the current president and by his Secretary of State, James Madison (see Chapter 20). Back then, Jefferson and Madison held that states could "interpose" between their citizens and the federal government, if a federal law violated the Constitution. Now, the same argument was used against them.

Some Federalists, including former Secretary of War and Secretary of State Timothy Pickering (see Chapter 18), pushed for New England and New York to secede from the union. Northeasterners were increasingly outnumbered because of western expansion, they said, and Republicans from the South and West would trample on their rights—Jefferson's Embargo was proof positive. When in power, Federalists had always trumpeted the importance of preserving the Union, fearful that southern and western states might break away to form their own confederacy. Now, out of power, Federalists were the ones threatening to walk away. The Embargo had divided rather than united the nation.

Politics, Same as It Ever Was

The Embargo Acts were repealed just as Jefferson left office in 1809. He had hoped they would prove to the world the strength of republicanism and the independence of America and keep the nation from war. Through the rest of his life he believed that the Embargo had been the nation's last, best hope to avoid bloodshed, and perhaps he was correct—three years later, America and Britain would be at war with each other.

In Jefferson's view, it was New England's intransigence and British interference that crushed an Embargo favored by a majority of Americans. He never did own up to the failures of his draconian enforcement procedures, which violated core principles of civil liberties and alienated the populace in affected regions. Eight years earlier, John Adams and the Federalists had limped from office, defeated in large measure by political overreach. Now, Jefferson and the Republicans had overreached, and though their party still won the presidency, people were roundly condemning a signature Republican program.

Framers of the Constitution who were still alive, had they not been partisans in the latest conflicts, might have found some comfort in these swings of power and ideology. Contentious debate was not destroying the nation, as they had feared. It was saving the nation from itself. No one person or party could ever deliver a final knockout blow, it seemed. An opposition always checked the deadly swing.

When a party was *not* in power, however, it thought about leaving the union. That would happen a half-century later, when self-regulating mechanisms failed and opposing factions from opposing regions went to war. The ultimate dispute, as it turned out, was not whether to favor Britain or France, or whether to enforce a temporary restriction of trade. No, it was whether slavery should extend to the West. Slavery was the one issue the Founders did not dare handle. Another generation, at a very great price, would attend to that.

The Least You Need to Know

- Once in power, Jefferson and the Republicans cut taxes, diminished the army and navy, and planned to pay down the national debt, hoping to limit the scope of federal government, but the Louisiana Purchase and Embargo Acts actually expanded the scope of government.

- In *Marbury v. Madison,* Federalist Chief Justice John Marshall declared the supremacy of the Supreme Court while avoiding a direct conflict with ruling Republicans.

- Republicans fought back by trying to impeach Samuel Chase, a Federalist Supreme Court Justice, but their failure helped establish the political independence of the judiciary.

- The Louisiana Purchase almost doubled the area of the United States and furthered the Jeffersonian notion of an "empire of liberty," an expanding nation of independent farmers who would spread republican values.

- Jefferson and the Republicans placed an embargo on all foreign trade, but when they applied stringent enforcement measures, they alienated the commercial Northeast and revived the struggling Federalist Party.

The American Way

"We have it in our power to begin the world over again," Thomas Paine wrote back in 1776. Paine said the budding nation was "a blank sheet to write upon," and by the time President Jefferson left office in 1809, Americans had been writing on that slate for a third of a century.

What did they have to show for it? In the early years of the nineteenth century, they began to take stock. Despite all the political squabbles, most everyday people were feeling more and more like *Americans*, with a unique national culture. In these final two chapters, we explore two aspects of the emerging American Way.

Socially, economically, politically, and culturally, old hierarchies were becoming less rigid. Formerly, a common man was a lesser man, but increasingly, commoners pointed to their humble roots with pride. Refined and educated elites, allegedly at the top of the heap, were passing out of style, while rough-hewn democrats were coming into their own. Women spoke in their own voices, and former slaves, now free, claimed America as their legitimate home. In Chapter 23, we will see these various groups take action.

Then, in Chapter 24, we will watch post-Revolutionary Americans proclaim an imaginative national heritage. Although their compelling account was not altogether true, it did help unite the nation.

Forgotten Founders and the Ideal of Democracy

Chapter 23

In This Chapter

- The rise of democracy in America
- People who pushed for political and economic equality
- Women who entered political and financial worlds
- Free blacks who formed independent communities
- The beginnings of a reform tradition

"All men are created equal." We know those words so well, and today, they exemplify the American creed. Back then, however, the people we regard as Founding Fathers did not always treat others equally. Many owned slaves. Few thought that a common laborer without property was really the equal of a gentleman farmer or wealthy merchant. None extended equality to women. The framers of the Constitution, almost to a man, opposed social equality, economic leveling, and political democracy.

But other men and women at the time *did* embrace these values, in deeds as well as words. Some pushed for universal suffrage, public education, and a genuinely free press. Others tried to end slavery and establish viable communities for free blacks. Some women, although not allowed to vote, stepped onto the public stage or acted on their own behalf in business and marriage. Such people, whom we meet in this chapter, were founders in their own right because they helped create a more just and equal nation.

"Democracy" Comes of Age

The framers of the Constitution used the word "democracy" with disdain, not respect. They complained there was already too much democracy. In the early 1790s, Federalists were actually *accusing* their opponents of being democrats, as if that were an insult. But by the mid-90s, only a few years later, the Federalists' critics embraced the term. They formed dozens of political clubs they called "Democratic-Republican" societies. They backed off the name, however, when President Washington accused the clubs of fomenting civil unrest (see Chapter 19), and by the late 90s, they called their groups "Republican" or "Constitutional" societies, or simply "town meetings."

Finally, when Republicans came to power in 1801, people who embraced democracy called themselves democrats and got away with it. Although Federalists still used it as a term of derision, others thought it was just fine. "We of the United States are constitutionally and conscientiously Democrats," Jefferson said in 1816. Here, unlike in other nations, people of all sorts were able to participate in their government. Congress, once effectively open to gentlemen only, now included people who worked with their hands, like butchers and printers. A dozen Irishmen took their seats, although the Irish had been treated as a decidedly inferior class in earlier years.

In a democracy, the people rule. They elect representatives to public office, but woe be to leaders who forget who's boss. In 1816, congressmen voted themselves a pay increase, from a $6 per day stipend to an annual salary of $1,500. (That sounds like a bigger deal than it was because they would still be receiving less than $10 for each day Congress was in session.) The move was ill conceived. Huge crowds across the country staged rallies and burned congressmen in effigy. The press talked of nothing else, disregarding more significant issues like the huge wartime debt, protective tariffs, and the national bank. Come election time, only 15 of the 81 congressmen who had voted for the pay raise were returned to office.

It was a new day. The original notion of republicanism—wise leaders make decisions for less educated constituents—was no longer in style. Democracy had arrived, for better and worse. (For the difference between republicanism and democracy, see Chapter 6.)

Founding Reformers

Democracy has many aspects, each championed in the early years of the nation by radicals and reformers who wished to broaden the promise of America. The most basic issue was suffrage, or the eligibility to vote, because those who couldn't vote couldn't weigh in on anything else. Most early state constitutions limited suffrage to men holding a certain amount of property (see Chapter 6). Those wanting to change that had to fight against people who feared losing control.

The battle for universal male suffrage was linked to that for public education. If commoners were to be full citizens, they would need to read and write and be able to make independent judgments so others couldn't easily manipulate them. That meant they should go to school. Public education also promoted equal opportunity, of course, because a man who learned mathematics or a trade could advance.

Radicals and reformers wanted to erase the glaring differences in wealth and opportunity so the nation could realize the promise of equality. The reformers generally started from the bottom and on the local level. Each step toward equality was small, but cumulatively, the results were grand. Witness, for instance, an effective struggle for democracy by two grassroots players.

Jedediah Peck Shakes Things Up

Born into a family with 13 children, the son of a farmer, Jedediah Peck was reared in humble circumstances. After serving in the Revolutionary War, he earned his way as a farmer—no surprise there—but also as a surveyor, a millwright, an evangelical preacher, and even as a county judge in Otsego, New York. A friend said that this self-made man "would survey your farm in the day time, exhort and pray in your family at night, and talk on politics the rest part of the time." Peck's increasing interest in politics led him to campaign for a New York senate seat.

Peck wasn't your typical candidate. His printed articles were filled with misspellings and he delivered speeches in "a drawling, nasal twang" that was "almost unintelligible." The common people didn't mind that, and they liked a candidate who addressed them as "my brother farmers, mechanicks [artisans] and traders" and publicly attacked lawyers and pompous officials. Though he lost that senate race, the farmers with small holdings, who could vote for state legislators (though not for the governor), knew Peck was their man and voted him into the state assembly two years later, in 1798.

THEIR OWN WORDS

Lawyers "wooled up the practices of the laws in such a heap of formality on purpose so that we can not see through their entanglements." Then, they "oblige us to employ them to untangle" the confusions they've created, "and if we go to them for advice they will not say a word without five dollars."

—Jedediah Peck

In that same year, Federalists in Congress enacted The Sedition Act, which was intended to end attacks on the government by hardscrabble critics like Peck. Arrested and put in irons, Peck was paraded off to New York City for trial, but that ploy backfired on his foes. Supporters created such a ruckus that Peck was set free. Now a folk hero, he continued to win seats in the assembly and then the state senate. His impressive victories increased the chances of other Republican candidates, who seized control of both houses in 1800. Recall that New York's turn from Federalist to Republican in 1800 was the major difference between the election of 1796, when Adams narrowly beat Jefferson, and the election of 1800, when Jefferson won (see Chapters 20 and 21). It was Peck, and men like him, who gave Republicans the presidency.

Peck's activism had a religious side. He called for school prayer and censured colleagues who did not believe in Biblical revelation. And a moral aspect: he wanted to emancipate slaves and increase penalties for adultery and gambling. Economics, too: he worked to abolish imprisonment for debt and protect landholders from eviction. Politically, he favored universal male suffrage and wanted to subdivide vast senatorial districts into smaller, more user-friendly ones. He also espoused state-supported education. Each of these, in its own way, was a people's issue. While public offices had once been the province of well-spoken and well-educated gentlemen, Peck proved that a self-made, rough and tumble fellow with a sweeping agenda could now make himself heard and have an impact.

Robert Coram Finds a New Way

Robert Coram had a vision. Society's ills, he believed, stemmed from the alleged "right to exclusive property" claimed by those who owned great amounts. But large holdings were originally obtained by conquest and therefore "arbitrary." Native American societies, based on communal property rights, actually provided for their people better than so-called civilized societies of Europe, in which "poor men have no rights."

We don't know where Coram, a native of South Carolina who moved to Delaware in the 1780s, came up with this idea, but we do know what he did about it. A schoolteacher, he joined the Wilmington Library Company and offered to house its books. After studying up on how others justified society's inequities, he wrote a pamphlet that showed how some basic changes could eliminate them. Although the communal arrangements in Indian societies might not work for the new nation, an equitable distribution of land would. "Every man should have property," Coram stated. And a man should have a trade on which he could "firmly rely for safety in the general storms of human adversity," when he might be "dispossessed" of property. Property and education were, like voting, basic rights, and government should provide both. Political democracy, equal economic opportunity, and public education all went hand-in-hand.

In 1791 Coram sent his pamphlet to President Washington, but he never heard back. He then was elected to the convention that revised Delaware's constitution, but there, instead of eliminating inequality, the delegates institutionalized it with stringent property requirements for public office. Defeated "in chambers," as people said, he took his ideas "out-of-doors." He started a newspaper, the *Delaware Gazette*, and in 1794 joined Wilmington's Patriotic Society, one of the political clubs formed to oppose Federalist policies (see Chapter 19). Now at last he found people who listened to his ideas. The society's first petition called for government-sponsored free education, a key element of his overall plan.

Coram died in 1796, at age 35. That same year, Delaware passed a School Fund Act to facilitate free education, the first step in a public education system that was finally completed decades later. Would government also distribute property equally, as Coram wished? Not exactly, but democrats like Coram did influence the homestead acts of later years, which made land affordable. Coram was a son of the Revolution and father to reforms he did not see, which would come in time because of democratic founders like him.

Founding Mothers

"What was done, was done by myself," said a Connecticut woman whose husband was often absent from their farm during the Revolutionary War. Running a farm without a husband was tough work, but it could change the way women viewed themselves. A farmwife from Massachusetts, whose loyalist husband had fled to England, reassured him in letters. "*Your* farm is doing well," she said at first. A little later it was "*Our* farm is doing well," and finally "*My* farm is doing well." She felt she had earned the right to claim it and she did, at least to her husband, privately. Publicly, few women dared.

One woman did dare to speak of the rights of women: the writer Judith Sargent Murray. In a three-volume collection of her writings she called *Gleaners*, she proclaimed that "the idea of the incapability of women" was "totally inadmissible … in this enlightened age." Educate women, she insisted, and they can be men's mental equals. That would make them independent, so they would not need to marry just for survival's sake. They could take their own place in the world, running businesses or, like her, writing and distributing their work.

A few women of the founding era, when given a chance, proved Murray's claim. Among them were Mercy Otis Warren and Abigail Adams, a most interesting pair. Both were in fact educated—Murray's key ingredient—and each in her own way made full use of the rare privilege.

Mercy Otis Warren Speaks Her Mind

As a child, when her two older brothers studied with a private tutor so they might attend Harvard, Mercy Otis convinced her father to let her crash the course. She devoured any and every text in reach, and when prominent Revolutionaries gathered in her home years later, she put her education to good use. With her brother James Otis, who had argued in court against the infamous writs of assistance (see Chapter 2), her husband James Warren, who joined the revolutionary fray during the Stamp Act disturbances, and close friends John and Abigail Adams, as well as several others, she spoke her mind freely on the pressing matters of the day. This was contrary to custom, yet the men seemed to listen, especially John Adams, who was impressed and encouraged her to take up her pen on behalf of the cause they both espoused.

She did just that. Writing anonymously (a common custom in that day), Mrs. Warren published a series of dramatic satires that audaciously attacked supporters of the Crown. After patriots dumped tea into Boston Harbor, John Adams asked her to employ "a certain poetical pen, which has no equal that I know of in this Country," to celebrate the event. She answered Adams's request, and she also responded when he asked her for words of advice when he went off to Congress. But during the war, the two parted ways. Adams sailed to Europe to represent America there, while Warren stayed home, supporting the war while hoping it would not take the life of her husband or any of her five sons. Warren and Adams parted politically as well. She became a fierce Anti-Federalist, convinced the new Constitution betrayed the values of the Revolution. (Her essay, published under the name of "A Columbian Patriot," was an Anti-Federalist mainstay.) And he, as we know, came to head the Federalist Party.

In 1805, using her own name this time, Warren published her three-volume magnum opus, *History of the Rise, Progress and Termination of the American Revolution, interspersed with Biographical, Political and Moral Observations.* The American Revolution had been a great and heroic struggle for republican values—"the natural equality of man, their right of adopting their own modes of government, the dignity of the people." As she sketched Revolutionary leaders, she was free with her praise but also criticized those she felt had abandoned republican values, men like her old friend John Adams. After "living near the splendor of courts and couriers," she wrote, Adams had "relinquished the republican system, and forgotten the principles of the American Revolution, which he had advocated for near twenty years." She even accused him of "a partiality for monarchy."

Adams fired back with an angry letter, then another, and yet another, ten in all within a six-week period, some as long as twenty pages. "Why am I singled out to be stigmatized?" he demanded. Unhinged by Warren's accusations, he accused her of pandering "to gratify the passions, prejudices, and feelings of the party who are now predominant," namely, the Jeffersonian Republicans. In the face of Adams's wrath, Warren stood firm. She observed that she had also said some favorable things about Adams in her history, but she refused to bend on political matters. Still, Adams continued his assault, writing additional letters even before she had answered the previous one. Finally she just cut him off.

Mercy Otis Warren was no modern feminist. She did not promote women's suffrage, but she did foster and model women's participation in the body politic through the promulgation of virtue in the public arena. She spoke her mind, wrote from her heart, and bowed to nobody—not even a former President.

THEIR OWN WORDS

"The lines with which you concluded your late correspondence cap the climax of rancor, indecency, and vulgarism. Yet, as an old friend, I pity you; as a Christian, I forgive you; but there must be some acknowledgment of your injurious treatment or some advances to conciliation, to which my mind is ever open, before I can again feel that respect and affection toward Mr. Adams which once existed in the bosom of MERCY WARREN."

—Mercy Otis Warren to John Adams, August 15, 1807, the final letter in their heated interchange

Abigail Adams Tends to Business

Like her good friend and mentor Mercy Otis Warren, Abigail Adams was not too shy to speak her own mind. But while Warren made waves in the public sphere, Mrs. Adams pushed her case only behind the scenes. We know about the famous appeal to her husband to "remember the ladies" (see Chapter 5), but like other American Revolutionaries, she did not simply make an appeal and wait for the powers-that-be to assent. She figured out what she wanted and got it.

A married woman in those days had no legal claim to her own personal property, all of which belonged to her husband in the eyes of the law. With no property to distribute, there was no point in making a will. But Mrs. Adams, at the age of 71, *did* make a will. "I Abigail Adams, wife to the Hon[ora]ble John Adams of Quincy in the county of Norfolk, by and with his consent, do dispose of the following property," it began, although it's not altogether certain that he had in fact consented. Then, in four pages, the will explained precisely who should get which item of property that she claimed she owned.

Had they known what she had done, contemporaries would have exclaimed, "A will! What ever possessed her?" One thing that did possess her was a sense of self-reliance, developed during a separation of about ten years from her husband. When Abigail was 29-years-old, John Adams went off to the First Continental Congress in Philadelphia, and she stayed behind to manage their Braintree farm and a family. Then he was off to France as a diplomat. In her husband's absence, Mrs. Adams became a business woman and investor.

Rather than having John send her a part of his salary from Paris so she could pay the bills, Abigail asked that he send goods, "some saleable articles … a small trunk at a time." These would go to a cousin of hers "who has lately come into trade, and would sell them for me." She would not make actual purchases—John would do that at her request—but she worked out the plan and she made the money. When 216 handkerchiefs and linen cloth arrived from Paris in 1780, she sold it all and put earnings aside in order to make a real estate deal, the first of many. She also put up $200 on a $300 carriage she wanted, and asked John for the remainder. Later on, she loaned money out and speculated in government bonds, picking them up for one third their face value and making a handsome interest (see Chapter 9). At one point, she spoke of "this money which I call mine." Another time, she gave "my pin money" to her son Thomas. "Mine" and "my"—she treated the money as hers, to dispense with as she pleased.

No one could keep such an independent woman from making a will. In it she gave most of her secret "estate" to granddaughters, daughters-in-law, female cousins, and female servants, but only a token to her two sons and nothing at all to other male relatives or male servants. She wanted the women to have something of their own, as she did.

When Abigail died, John was under no legal obligation to honor his wife's will. In the eyes of the law, her property was still his. But the man Abigail called "my much loved friend" knew the property was *really* hers, if not legally so, and he did execute her estate as she wished. This was the kind of private battle for economic independence that many women waged, and some won. Because they did, the practice of *coverture* eventually ended, and all women gained.

DEFINITIONS

According to the legal doctrine of **coverture,** which prevailed in the Founding Era, a married woman could not possess personal property, control her real estate holdings, engage in contracts, or sign legal documents. Legally, she had no separate existence. A married couple was one person in the eyes of the law, and that person was the husband. Coverture remained embedded in state laws through much of the nineteenth century.

Free Black Communities

In the early days of the nation, free blacks stood up for others of their race. Some had escaped from slavery, some had purchased their own freedom from white "owners," and some had been legally emancipated, but they all understood slavery and racism from a perspective that no white person could fully comprehend. Feeling personally and passionately that slavery was wrong, they reminded their nation again and again of the obvious: slavery contradicted the country's fundamental pledge to liberty, and Christians who tolerated bondage were turning their backs on the Christ they prayed to. Many free blacks did what they could to liberate those who remained in bondage, either by purchasing their freedom or helping them flee.

Aside from helping others, free blacks helped themselves. They had to, because few others did. Faced with rampant discrimination, they created safe havens within a predominately white world, including black churches or social organizations or schools that unified and empowered their members. Working together, they created viable communities around these new institutions. They also created rich cultural expressions based on shared values, a history of oppression, and their African roots. The people who managed to pull this off, amidst extremely adverse circumstances, deserve to be counted among our nation's founders. Two exemplary men will represent the rest.

BY THE NUMBERS

The free black population was rapidly expanding at the close of the Founding Era, but so was the slave population:

- According to the federal census, there were 59,150 free, nonwhite people in 1790, 104,294 in 1800, and 229,620 "free colored persons" in 1820 in the United States.

- The same census reports show there were 694,280 enslaved people in the United States in 1790, 893,605 in 1800, and 1,529,012 in 1820. (The 1820 figures do not include slaves in territories that were not yet states.)

Prince Hall Becomes a Mason

Prince Hall ran his own leather business in Boston, owned property, paid taxes, and was a registered voter and a married man—exactly the sort of person who would seem eligible for membership in a Masonic Lodge. But Boston's white Masons, who allegedly loved freedom, did not allow Hall entry in their lodge because he was black. Not to be denied, Hall sought membership in a lodge attached to the British Army in 1775, although by then the British were the enemy. He and fourteen other free blacks were in fact initiated into Military Lodge No. 441, but that did not mean these men had become Tories. Hall supplied American forces with leather during the war, and historians think he fought at Bunker Hill. (Because others shared the name Prince Hall, it isn't possible to certify that.) Politically, Hall seems to have been an American patriot, but his allegiance to one side did not stop his seeking racial respect and his rights from another.

When the British departed Boston in 1776, Hall and his black companions continued to gather as Masons in what they called "African Lodge No. 1." In 1784, the Premier Grand Lodge of England granted the lodge official recognition, naming it African Lodge No. 459. This soon became the "Mother Lodge" for others in Newport, Providence, Philadelphia, and New York. In 1791 black freemasons convened in Boston to form the African Grand Lodge of North America, with Prince Hall as Grand Master. Years later, in 1827, black freemasons declared independence from the Grand Lodge in England and formed their own organization, known as Prince Hall Lodges, which existed parallel to America's white Masonic Lodges.

Each African Lodge functioned as a sanctuary, where blacks found the respect they were denied in white society. The lodges also provided a communal infrastructure for protest and reform. Masonic blacks acted in concert, not alone. Hall, alongside others, submitted numerous petitions to the Massachusetts legislature. One demanded that the state abolish slavery. Another asked for an African American school. (When their petition was denied, the Masons created one, which started out in Hall's leather shop.) A third asked the legislature to sponsor a "return to Africa," where blacks could "live among our equals." This was a divisive issue among free blacks, but Hall believed Africans should embrace their African heritage, not deny it.

In Boston, Prince Hall and the African Lodge paved the way for other black institutions. An African Baptist Church was founded in 1805, and an African Meeting House, home to the church, the following year. This building, still standing, has through the years been called the African Church, Abolition Church, and Black Faneuil Hall. The names tell the story—blacks came together, and with purpose.

Richard Allen Founds a Church

"All of a sudden my dungeon shook, my chains flew off, and, glory to God, I cried. My soul was filled. I cried, enough, for me the Saviour died." These were Richard Allen's words as he described being born again (converted to Christ). Religion gave him strength in a period of despair, following the sale of his mother and father and three younger siblings by "a good master," who was in financial trouble. He attended Methodist instructional meetings, and after purchasing his own freedom, he started preaching. Traveling by foot through Maryland, Delaware, New Jersey, and Pennsylvania, he inspired interracial crowds. Back in Philadelphia, St. George Methodist Church asked him to preach, hoping to attract black converts.

But St. George built a separate, segregated section for blacks, and that sparked a dramatic walkout by Allen, fellow black preacher Absalom Jones, and the men and women they had brought into the church. "We never entered it again," said one of the protesters years later. Black worshipers then formed two churches of their own, the African Episcopal Church headed by Jones, and an African Methodist Episcopal Church, called Bethel, headed by Allen.

These churches were officially sanctioned by their denominational organizations, but therein lay a problem: blacks still worshiped under white authority. Further, white elders at St. George's claimed that the Bethel Church property was by rights theirs, even though blacks had purchased the property and built the church themselves. Allen took the case to court and won. Also, in 1816, Allen organized a meeting of 60 African American church delegates from four states, and this group established an autonomous African Methodist Episcopal (AME) denomination, beholden to no higher authority. Today, AME churches claim some two-and-one-half million members.

Allen was more than a religious leader. He used any and every avenue that allowed blacks to counter discrimination and build communities. With Jones and others, he created the Free African Society, a benevolent association that came to the aid of widows and orphans, and a black Masonic Lodge for Philadelphia, sanctioned by Prince Hall's lodge in Boston. He helped establish a day school, a night school, and a Free Produce Society, which boycotted goods produced by slave labor. During the War of 1812, Allen and the free black community formed the Black Legion, a force of 2,500 men dedicated to the defense of Philadelphia.

Unlike Prince Hall, Richard Allen opposed the colonization of American blacks in Africa. He prophesized the dangers of such an exodus, a prophecy that proved terrifyingly true. He also argued that people of African descent had a perfect right to stay in America, the country they had helped to build. "This land which we have watered with our tears and our blood, is now our mother country and we are well satisfied to stay where wisdom abounds, and the Gospel is free," he said.

THEIR OWN WORDS

"We have tilled the ground and made fortunes for thousands. Why should they send us into a far country to die? See the thousands of foreigners, emigrating to America every year. If there be ground sufficient for them to cultivate, and bread for them to eat, why would they wish to send the first tillers of the land away?"

—Richard Allen, 1827

A Tradition of Reform

The class, gender, and racial inequalities of the Founding Era are something of an embarrassment. School texts admit to the problem but try to rescue the situation as best they can. "All people were not treated equally in America in 1776," says a typical textbook, "but the Declaration of Independence set high goals for equal treatment in the future." The Founding Fathers, the theory goes, made a "promise" that Americans of the future would later fulfill. Unfortunately, however, the traditional founders made no such promise. With few exceptions, they opposed popular democracy and gender and racial equality.

But there is a way to both save face and stay honest because *some* pioneering founders, represented by the ones we've met in this chapter, *did* promote the democratic ideals we embrace today. Most textbooks, however, ignore these pioneering founders. They claim democracy started with Andrew Jackson a generation later, women did not find a voice until the mid-nineteenth century, and the idea of economic justice was immaculately conceived by trade unionists and Populists at the end of the century. In truth, the radical reformation of American society along more equal lines had its roots at the nation's founding, even if the people who planted those seeds have not become household names.

The Least You Need to Know

- Although Federalists used the term "democracy" as an insult, Americans increasingly embraced the idea that common people could make political decisions on their own.

- When ordinary folks like New York's Jedediah Peck and Delaware's Robert Coram pushed for political democracy, public education, and equal economic opportunities, they made preliminary gains and paved the way for others.

- While there was no organized movement for gender equality, individual women like Judith Sargent Murray, Mercy Otis Warren, and Abigail Adams took strides in achieving intellectual or financial independence.

- Cast aside by white society, free blacks in the North created vibrant communities around such institutions as Masonic Lodges, pioneered by Prince Hall of Boston, and African American Churches, such as those formed by Philadelphia's Richard Allen and Absalom Jones.

- The reform tradition in America, which we usually date from the mid-nineteenth century, had its roots in the Founding Era.

Enshrining the Founders

In This Chapter

- Recreating the past to unite the nation
- Developing founding mythologies
- The death of two presidents as the nation turns 50
- "Signers" of the Declaration of Independence and "Framers" of the Constitution
- The familiar Founding Fathers, and why we need to meet others

All nations like to celebrate their origins, but the birth of our nation makes a particularly gripping drama. The United States has a clearly defined "founding," the work of a single generation. Not all nations are so fortunate. The story of Britain's founding unfolds over centuries—the Norman invasion in 1066, Magna Carta in 1215, Glorious Revolution in 1688, and Act of Union in 1707. China's founding dates back to the rise of the ancient dynasties and continues through the Nationalist Revolution in 1911 and Communist Revolution in 1949—a lot to tell in one story. Mexico has two founding moments, independence in 1821 and a revolution in the early twentieth century, but these were separated by 90 years. Canada eased into nationhood so gradually that it hardly has a story to tell.

Our story, by contrast, is simple yet grand. Its plotline is easy to follow. American colonists resisted British oppression, declared independence and defended it, then established a lasting government. By telling this story over and over, Americans affirm a national identity.

But since the beginning, Americans have imaginatively embellished the tale. They didn't have to—our history is powerful enough as it stands—but they did. In this chapter, we will see how patriotic promoters in the early nineteenth century created a romanticized national narrative that we still repeat today.

Erasing and Recreating the Past

Our history texts tell us that colonists became "Americans" by sharing the experience of the Revolutionary War. This is partly true, but it's also misleading. Soldiers and civilians, Northerners and Southerners, whites and blacks—these people experienced the war in very different ways. A few years later, supporters and opponents of the Constitution divided sharply and painfully (see Chapter 14), and after that, Federalists and Republicans competed fiercely for the soul of the nation (See Chapters 19–22). Unity was not a direct consequence of the Revolutionary War, nor was it a foregone conclusion.

To create the image of a unified America, people first had to learn to forget. The true past needed to fade from view, so a brighter image could emerge. Naturally, time was an ally in this. In the words of historian John Shy, "Memory, as ever, began to play tricks with the event." Only one thing stood in the way: the actual historical record.

Charles Thomson Burns His Papers

The cold, hard, factual record created a serious dilemma for Charles Thomson, who was secretary to the Continental Congress through its entire existence, from 1774 to 1789, and who documented it all. Theoretically, enlightened leaders governed the nation in those critical years and exercised cool judgment under adverse circumstances. In fact, Thomson witnessed a steady stream of petty bickering and contentious debating.

Thomson knew too much, and that was the problem. He wanted to write a tell-all account of what had transpired during the nation's laborious birth, and in fact he started to do so. But then, surprisingly, he gave the project up. "I shall not undeceive future generations," he later explained. Before he died, Thomson burned his papers so "future generations" would not be burdened by the knowledge of what had actually happened.

THEIR OWN WORDS

"I could not tell the truth without giving great offense. Let the world admire our patriots and heroes. Their supposed talents and virtues (where they were so) by commanding imitation will serve the cause of patriotism and our country."

—Charles Thomson, explaining why he did not want to tell what he knew.

Noah Webster Calls for Heroes

When people like Thomson decided to discard factual accounts, people like Noah Webster stepped in, promoting self-congratulatory national chronicles. "Every child in America, as soon as he opens his lips, should rehearse the history of his country," Webster declared in 1790. "He should lisp the praise of liberty and of those illustrious heroes and statesmen who have wrought a revolution in their favor."

Where would children learn how to become good patriots? In public schools, to be attended by all future citizens. Promoting public education attracted strange political bedfellows: elite nationalist leaders like Noah Webster, a diehard New England Federalist who wanted to inculcate patriotism, and radicals and reformers who pushed for political democracy and equal economic opportunity (see Chapter 23).

Webster was relentless. "Every engine should be employed," Webster wrote, "to render the people of the country national, to call their attachment home to their own country, and to inspire them to the pride of national character." One of Webster's engines was the development of a uniquely "American" language, and this is how we know Webster best.

FOUNDER ID

Noah Webster (1758–1843). Author of *American Spelling Book* (1783), *American Grammar* (1784), *American Reader* (1785), *Sketches of American Policy* (1785), *Dissertation on the English Language* (1789), *A Collection of Essays and Fugitiv Writings* (1790), *Effects of Slavery on Morals and Industry* (1793), *Elements of Useful Knowledge* (1802–1812), *A Compendious Dictionary of the English Language* (1806), *Education of Youth in the United States* (1807), *A Dictionary of the English Language, Compiled for the Use of Common Schools in the United States* (1807), *American Dictionary of the English Language,* (1828), *History of the United States* (1832). Editor, *American Minerva/Commercial Advertiser* (1793–1797) and *The Herald: A Gazette for the Country* (1794–1797). Connecticut House of Representatives, 1800, 1802–1807.

Like other Federalists, Noah Webster wanted to turn diverse states and regions into a nation, but he had a special plan for doing this. If schoolchildren learned their common history and an American adaptation of the English language, they would come to share a national culture. Literally, people from all regions would speak the same language. He started with spelling and grammar texts that reflected the way words were used by common people in America, not by the educated elite in England. To make words easier to learn, he cut out extraneous letters, turning "labour" to "labor" and "publick" to "public." He followed this with a reader that featured glowing renditions of the American Revolution rather than the usual Biblical texts. His schoolbooks were a success, particularly the speller, which went through 385 printings and sold some 24 million copies during his lifetime. At age 70, after "laboring" (without the "u") for decades, Webster published his monumental *American Dictionary of the English Language.* Of its 70,000 entries, 12,000 had never appeared in a dictionary, even though they were in common use. Noah Webster declared linguistic independence from the Mother Country, and Americans ever since have followed his path.

Children's Stories

Promoting patriotism was the aim of several schoolbook authors. One, Selma Hale, won a prize of $400 plus a solid gold medal for his history text. The point of his book, he explained, was "to produce virtuous and patriotic impressions on the mind of the reader." The best way to accomplish this, he and others believed, was to extol the "fortitude" and "courage" of the "illustrious" heroes of Revolutionary times, times that were fading from memory.

Mason Weems Lies about a Cherry Tree

The most amusing of these writers, and among the most successful, was Mason Weems, an itinerant preacher and traveling book salesman who could deliver a sermon, fashion a speech, or play the fiddle—whatever would draw an audience. Peddling his "Flying Library" from New York to Georgia, Weems worked the crowds at court days and revival meetings.

Weems knew what people wanted: "quarter dollar books" on "men whose courage and abilities have won the love and admiration of the American people." Men like George Washington, for instance. Weems started with a short biography of Washington that sold "like flax seed," in his words. The demand was so great that he printed edition after edition, expanding his material as he went to quench the popular thirst. It was Weems who wrote that Washington, after chopping down a cherry tree, confessed his evil deed because he could not tell a lie. We do not know whether this was local folklore or whether Weems made it up from scratch, but there is no evidence it happened. If Washington couldn't tell fibs, Weems could. To gain credibility, "Parson Weems" said he was "formerly Rector of Mount-Vernon Parish," although there never was a Mount Vernon Parish.

William Wirt Channels Patrick Henry

Mason Weems's cherry tree tale has disappeared from our textbooks, but William Wirt's fictive tale about Patrick Henry has not. Believing that "the present and future generations of our country can never be better employed than in studying the models set before them by the fathers of the Revolution," Wirt resolved to write a biography of his fellow Virginian, Patrick Henry. As he cast about for material, however, he quickly perceived a problem—he did not have enough. Henry was a speaker, not a writer, so it was hard to get a grip on the details of his life. "He was a blank military commander, a blank governor, and a blank politician, in all those useful points which depend on composition and detail," Wirt grumbled. "In short, it is, verily, as hopeless a subject as a man could desire."

THEIR OWN WORDS

"It was all speaking, speaking, speaking. 'Tis true he could talk—God knows how he could talk! But there is no acting the while. And to make matters worse, from 1763 to 1789, not one of his speeches lives in print, writing or memory. All that is told to me is, that on such and such an occasions, he made a distinguished speech."

—William Wirt in 1815, complaining on the lack of material for his biography of Patrick Henry.

Not wanting to be "fettered by a scrupulous regard to real facts," Wirt simply filled in the blanks according to his own discretion. He knew that on March 23, 1775, just before the outbreak of war, Henry had made a "distinguished speech" calling for military preparations. All Wirt had to do was supply the "composition and detail"— in this case the *words*, all 1,217 of them, culminating in the unforgettable last line that immortalized the subject of his biography (see Chapter 3). For a century to follow, schoolchildren memorized and reenacted the speech, throwing their arms to the sky for the dramatic conclusion: "I know not what course others might take; but as for me, give me liberty or give me death!" To this day, textbooks celebrate Wirt's words as if they were Henry's, just as their author had hoped.

A Poet Takes History for a Ride

Thanks to tales such as these, kids *did* think of themselves as Americans. The most successful tale of all was conjured by Henry Wadsworth Longfellow 86 years after the fact. In 1861, sounding the alarm to a nation that was on the brink of war, Longfellow embellished a local tale and created the unforgettable story of how one man and his horse had saved America from certain destruction: "Listen, my children, and you shall hear/Of the midnight ride of Paul Revere."

Writing in the cadence of a galloping horse, Longfellow took full advantage of poetic license and contradicted Revere's very own account. In his version, for sixteen lines, Revere stands on the opposite bank waiting to see lanterns in the belfry of the Old North Church. He pats his horse, gazes across the landscape, and stamps the earth, fretfully passing the time until he sees "a glimmer, and then a gleam of light." But according to Revere, who we can consider an expert in the matter, he was never there. Someone *else* waited for that signal.

Longfellow's poem, with its many distortions of fact, trumped history. Schoolbooks and even scholarly histories adopted the yarn as-is. One late-nineteenth century text told flatly how Revere "waited at Charlestown until he saw a light hung in a church-steeple, which was a signal to him that the British were moving." This writer then dutifully cited his source—"Longfellow's famous poem on the subject."

America Turns Fifty and Two Founders Die

Every year America celebrated its defining moment: independence. The Fourth of July was "the Sabbath of our Freedom," the only day in the year that ordinary people neither worked nor went to church. Each year's festivities were grand, but one stood out. In the spring and early summer of 1826, Americans prepared to commemorate the fiftieth anniversary of their nation's birth. They called this unique Fourth their "Jubilee" (after the biblical Jubilee, which came every 50 years), and it was special, but in an unexpected manner.

Amazingly, on the very day of the Jubilee, both John Adams and Thomas Jefferson passed away. It was "too marvelous to be true," proclaimed one of the countless joyful eulogies. The simultaneous passing of two such illustrious patriots at such a providential moment proved beyond all doubt the existence of God, "who with wisdom inscrutable, and immeasurable power, controuls the fate of individuals, and overrules the destiny of nations."

It further proved that God favored America and the ideals embedded in the document that Thomas Jefferson had written and that John Adams had marshaled through Congress. Because it was God's chosen nation, the United States had a divine calling or "Manifest Destiny" to spread far and wide. But that is a story for another chapter in another book. With the Jubilee this book nears its end. Americans at the time felt that the passing of Adams and Jefferson signaled an official end to the Founding Era.

> **THEIR OWN WORDS**
>
> "Yes, fellow-countrymen! The principles proclaimed in the Declaration of Independence have not only produced their fruits on this wide continent, and been disseminated on the wastes of Europe, but before the revolution of another jubilee [another fifty years], they will take root and flourish in every soil and climate under Heaven! The march of Light, of Knowledge, and of Truth, is irresistible, and Freedom follows in their train."
>
> —William Alexander Duer, *A Eulogy on John Adams and Thomas Jefferson at the Public Commemoration of Their Deaths,* July 31, 1826, Albany, New York.

Our Founding Fathers: Five Drafts

The countless orators who eulogized Adams and Jefferson did not dwell on their "momentary" rivalry. That would be "sacrilege." When God took the second and third presidents of the United States on the same day, it seems, He also reshaped our history's telling. Henceforth, America's Founding Fathers would be friends, not foes, and their tumultuous days disremembered.

If God didn't *actually* set to work on this project, selective memory did. And, given time, selective memory had an easier and easier time of it. Over decades, the "Founding Fathers"—Federalists and Republicans alike—would blend into a single generic composite. Today, we rarely identify *which* group we are even talking about. In their time, our second and third presidents, Adams and Jefferson, were polarizing political figures, forcefully vilified by one side or the other. Today the general public reveres the two of them, no questions asked. It is difficult for us to imagine it was not always that way.

Take 1: Local and Military Heroes

History adjusts to time's passage, sanctifying some heroes in one time, other heroes in another. During and following the Revolutionary War, two national figures stood head-and-shoulders above the rest: The General (George Washington) and The Doctor (Benjamin Franklin). But Americans then also had other heroes who might stake claim to the term "Founding Father."

In Boston John Hancock, Samuel Adams, and Joseph Warren were a revered triumvirate. In fact, the resistance movement included a much larger cast, but by chasing Hancock and Adams to Lexington and by martyring Joseph Warren at Bunker Hill, the redcoats made champions of these three.

Throughout New England, "Old Put" was a popular favorite. Almost forgotten today, Israel Putnam was already a folkloric hero for his exploits in the French and Indian War, but one incident closed the deal. Supposedly, he was plowing his field in Connecticut when he heard that the British had marched on Lexington; immediately he dropped his plow, mounted his horse, and sped away to answer the alarm, not even returning to his house. Then, shortly after, he made the British pay at Bunker Hill. Such is the stuff of legend, and it earned Old Put a unique place in the hearts of his countrymen.

Two other New Englanders also became famous generals and household names: Henry Knox (see Chapter 15) and the "fighting Quaker" from Rhode Island, Nathanael Greene. In a militarized society that had fought for its very survival, valiant warriors achieved instant fame. New York's Richard Montgomery, a dazzling Irishman who rose quickly in the ranks, led the charge against Quebec. There he lost his life and entered the history books. Henry "Lighthorse Harry" Lee, commander of the fabled "Lee's Legion," was more celebrated than his second cousin once removed, Richard Henry Lee, who made the motion for independence in Congress. Francis Marion, the "Swamp Fox," and Thomas Sumter, the "Gamecock," achieved great renown for harassing the British Army in the South. Even the great orator Patrick Henry rose to fame in part because he was such a firm friend of war.

Take 2: 56 "Signers" of the Declaration

Around the time of the Jubilee, the nation settled on a more cohesive group of Founding Fathers—the cadre of patriots who had signed the Declaration of Independence. It started in 1817, when Congress commissioned John Trumbull to paint a giant canvas, based on a smaller one he had painted three decades earlier, commemorating the men who declared independence. Before settling into its final home in the rotunda of the capitol in 1826, Trumbull's painting toured the country, attracting huge crowds in Boston, New York, Philadelphia, and Baltimore. Simultaneously, Congress distributed facsimiles of the engrossed copy of the original document, complete with signatures (see Chapter 4).

As a group these 56 men became known as the "Signers," and Americans hungered to know more about them. In the 1820s John Sanderson, with the help of Robert Waln, published a nine-volume work called *Biography of the Signers of the Declaration of Independence*, and in 1827 Charles Goodrich came out with the bestselling *Lives of the Signers of the Declaration of Independence*. Others followed in a similar vein, and America had found its most hallowed men. Every detail of their lives was uncovered (and a few additional details invented). The Signers ruled through much of the nineteenth century.

Take 3: 55 "Framers" of the Constitution

But what about the people who framed the Constitution? This is not a trivial question because "Signers" and "Framers" were two very different sets of people. In fact, few Framers had argued in favor of independence in 1776. Only six men signed both documents, and of these, only three had voted to form a separate nation.

Somehow, the Framers had to enter the picture, and without conscious design, Americans began to apply the term "Signers" to men who affixed their names to *either* document. Today, if you hear people talking about the Signers, try asking them which of the two documents they are referring to. You will probably get blank stares. In the popular mind, the Declaration and Constitution have almost merged into one, and people don't really care who signed what.

BY THE NUMBERS

Although the "Signers" of the Declaration of Independence and the "Framers" of the Constitution are often lumped together, they were two distinct groups of people. Each group had a special purpose, and there was only a minimal overlap between the two. Consider these facts:

- Of the 56 "Signers" of the Declaration of Independence, 14 did not vote on its passage because they were not there.
- Of the 55 "Framers" who attended the Constitutional Convention and contributed to the discussions, 39 signed the final document, 3 refused, and the remaining 13 were not present at the end.
- Of those who signed the Constitution, only 6 had signed the Declaration of Independence.
- Of these Signers/Framers, only 2 (Benjamin Franklin and Roger Sherman) were firm advocates of independence and voted for it. One (James Wilson) had opposed independence almost to the end, but wound up voting for it. Two (Robert Morris and George Read) actively opposed independence but signed the Declaration later. One (George Clymer) was among those who were not present on July 4, 1776.
- One Framer (Elbridge Gerry) had supported independence and signed the Declaration, but refused to sign the Constitution.

Take 4: A Smaller Crew, the Ones We Remember

The Signers and Framers, taken together, number over a hundred individuals, most of whom are *not* household names. Try these: James Smith, Jacob Broom, William Few, William Ellery, and Daniel of St. Thomas Jenifer. Unless you are related to one of these men, or they lived nearby, these are not the people you think of when you hear the term "Founding Fathers."

Most likely, you think instead of Washington, Adams, Jefferson, Madison, Franklin, and Hamilton, with a few others making cameo appearances. The list has become rather short. Through successive filtrations, Americans have reduced a sweeping epoch to a manageable size, but the real story of our nation's founding extends far beyond the lives of these important personages.

Take 5: The Revolutionary Generation, Founders All

Historians over the last few decades have reversed the trend and rediscovered "the body of the people," those commoners who drove the Revolution from below. They've investigated the lives of privates like Joseph Plumb Martin (see Chapter 8) as well as famous military officers. Some may think commoners are now getting *more* than their fair share of attention, but the story has only become more balanced and accurate. The traditional Founding Fathers have not lost out; their biographies still sell by the tens and hundreds of thousands.

The 56 "Signers" were not solely responsible for the Declaration of Independence, historians now note. Not until they were pushed from below by thousands of others did they dare to break from Britain. Similarly, the 55 "Framers" certainly *wrote* the Constitution, but the nation at large had to *approve* it, and without the Framers' opponents, we would be without a Bill of Rights. Even the partisan bickerings of the 1790s can't be understood just by looking at Jefferson and Madison, Hamilton and Adams. In the press, in the streets, in state legislatures, and at the ballot box, people from every level of society played politics. The entire nation was involved.

"The entire nation"—that is the most important message. In the words of Abraham Lincoln, American patriots established a nation "of the people, *by the people*, and for the people." If we say that the United States was created not "by the people" but just "by a few important men," we sell the Founders, and ourselves, short.

The Least You Need to Know

- In order to fashion a story that would unite the nation, Americans enshrined the Founders and hid their partisan past.
- Early histories, written for children, freely distorted actual events.
- The first "Founding Fathers" were local and military heroes because national political figures like Adams, Hamilton, Jefferson, and Madison were deemed too controversial.
- In the 1820s Americans treated the "Signers" of the Declaration of Independence as their Founding Fathers, but later, when the "Framers" gained more notice, the cast grew to over a hundred.
- This large crew was reduced to a familiar few, but recently historians have enlarged it once more by recovering the popular roots of our nation's founding.

Internet Sources for Primary Materials

The Web is an incredible source of information, but also an incredible source of misinformation because anybody can post anything online. So it's "browser beware" when it comes to finding out about American history there. On the other hand, more and more primary source materials are available online and these, straight from the horse's mouth, are generally reliable. The selected archival sites I've listed in this appendix certainly are. Beginning here and ending where you will, you can discover more than any single volume can give you—thousands of voices from those who actually participated in our nation's founding.

To access any of these sites, either place the title words in your browser or go directly to the URL address on the following line. You can navigate within each major site by clicking the words I've italicized.

A Century of Lawmaking for A New Nation (Library of Congress)

memory.loc.gov/ammem/amlaw/

This is an amazingly rich source for political life in the Founding Era, starting with the Continental Congress in 1774 and continuing through the Jefferson years and beyond. All items are searchable, but selective browsing can sometimes yield great results. Here's how. For the years before the Constitutional Convention in 1787, click *Journals of the Continental Congress* and then *Browse*. That leads you to a listing of all the volumes and years, and at the bottom, a *contents* and *index* for each year. If you want to learn about lotteries, for instance, click the index for each year, then look for "lottery." You'll find enough information for at least a term paper. Or you can find all drafts of the Articles of Confederation and track the debates. Similarly, look up any delegate and follow his progress. To access any page (the numbering starts new each year), find and click the appropriate volume and on that page click *Navigator*, which lists dates. Click *page image*, which gives you a visual image of the printed journal, and in the box at the top, enter the page you want. Once you're on a page or date, click *link to date-related documents* to see what people were writing about on that day. (For additional context, do this for a few days before and after.) An alternate way to access these letters is to return to the home page and on the top menu click *Letters of Delegates to Congress.* This route is difficult to browse by date but doable by trial and error. You can also try *search*, but the entries do not come up in chronological order.

There are four more very useful items at the *Century of Lawmaking* site. On the home page menu, *Farrand's Records* contains all notes and journals of the Constitutional Convention, Madison's included but also several others. These are organized by date, and again, click *Navigator* to start. *Elliot's Debates* leads you to a host of documents relating to the debates over ratification of the Constitution, including proceedings at the various state conventions. On the right side of the home page menu you'll see the official House and Senate Journals, but these contain only the official proceedings, which are sometimes difficult to interpret. The *Annals of Congress*, however, has the juicy debates. Also, for the first federal Congress, *Maclay's Journal* reads like a rich novel. William Maclay was an avowedly partisan Anti-Federalist within an over-whelmingly Federalist Senate, so his journal must be read in that context.

The Founders' Constitution (University of Chicago Press and Liberty Fund)

press-pubs.uchicago.edu/founders/

If you want to know what the founders had to say about any particular part of the Constitution or Bill of Rights, this is the site for you. It's broken down article-by-article, section-by-section, and clause-by-clause. First, click *Contents*, then *Fundamental Documents*, then *Constitution of the United States and the First Twelve Amendments 1787–1804* (or consult the Constitution from any other source). Locate the number for the article, section, and clause you're wondering about, then go back to *Contents* and click that number. There you'll find what John Locke or the English jurist William Blackstone or various people of the Founding Era, both Federalists and Anti-Federalists, had to say about the matter before, during, and after the framing of the Constitution. You'll also find relevant court decisions. Congress can regulate commerce? The president can call up the militia? The right to keep and bear arms shall not be infringed? You name it, then read about it. Particularly if you prefer to interpret the Constitution according to either the "original intent" or "original mean-ings" method (see Chapter 12), this site is a must.

Avalon Project (Yale Law School)

avalon.law.yale.edu/

This site includes a wide range of documents in law, history, and diplomacy. There are two ways to approach it. On the home page, you can click *18th Century Documents*, but this leads to an alphabetical list that is not exactly user-friendly. (Hamilton's argument for his bank, for instance, is listed under "A" for "Alexander.") I'd suggest instead clicking *Document Collections*. On the long list that comes up, a few items stand out. *Colonial Charters, Grants and Related Documents* brings up a list of colonies, and when you click one, you get a complete list of that colony's founding documents, chronologically arranged. *The American Constitution—A Documentary Record* leads to a variety of documents relating to the Constitution, arranged chronologically. These include, among a host of others, the Magna Carta (1215), the confederation of the United Colonies of New England (1643), the Articles of Association, generally known as the Continental Association (1774), the Articles of Confederation (1781), the various notes of the Federal Convention, including Madison's (1787), the Federalist Papers (1787–1788), and the Virginia and Kentucky Resolutions (1798–1799). *Madison's Notes on Debates* and the *Federalist Papers* can also be accessed on the *Document Collections* page, and they appear in very easy-to-use formats.

Several other document collections on the Avalon site are useful if not always complete. These include, in alphabetical order: *American Diplomacy: Bilateral Treaties, American History: A Chronology 1492–Present* (this is very handy), *American Revolution— A Documentary Record, Inaugural Addresses of the Presidents, The Jefferson Papers, Journals of the Continental Congress, Native Americans: Treaties with the United States, Presidential Papers, The Quasi-War with France, Slavery: Statutes and Treaties*, and *United States Statutes Concerning Native Americans*. Perhaps because the site is hosted by legal scholars rather than historians, it posts the disputed *Mecklenburgh Resolutions* of 1775, for which there is no contemporary documentation.

Note: You can search the Avalon site on the upper right corner of any page. When you plug in a term and a list comes up, it will include references from the Avalon site. If you click "search the web," you'll be out on a global browser, tapping into everything under the sun.

First Federal Congress Project (George Washington University)

www.gwu.edu/~ffcp/

This site helps you understand how the new government under the Constitution was launched. It provides brief sections of original documents with contextual explanations. Click *Online Exhibit*. From there, you can view the exhibit sequentially by clicking *next*, or you can select topics from the list farther down the page, or you can click *Contents* at the bottom. If you're a teacher, you'll naturally want to click *Teacher's Guide* as well.

Online Library of Liberty (Liberty Fund)

oll.libertyfund.org/

This site is jam-packed, but you need to navigate it carefully to get to the good historical materials from the Founding Era. College student alert: find a topic for your paper here! Start by clicking *Groups & Collections* on the left menu of the home page, then click *The American Revolution and Constitution*. The very first item on the list, a two-volume set called *American Political Writings During the Founding Era*, contains many lesser known but very revealing documents such as *A Discourse at the Dedication of the Tree of Liberty*, *The People the Best Governors*, Benjamin Rush's *Plan for the Establishment of Public Schools*, Robert Coram's *Political Inquiries* (see Chapter 23), John Leland's *Connecticut Dissenters' Strong Box* (see Chapter 17), and Noah Webster's 1802 *Oration on the Anniversary of the Declaration of Independence* (see Chapter 24). Down the list, look for the collected papers or works of important but less celebrated founders James Wilson, John Jay, and Gouverneur Morris, as well as Thomas Paine. You will also find John Dickinson's *Letters from a Farmer in Pennsylvania* (see Chapter 7), the *Pacificus-Helvidius Debates* between Hamilton and Madison (see Chapter 19), Paul Leicester Ford's collection of *Pamphlets of the Constitution* during the ratification debates (see Chapter 14), and three of the four histories of the American Revolution written at the time: David Ramsay's *History of the American Revolution*, Mercy Otis Warren's *History of the Rise, Progress and Termination of the American Revolution* (see Chapter 23), and John Marshall's *Life of George Washington*. (The fourth, not available here, is William Gordon's *History of the Rise, Progress, and Establishment of the Independence of the United States of America*.) Finally, you will find older collections of the works of Hamilton, Adams, Jefferson, and Madison that served as standard references until the middle of the twentieth century. While most of the newer collections are available on the Net only by subscription, and while several new collections are not yet completed, the dated collections here are handy and therefore welcomed. Most of the important letters and public writings are included.

George Washington Resources (University of Virginia Library)

etext.virginia.edu/washington/

The prime resource on this site is on the main menu: *The Writings of George Washington from the Original Manuscript Sources, 1745–1799*, edited by John C. Fitzpatrick, 1931–1944. Through the middle years of the twentieth century this was the standard Washington printed reference. The digitized version here is searchable. Unfortunately, the index for each volume does not include page references to the printed edition. This makes tracking down citations from scholarly works a bit time-consuming, but you can still do it by focusing on dates. The home page will also whet your appetite by taking you to the digital edition of the updated and more complete *Papers of George Washington*, still in process. But it's look-don't-touch because access is limited. Research libraries purchase access, and unless you are independently wealthy, you'd probably have to go through them.

Jefferson Digital Archive (University of Virginia Library)

guides.lib.virginia.edu/TJ

There are several threads to follow here. First, click *Jefferson Quotations*. This will take you to the *Jefferson Cyclopedia*, a remarkable collection of key quotations on topics that are easily searchable. Enter "embargo," for instance, and you will see the story as it evolves through his eyes. Or click *Thomas Jefferson Encyclopedia: Quotations* for a less comprehensive but still interesting collection. Back on the home page, click *Texts by Jefferson*, then *The Papers of Thomas Jefferson—Digital Edition*. When that page comes up, click *Enter* and you seem to have access to the entire new collection of Jefferson Papers, fully indexed and searchable. But alas, again, it's look-don't-touch. You need to buy in or go through a research library to call up any documents. There are exceptions, though. Click *The Founding Era Collection*, then *Founders Early Access*, and you will gain access to volumes of the Washington, Adams, and Madison papers that are still in the process of being edited for publication.

American Memory (Library of Congress)

memory.loc.gov/ammem/index.html

Click *Presidents* to get to the original papers of Washington, Jefferson, and Madison—and by "original" I mean handwritten, not transcribed. Unfortunately, the reproduction and digitizing processes compound the difficulty in reading handwritten sources such as these, so good luck deciphering them. Washington's diaries, though, are transcribed. Also on the American Memory home page, you can browse by topic (*Government and Law, Religion, Presidents,* etc.) or click *Browse* and then, under *Browse Collections by Time Period,* select *1700–1799.* Either way will lead you to several useful collections, all searchable and indexed. In particular, look for collections under these categories: *African-American Odyssey, Broadsides and Printed Ephemera, Continental Congress and Constitutional Convention, Louisiana Purchase, Manuscript Division, Ohio River Valley, Presidential Inaugurations, Religious Petitions (Virginia), Revolutionary Era Maps, Slavery and Law, Southern Black Churches,* and the presidential papers mentioned previously. If you're a teacher, be sure to click *Teachers* on the home page, then *Classroom Materials.* Here you'll find a wealth of lesson plans, primary sources selected for classroom use, and so on.

Religion and the Founding of the American Republic (Library of Congress)

www.loc.gov/exhibits/religion/religion.html

Religion was a key part of the lives of most people in the Founding Era, and this site gives a survey history bolstered by a wide variety of documentary evidence. It includes engravings and other graphics from the time period, along with the Library's text and explanation.

Religious Liberty Archive (The Religious Institutions Group)

www.churchstatelaw.com/

On the home page click *Historical Materials* to find colonial charters, state constitutions, bills and legislation, Congressional debates on the First Amendment, and all manner of primary documents from people like Roger Williams or John Locke, and from our first presidents.

History Matters (American Social History Project, CUNY and George Mason University)

historymatters.gmu.edu/

This site broadens history's perspective. On the home page click *many pasts*. Over 1,000 first-hand documents appear in vaguely chronological order. This allows you to find the few dozen from the Founding Era. Here you can read several accounts from those who were not legally citizens at the time, including slaves, women, and Native Americans. Look also for shoemaker George Hewes's accounts of the Boston Massacre and Boston Tea Party, the journal of Quaker abolitionist John Woolman, Herman Husband's case for the North Carolina Regulators, and Benjamin Franklin Bache's defense of the French Revolution (see Chapter 20). Alexander McDougall, on behalf of New York City's workingmen, calls upon rich merchants to honor a Nonimportation agreement, and a fearful slaveowner worries that the black Haitian Revolution might spread to the United States. You get the drill—this site helps round out the story.

Back on the home page, click *making sense of evidence* for an informal, online course on how to deal with documentary sources. This is particularly helpful for teachers. Also, click *www.history* and then *Revolution & the New Nation* for a potpourri of external links. These include the ones mentioned here but also several others. From here, though, you're on you own. Take off and have some fun.

Concluding Research Tips

When conducting Internet research, you will likely discover that a few quotes from founders are used over and over because they appear to support a particular viewpoint. If you want to find out the context for a quotation, or if you want to cite it for a term paper, try typing several exact words, within quotation marks, into your search engine. You'll get numerous hits, but try to find one from an academic book or paper that cites the original source. Then, by looking up that citation, you can place the quotation in its proper context.

If you want to take your research further, you might want to go to a university library and take advantage of tools there. Most will have the recently edited works of the most famous founders, with very helpful notes that contextualize the documents. Many also subscribe to services unavailable at home to the unaffiliated researcher. Usually, they allow people to use these onsite at designated computers. That's how you can access the *Early American Newspapers* collection, and newspapers were the major medium for politics in those days. (This series is on microfilm as well.) Also at these libraries, you can access the digital version of Charles Evans's very thorough collection of printed material prior to 1800, known as *Early American Imprints, Series 1.*

One final note. Although you can do much of your research at home and online, and more yet at university libraries, there are limits. Several very important sources are *not* online, and we don't want history to be driven exclusively by what gets digitized. In the National Archives, thousands upon thousands of depositions from Revolutionary War veterans await serious researchers. Similarly, the records of countless town meetings and Revolutionary committees, conventions, and congresses have not crossed the digital divide. If we leave all these out of the picture, we will lose a large portion of our Revolutionary heritage. We will also skew history in favor of the few famous figures whose words are more extensively available.

So I end with this plea. If you really get into this stuff, make at least one visit to some archive with *real* original sources, the stuff that's not out there yet on the Internet. It's a special feeling and can yield extraordinary results.

Founding Fathers Index

General Index

CHECK OUT
THESE BEST-SELLERS

More than 450 titles available at booksellers and online retailers everywhere!

978-1-59257-115-4

978-1-59257-900-6

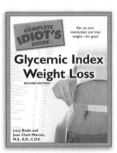

978-1-59257-855-9

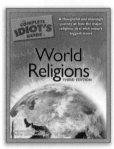

978-1-59257-222-9

978-1-59257-957-0

978-1-59257-785-9

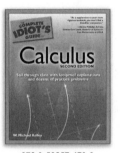

978-1-59257-471-1

978-1-59257-483-4

978-1-59257-883-2

978-1-59257-966-2

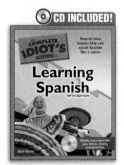

978-1-59257-908-2

978-1-59257-786-6

978-1-59257-954-9

978-1-59257-437-7

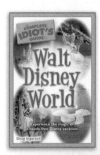

978-1-59257-888-7

ALPHA   **idiotsguides.com**

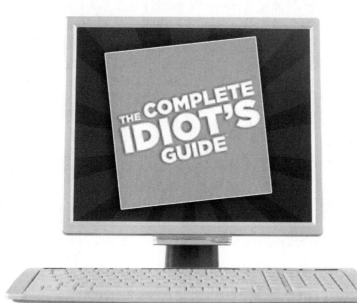